Robert Todd Lincoln

Robert Todd
LINCOLN

A Man in His Own Right

by John S. Goff

Friends of Hildene, Inc.
Manchester, Vermont

Library of Congress Catalog Card Number: 68 - 15686

Copyright 1969 by the University of Oklahoma Press, Publishing Division of the University. Composed and printed at Norman, Oklahoma, U.S.A, by the University of Oklahoma Press. First Edition.

Second edition printed by Academy Books, Rutland, Vermont, for Friends of Hildene, Inc., Manchester, Vermont.

Third edition printed by WF Sharp and Company Printers, Rutland, Vermont, for Friends of Hildene, Inc., Manchester, Vermont.

Introduction to Third Edition

Nestled at the foot of Mount Equinox in Manchester, Vermont is Robert Todd Lincoln's 24-room Georgian Revival mansion. He built his "summer" home in 1902 and named it Hildene, which means, hills and valley. Loving the home and location, Bob Lincoln spent his summers here even before retiring from his service with the Pullman Palace Car Company.

It was a long way from Springfield, Illinois, and the boarding house where he was born – the first son of Abraham and Mary Todd Lincoln. Lincoln could not help but reflect on his days in Springfield – a dusty, muddy town established only a few years before his birth. His father, an aspiring lawyer, doted on Bob and the other boys – Edward Baker ("Eddie"), William Wallace ("Willie"), and Thomas ("Tad" or "Taddie") – as did his mother, the society belle from Lexington, Kentucky.

Every mention of Robert Lincoln in reference works prominently cities his service as Secretary of War and Minister to Great Britain, as well as being the eldest son of Abraham Lincoln – an aspiring politician and lawyer who became the 16th President of the United States. As Robert Goff points out, however, Robert Lincoln was, also "A man in his own right."

His early life was much easier than his father's who had grown up in the immediate post-frontier period. His parents reared him with the etiquette that his mother knew so well. Having the looks of a Todd, Bob was different from his father in many ways. During his boyhood, his father rose from frontier insignificance to national prominence, so that every effort was made to give Robert the formal education that Abraham lacked. Tutored at home and in private schools, he attended Phillips Andover Academy in preparation for entrance to Harvard College in the Fall of 1859. He brought a note of introduction to the college's president from Abraham Lincoln's political nemesis, Stephen A. Douglas, who characterized Robert as the son of his friend, "with whom I have lately been canvassing the State of Illinois." He graduated from Harvard in 1864 and then studied briefly at its law school during the final months of the Civil War.

Only seventeen years old when his father became President, Robert Lincoln was "subjected to" almost constant attention from the press and the population in general (p.39). President Lincoln felt an obligation to have him serve in the Union army. However, after losing two of their sons to illness, the Lincolns did not want to send their eldest son into combat. Instead the President requested General Ulysses S. Grant find a place for him on his staff and the commanding general agreed. So Robert served as a Captain during the last two months of the war as a member of General Grant's staff.

The assassination of his father in April 1865, combined with the increasing mental instability of his mother, left Robert Lincoln the head of the family at twenty-one years of age. He handled the burden well, establishing the reputation that the Chicago Tribune described a quarter of a century later, "In all walks of life, public and private, he has been conspicuous for his good judgment, tact, prudence, and discretion" (p.174). Following a clerkship and some law classes at the University of Chicago, Robert would practice law in Chicago off and on for forty-five years.

He married Mary Harlan, daughter of Senator James Harlan of Iowa on September 24, 1868. Of the three children of this marriage, two daughters would survive him.

As Goff aptly demonstrates – Robert Lincoln was determined to remain a private person and prevent others from using his name for political of financial gain. These may have been unrealistic objectives for Abraham Lincoln's only surviving child.

Newspapers across the nation publicized the trying experience of having his mother declared mentally ill in 1875. Building on a substantial inheritance, Robert accumulated great wealth during his career. He gained profitable clients among railroad and other corporate interests, and his name appeared as a charter member of the Chicago Bar Association in 1874.

He was often mentioned by political leaders as a potential candidate for the American presidency as they were not averse to profiting from his name. But he generally kept aloof. He went to the State of Illinois republican convention, however, in 1880 as the head of a Ulysses S. Grant delegation from Chicago and was allied with the efforts of Senator John Logan to procure a third term for Grant. Logan repaid him, when he switched his allegiance to James A. Garfield because of a lack of support for Grant, by persuading Garfield to appoint Lincoln to his cabinet. Lincoln became Secretary of war without enthusiasm, serving an uneventful term of office. The army was dominated by his father's old generals. The Great retirement bill became the most controversial matter to come before him save for the perennial case of General Fitz-John Porter who sought exoneration for his ignominious dismissal from Civil War service.

Reluctant to hold high public office, Lincoln nevertheless remained in the cabinet after the assassination of President Garfield. He was the only member of the cabinet to serve the full four-year term in the administration of President Chester A. Arthur.

While Lincoln served as Secretary of War, the army of only twenty-five thousand officers and soldiers entered the last decade of its continuing campaign against the Indians and took the first steps into the modern area. In 1881, the army launched a program of specialized training for cavalry and infantry officers at Fort Leavenworth, Kansas. The following year, the army began to change the composition of the officer corps by making retirement mandatory at age sixty-four. Lincoln may have spent most of his time performing what has been described as "routine" duties, but he built his reputation among the intellectuals in the Northeast – the "mugwumps" – and other republicans who favored any candidate rather than James G. Blaine for the presidential nomination in 1884. Though he refused to campaign for the presidential nomination for himself, Lincoln received four votes on the first ballot. Instead, he supported Blaine's most serious rival for the nomination, President Arthur.

Lincoln returned to his practice of law in 1885, but was recalled to public service in 1889 by President Benjamin Harrison who sent him to London as Minister to the Court of Saint James. Lincoln had received three votes on the first ballot for the presidential nomination in 1888.

In England, Lincoln's name served him well, and he resisted the charms of British society. Theodore Roosevelt characterized "all of our ministers to England [as] pro-British except Bob Lincoln." He continued to keep his name out of the papers and gain none of the distinction as spokesman for the United States that has come to many of the American ministers at the British court. While in England, Lincoln stoically endured another family tragedy, the death of his son, Abraham Lincoln II, who was most like his grandfather and namesake, from "blood poisoning." While Secretary of State Blaine and President Harrison took charge of the drawn-out dispute with Great Britain over the seal herd in the Bering Sea, Lincoln did little more than relay correspondence. Service in London marked the end of his public career.

For nearly twenty years after his return from England, Lincoln continued his work as counsel for business interests. He would permit no intrusion into his semi-reclusive life. One of his chief clients was the Pullman Company and when the founder, George M. Pullman, died in 1897, he became first its acting executive and then its president. After the Pullman strike of 1894 and his use of a court injunction against the workers, some contrasted his harsh treatment of his employees with his father's humanity in the emancipation of the slaves. Nonetheless, he paid no public attention to the criticism. In 1911, he was forced to resign the Pullman presidency due to ill health, though he remained Chairman of the Board of Directors.

In 1912 Lincoln moved to Washington, D.C. but remained almost unknown as he advanced in years. He divided his time between his Georgetown home and Hildene, where he found privacy and the opportunity to golf. He also maintained an interest in astronomy and found pleasure working on algebraic problems. His father's papers, which John Hay and John Nicolay had worked with in the 1880s for their multi-volume biography of President Lincoln and his administration, remained in his possession until near the end of his life when he gave them to the Library of Congress for opening twenty-one years after his death.

He participated in the dedication of the Lincoln Memorial in Washington on May 30 (Memorial Day), 1922. Four years later, he died in Vermont on July 26, 1926 at his beloved Hildene.

Robert Lincoln's papers covering 1865-1912 are on microfilm in

Introduction

the Henry Horner Lincoln Collection of The Abraham Lincoln Presidential Library and Museum in Springfield, Illinois. The Library holds an additional 170 letters covering the period 1859-1924, and there are some forty letters in the Manuscript Division of the Library of Congress. John Goff's biography remains the only one of Robert Todd Lincoln, so it richly deserves this new edition.

Frank J. Williams
Hope Valley, Rhode Island
January 26, 2005

Frank J. Williams, founding chairman of The Lincoln Forum, is Chief Justice of the Supreme Court of Rhode Island. He has been a leader in the Lincoln community for 40 years, first as president of both the Lincoln Group of Boston and the Abraham Lincoln Association. In addition, he is a major collector of Lincolniana, a peripatetic lecturer before Lincoln and Civil War groups, and a scholar whose books include Abraham Lincoln: Sources and Styles of Leadership (1994) and Abraham Lincoln Contemporary (1995). He is a member of the U.S. Lincoln Bicentennial Commission. He is also Literary Editor of the Lincoln Herald and writes an annual survey of "Lincolniana" for Lincoln Lore. His latest book, Judging Lincoln, is a collection of his lectures and essays. Chief Justice Williams has been a participant at every conference held at Hildene since its restoration.

Contents

	Introduction to Third Edition	_v_
I	The Years in Springfield	3
II	Widening Horizons	22
III	College Years	41
IV	Changing Roles	59
V	Family Matters	76
VI	Chicago Attorney at Law	91
VII	An Entry into Politics	106
VIII	The War Department	125
IX	Lincoln for President	142
X	Another Presidential Election	159
XI	Literary Matters	178
XII	The Years in London	192
XIII	Return to Chicago	209
XIV	Politics and Personal Life	227
XV	The Final Decade	244
	Bibliography	266
	Index	280

Illustrations

Robert T. Lincoln as a College Student   *following page*   96
At the Caton Wedding, 1867
An Early Photograph of Robert T. Lincoln
Mary Harlan Lincoln, 1868
The Lincoln Children, Mary, Abraham II, and Jessie
Lincoln's Beloved "Hildene"
The Lincoln Home in Chicago
Robert T. Lincoln with Edwin M. Stanton, Jr., and
   Edgar T. Welles
Robert T. Lincoln, 1889
Robert T. Lincoln, 1905   *facing page* 224
Robert Lincoln's Favorite Photograph of His Father   225
Letter About Abraham Lincoln Photograph
The Lincoln Family Arriving at Dedication of
   Lincoln Memorial   240
Taft, Harding, and Robert T. Lincoln at Dedication of
   Lincoln Memorial
Robert T. Lincoln at Dedication of Lincoln Memorial, 1922 241

xiii

Fathers and Sons

THE FIRST THIRTY-FIVE PRESIDENTS of the United States col-
lectively fathered between sixty and seventy sons. These presidential offspring have had vastly varied and different careers. Some
of them were great disappointments to their sires; others have led
important lives in their own right. Of these sons almost no one
would dispute the fact that John Quincy Adams, son of the second
Chief Executive, was the most distiguished. Who should then rank
next? Some might suggest Robert A. Taft, United States senator
from Ohio; some General Richard Taylor of the Confederate Army;
and still others James R. Garfield, an important Progressive leader
and Secretary of the Interior. Almost certainly the name of
Abraham Lincoln's eldest child would be mentioned. Robert Todd
Lincoln was in many respects unique among the sons of Presidents.

In his monumental life of George Washington, Douglas Southall
Freeman observed that it was in a way fortunate that the father
of his country, though he desired children, had none. "A boy
scarcely could have lived up to the name of George Washington,
Jr."[1] It was certainly no easier and probably more difficult to be
"Abraham Lincoln, Jr.," but Robert T. Lincoln somehow had to
manage.

The Lincoln legend is seemingly unending and ever develop-

---

[1] Douglas Southall Freeman, *George Washington*, III, 263–64.

ing. Each year brings the production of books, stories, plays, and articles dealing with the life and times of the sixteenth President of the United States and with members of his family, friends, associates, and enemies. Yet for the most part, Robert T. Lincoln has been ignored. This is all the more unusual when one considers the impressive career that the man himself had. Cabinet member, diplomat, and businessman, he has been worthy of study.

Two explanations for the ignoring of Lincoln's eldest son might be advanced, one tangible and the other less obvious and more subtle. It is axiomatic that a biographer's chief tools are the letters and other written records of his subject. Those who wish to be later written about should be careful to preserve extensive documentation of their lives. In this case not only did Robert T. Lincoln not care to aid a future biographer, but there is a rather persistent tradition that he never wished to be the subject of a "life." Ironically the Robert Todd Lincoln Papers in the Library of Congress, so often mentioned in historical literature, take their name from the long-time custodian of the collection and not from their subject. If the letterpress books of his own writings, which the younger Lincoln is known to have kept for a long period, still survive, their whereabouts is unknown. There is another, quite different reason that this man has been ignored, except for the many pot shots taken at him by the worshippers of his illustrious father. Robert Lincoln does not fit well into the Lincoln legend. A millionaire corporation lawyer and businessman of decidedly conservative views is difficult to reconcile with the almost universally held myths about Abraham Lincoln. Ida Tarbell long ago concluded that he was "all Todd," and it is true that in physical stature he more closely resembled the distaff side of his heritage, but being a "Lincoln-Todd," he had many of the characteristics of his paternal relatives.

Robert T. Lincoln has always suffered at the hands of writers, particularly his father's biographers. Inevitably he is compared to the Great Emancipator and always unfavorably. There is no escaping the fact that there is a "Lincoln major" and a "Lincoln minor," but the comparison is not entirely fair. How well would Abraham Lincoln be remembered today if he had been President of the United States, not in the period from 1861 to 1865, but say in the period his son served as secretary of war, 1881 to 1885? Albert J. Beveridge, while working on his impressive study of the President, wrote "it is already clear that the Lincoln of youth, early and middle manhood showed few signs of the Lincoln of the second inaugural."[2] The same writer also observed, "The cold fact is that not one faint glimmer appears in his whole life, at least before his Cooper Union speech, which so much as suggests the radiance of the last two years."[3] Any attempt to compare Abraham and Robert Lincoln is difficult. To be sure, their personalities, physical appearance, and the like may be compared and contrasted. However, the fact that these two men lived in different worlds cannot be denied. One began his career almost at the same time that the other ended his. In other ways their worlds could never be the same. Abraham Lincoln had to use all the resources at his disposal to rise in his world; Robert Lincoln was born into the results of that successful struggle and he inherited the worldly goods, as well as the name, of his father.

The life that Robert T. Lincoln was forced to lead as the son of his father was not an easy one. In some ways even a George Washington, Jr., would have had an easier time of it. He would probably have been born in the early 1760's and would have died perhaps no later than 1840. In that period of American history, with its difficulties in transportation and communication, he would doubtless have remained at Mount Vernon and led the quiet life of a Virginia planter. He would not have been asked constantly to make a speech here or there, or ever have been besieged by prying reporters looking for a good story. In addition to the ever-present comparisons to his father, Lincoln's son found himself in the uncomfortable position of being criticized for any attempt to capitalize upon his father's name, while if he at-

2 Albert J. Beveridge to Edward Channing, Dec. 19, 1923, in Claude G. Bowers, *Beveridge and the Progressive Era*, 565.

3 Beveridge to Ferris Greenslet, Feb. 2, 1924, *ibid.*, 566.

tempted to avoid the public gaze, he was considered snobbish, cold, aloof, and aristocratic. Those who reside at any time in the public mansion on Pennsylvania Avenue find themselves considered public property, at least while they live there and in some ways for the rest of their lives. The treatment they receive can be most unfair. During the Civil War it was despicable to have the President's son in college while other youths were out fighting, but no one ever mentioned that the sons of Secretary of War Edwin M. Stanton and Secretary of the Navy Gideon Welles also remained in school and never saw any military service.

Measured in the traditional American materialistic terms, the life of Robert T. Lincoln was one of great accomplishment. Essentially it was one of great tragedy. One by one his brothers died; his father was cut down by an assassin's bullet; and his mother was mentally ill for years if not decades. Few have speculated in print about the success of the Robert Lincoln–Mary Harlan marriage, but there are persistent rumors that even though it lasted for nearly sixty years, it was subject to more than the usual difficulties accompanying adjustment to that social institution. It is impossible to calculate the effect on a man when his only son, to whom he was obviously devoted, dies just as the boy is approaching manhood. In the words of a physician:

> I hold the opinion that Robert Lincoln was sensitive—in fact, supersensitive; that he was emotional under certain influences. . . . There was much in life that gave him pain . . . . While his personality was somewhat abnormal, the trials to which he was subjected never even threatened to push him beyond the limits of his endurance.[4]

Four decades after his death, there are not many persons living who had extensive personal acquaintances with Robert T. Lincoln, and certainly not many who had contact with him during the prime of his life. Those who remember him thought well of the man. Recorded statements of contemporaries, particularly those by persons who spoke from a degree of personal acquaint-

[4] W. A. Evans, *Mrs. Abraham Lincoln*, 53.

ance, are almost all favorable. Mrs. Henry Adams' observation that the younger Lincoln was "a quiet, gentlemanly, attractive man"[5] was typical. Probably the following is the most critical recorded comment by a contemporary:

> Robert T. Lincoln . . . was a man of mediocre attainments, puffed up with pride almost to the exploding point by the brilliance of his parentage, who, left to his own devices, never would have risen above the ranks of the commonplace.[6]

It is ironic that the author of this estimate was Carter H. Harrison, Jr., who was elected to succeed his murdered father as mayor of Chicago.

Robert T. Lincoln lived during the age of enterprise and industrialization that followed the Civil War and continued largely unchecked by political restraints until the advent of the twentieth century. For the last quarter of a century of his life, he was philosophically a living relic of a bygone era. If he is judged by the standards of a later, perhaps more individual, and less property-conscious time, he is found wanting. However, his personal traits of honesty, integrity, and quiet dignity have a meaning for all ages.

Hopefully, Robert T. Lincoln will, by word and by action, speak for himself here. In a period when that semi-science, psychology, seems to be making an illicit alliance with the mother art, history, it is well to remember that the practitioners of the former cannot agree among themselves on the thinking, notions, and motives of an individual when they have him before them. How then can they deal with a person who has long been dead and has left little to survive him? The biographer must always remember that most of the time he can only describe what happened, and that to delve more deeply is to invite disaster.

5 Mrs. Henry Adams to her father, Dr. Robert W. Hooper, Feb. 20, 1881, in Ward Thoron, ed. *The Letters of Mrs. Henry Adams*, 269.
6 Carter H. Harrison, *Stormy Years*, 276.

Robert Todd Lincoln

Chapter 1

The Years in Springfield

ABRAHAM LINCOLN, sixteenth President of the United States, is perhaps the best known and most widely discussed figure in all of the history of the United States. It will therefore suffice to review only a few facts concerning him. He was the son of Thomas Lincoln (1778–1851), a descendant of Samuel Lincoln, who came from England in the 1630's, settled in Massachusetts, and there raised a large family.[1] Thomas Lincoln, a semiliterate carpenter and farmer, was a member of that branch of the family that, after living for a time in Berks County, Pennsylvania, settled in Rockingham County, Virginia, where Thomas was born.[2] When the President's father was a boy of six, the family pushed on to Kentucky, where Abraham Lincoln, father of Thomas, was killed by the Indians.[3] Thomas Lincoln's wife, whom he married June 12, 1806, was Nancy Hanks (1784–1818). She was descended from Thomas Hanks who migrated from England to Virginia in 1644. Her mother was Lucy, or Lucey, Hanks, but her paternity is open to doubt. It has been said that she was illegitimate, although her mother was later married to Henry Sparrow.[4] To Thomas and

1 John G. Nicolay and John Hay, *Abraham Lincoln*, I, 2.

2 "Autobiography of Abraham Lincoln," ms. in the Library of Congress, quoted in David C. Mearns, *The Lincoln Papers*, I, 141.

3 Nicolay and Hay, *Lincoln*, I, 21.

4 For a summary of the various schools of thought regarding the background of Nancy Hanks, see Louis A. Warren, *Lincoln's Parentage and Childhood*, 17–37.

3

Nancy Lincoln were born three children. The eldest, Sarah,[5] was born February 10, 1807, married Aaron Grigsby on August 2, 1826, and died January 20, 1828.[6] The second child was Abraham, born February 12, 1809, and the youngest was Thomas, who died in infancy.[7]

Abraham Lincoln's early life is well known. His family took him from his birthplace in Kentucky, first to Indiana and then in 1830 to Illinois. His mother died when he was nine, and his stepmother, Sarah Bush Johnston Lincoln, had a great influence upon him. He split rails, helped clear land for farming, and operated a general store, which went bankrupt. After serving in the Black Hawk War, he had a choice between learning blacksmithing or the law and chose the latter. While studying law, he served in the Illinois state legislature, and in 1836 he was licensed to practice his profession. Abraham Lincoln had lived in many places before he settled in Springfield, Illinois, in April of 1837, where he remained until the spring of 1861. He was a junior partner in two law firms before becoming the senior half of Lincoln and Herndon in 1844.

Mary Todd Lincoln, wife of Abraham Lincoln, had quite a different background from that of her illustrious husband. She was born in Lexington, Kentucky, December 13, 1818, the daughter of Robert Smith and Eliza Ann (Parker) Todd of that city. The Todds and the Parkers were substantial citizens who played an important role in community affairs.[8] In 1825, Mary's mother died in childbirth, leaving six young children, and, after a respectable waiting period, Mr. Todd remarried and continued expanding his family. Mary Todd was educated in the traditions of her time at a private academy in Lexington, which was attended by the children of the leading families of the area. In the fall of 1839, Mary, a young lady of twenty-one, went to make her

---

[5] Sarah Lincoln was generally known as "Sally," according to a statement by Nat Grigsby, brother of her husband, to William H. Herndon, quoted in Emanuel Hertz, *The Hidden Lincoln*, 353–57.

[6] Warren, *Lincoln's Parentage*, 140.

[7] *Ibid.*, 154–55.

[8] Thomas Marshall Green, *Historic Families of Kentucky*, 208–20, 274.

4

home with her sister, Mrs. Ninian Wirt Edwards, in Springfield, Illinois.[9] Mrs. Edwards' husband was the son of Governor Ninian Edwards; their home was the "center of the aristocratic 'Edwards clique' and all distinguished visitors to the town . . . found their way up the gentle slope to the house on the hill where hospitality was on a lavish, old-fashioned scale."[10]

Since it is so obvious that Abraham Lincoln and Mary Todd came from two entirely different backgrounds, it is often observed that they had very little in common. How then did they meet and eventually marry? No one knows exactly how or when they first met. It is suggested that they first became acquainted at a cotillion held at the Edwards' home.[11] At any rate, during the winter of 1839–40, the two began seeing one another regularly.[12] With the passage of time, it became evident that Mr. Lincoln was paying court to Miss Todd. Of course the lady had other callers, including, legend has it, Stephen A. Douglas. Further, tradition indicates that Mr. Lincoln wrote to the lady's father asking for permission to "pay his address" to the gentleman's daughter. Mr. Todd, so the story goes, promptly wrote Ninian W. Edwards to inquire about this Mr. Lincoln.[13] About the end of the year 1840, the couple was engaged.[14] Then something happened—the famed "broken engagement." It is not relevant to this story to delve into that question, but in time the couple was reconciled and the association renewed.[15] On the evening of November 4, 1842, at the Edwards' mansion, Abraham Lincoln and Mary Todd were married. A few days later, the groom in a letter to a friend wrote, "Nothing new here, except my marrying, which to me, is a matter of profound wonder."[16]

9 Ruth Painter Randall, *Mary Lincoln*, 4.

10 *Ibid.*, 5.

11 Katherine Helm, *Mary, Wife of Lincoln*, 71–75.

12 Statement of Mrs. Ninian W. Edwards to William H. Herndon, n.d., Herndon-Weik Manuscripts, Library of Congress.

13 Randall, *Mary Lincoln*, 17.

14 Mrs. Edwards to Herndon, Sept. 27, 1887, Herndon-Weik Mss.

15 Randall, *Mary Lincoln*, 36–51, discusses the "broken engagement" at some length.

16 Abraham Lincoln to Samuel D. Marshall, Nov. 11, 1842, in Roy P. Basler, ed., *The Collected Works of Abraham Lincoln*, I, 304–305.

Mr. and Mrs. Lincoln lived in the Globe Tavern in Springfield during the first year of their marriage. They had to be extremely careful with money and could not yet afford a home of their own. During the year 1843, Lincoln wrote several interesting letters to his friend Joshua Fry Speed of Kentucky, in which he discussed his new life. Regarding the living quarters, he told Speed, "We are not yet keeping house; but boarding at the Globe Tavern, which is very well kept by a widow lady of the name of Beck."[17] In the same sentence he mentions that their board was only four dollars a week. When Speed wrote Lincoln about the prospect of there being an addition to the family, the latter, in March, 1843, answered, "About the prospects of your having a namesake at our house, cant say, yet."[18] Certainly by that time the Lincolns knew of their impending parenthood, but perhaps the father-to-be was merely indicating the obvious fact that the baby might be a girl and there would be no Joshua Lincoln. However, perhaps he was hedging on the name even if it was a boy. In the late spring Speed wanted the Lincolns to visit Kentucky, but his friend declined, giving as one of his reasons "those 'coming events.' "[19] "We are but two, as yet," wrote the expectant father on July 26.[20] The baby was born in the Globe Tavern on August 1, 1843. It was a boy and he was named Robert Todd Lincoln. Thus he would always be known, for many have enjoyed emphasizing the Todd name. He himself never at any time used his middle name, but, rather, always signed himself Robert T. Lincoln or simply R. T. Lincoln.

Although Robert Lincoln was born into somewhat humble surroundings, they were certainly not similar to those into which his father was born. Fortunately for the mother's peace of mind, the father was in town when the baby arrived. Frequently, though, such was not the case, for Lincoln would be away "on circuit" practicing his profession. For example, he was absent from Springfield during the period April 5 to May 5 of the year

17 Lincoln to Joshua F. Speed, May 18, 1843, *ibid.*, I, 323–25.
18 Lincoln to Speed, Mar. 24, 1843, *ibid.*, I, 319.
19 Lincoln to Speed, May 18, 1843, *ibid.*, I, 323–25.
20 Lincoln to Speed, July 26, 1843, *ibid.*, I, 328.

in which Robert was born.[21] Mrs. Lincoln's biographer, Ruth Painter Randall, feels it strange that Mary was not taken to the Edwards' mansion or to the home of one of her other sisters then living in the town, but she suggests that possibly there was still resentment over the fact that Mrs. Lincoln may have married against her family's wishes.[22] Mr. Todd came up from Lexington to bestow his best wishes on the new arrival. Robert Lincoln once confirmed the source of his name with the comment that "I was named for my maternal grandfather . . . , and not for any connection with any Lincoln bearing the name."[23] The evidence indicates that Mr. Todd felt differently toward his son-in-law than did some other members of the clan. Well aware of the fact that the Lincolns were not yet well off financially, he on several occasions advanced them money.[24] It is estimated that during the decade of the 1840's, Lincoln's law practice yielded him about fifteen hundred to two thousand dollars a year, and it must be remembered that he still had the "New Salem debt," money owed from an earlier period when his business venture failed.[25]

The fact that Robert Lincoln was the son of Abraham Lincoln yields certain advantages to the biographer in that ordinarily the early life of a person is clouded, and long-forgotten details of happenings are not available. This is not so in this instance; Robert's childhood years are quite well documented. The evidence is conflicting and leaves some questions unanswered, but, taken altogether, it indicates that Robert had a generally normal childhood.[26] Fellow guests at the Globe Tavern recalled the first few weeks in the life of the baby. "Mrs. Lincoln had no nurse for herself or the baby. Whether this was due to poverty or more probably to the great difficulty of securing domestic help, I do

21 Harry E. Pratt, *Lincoln, 1840–1846*, 171–75.

22 Randall, *Mary Lincoln*, 82.

23 Robert T. Lincoln to Ida Tarbell, Aug. 6, 1920, Tarbell Lincoln Collection, Allegheny College Library.

24 Upon the death of Robert S. Todd, it was found that the amounts totaled $1,157.50. William H. Townsend, *Lincoln and His Wife's Home Town*, 90.

25 Harry E. Pratt, *The Personal Finances of Abraham Lincoln*, 14, 84–85.

26 Harry E. Pratt, Review of *Lincoln's Sons*, by Ruth Painter Randall, *Saturday Review*, Vol. XXXIX (Jan. 26, 1956), 26–27.

not know," was the observation of a woman who was six years old at the time of the birth of the eldest Lincoln son. She was Sophie, daughter of Mr. and Mrs. Albert Taylor Bledsoe, and she recorded that her mother went every day to Mrs. Lincoln's room and washed and dressed the new arrival. Sophie also noted:

> I was very fond of babies, and took on myself the post of amateur nurse. I remember well how I used to lug this rather large baby about to my great delight, often dragging him through a hole in the fence between the tavern grounds and an adjacent empty lot, and laying him down in the high grass, where he contentedly lay awake or asleep, as the case might be. I have often since that time wondered how Mrs. Lincoln could have trusted a particularly small six year old with this charge.[27]

In the fall of 1843 the Lincolns moved from the tavern to a small frame house located at 214 South Fourth Street in Springfield.[28] There they spent only a few months, for in January of the next year, Abraham Lincoln purchased a house located at the corner of Eighth and Jackson Streets and convenient to his law office.[29] In May the three members of the household moved into the house that they occupied for the next sixteen years. Later given by Robert Lincoln to the state of Illinois as a public monument, it bore little resemblance to its later-day appearance when the family first occupied it. Then a rather small, story-and-a-half dwelling, it grew as the needs and resources of the family grew.

In all, four sons were born to the Lincolns. The three younger children were: Edward Baker Lincoln, born March 10, 1846; William Wallace Lincoln, born December 21, 1850; and Thomas Lincoln, born April 4, 1853.

Many people have left their recollections of the family in Springfield in the 1840's and 1850's, and it is from them, plus other surviving documentation, that a picture is formed of Robert Lincoln in his early years. In October, 1846, Robert's father

---

[27] Quoted in Pratt, *Personal Finances*, 84.
[28] There is a sketch of this cottage in W. A. Evans, *Mrs. Abraham Lincoln*, 138.
[29] Pratt, *Personal Finances*, 63.

wrote to Joshua Speed to tell him of Edward's arrival. His comments in the same letter about his first-born are interesting:

> Bob is "short and low," and, I expect, always will be. He talks very plainly—almost as plainly as any body. He is quite smart enough. I sometimes fear he is one of the little rare-ripe sort, that are smarter at about five than ever after.[30]

This oft-quoted letter is unusual and many have wondered about its meaning. Is it indicative of a lack of warmth toward the child on the father's part? Certainly some have interpreted it in such a manner. Or was it simply a proud parent, who, rather than boast too much, joked about a first-born son of whom he had already said, "He is quite smart enough." Only Abraham Lincoln could answer this and any inference drawn from the statement is pure conjecture.

The same letter continues with the observation that the boy "has a great deal of that sort of mischief that is the offspring of much animal spirits." Lincoln was evidently writing to Speed from his law office:

> Since I began this letter, a messenger came to tell me, Bob was lost; but by the time I reached the house his mother had found him, and had him whiped [*sic*]—and, by now, very likely he is run away again.

Apparently, young Robert's running away from home was a relatively common occurrence. At least it happened often enough that a neighbor of the Lincoln family could recall the mistress of the household on several occasions, dashing out to the front of the house and screaming, "Bobbie's lost! Bobbie's lost!"[31]

The home life of the family has received much attention. According to William H. Herndon, "Mr. and Mrs. Lincoln never lived a harmonious life."[32] He observed that Lincoln "exercised no government at all over his household. His children did much

---

30 Lincoln to Speed, Oct. 22, 1846, *Collected Works*, I, 389–91.
31 Randall, *Mary Lincoln*, 118.
32 Herndon to Weik, Nov. 19, 1885, Herndon-Weik Mss.

as they pleased. Many of their antics he approved, and he restrained them in nothing. He never reproved them or gave them a frown."[33] Of course, it should be noted that Herndon hated Mary Lincoln and could hardly be called an unbiased witness. Still, despite the efforts of Ruth Painter Randall and others, the Herndon view of Lincoln's home life is the popularly held one, and it cannot be denied that the day-to-day life was far from quiet. Mary Lincoln was often nervous and her temper tantrums and outbursts shattered the normal calm of family living. At times she was unable to meet the problems that raising a normal active boy created. On one occasion when Bobbie was playing in the yard, he got into the lime box, which was a necessary accessory to the outside toilet, and put some lime into his mouth. While his mother screamed "Bobbie will die!," a neighbor rushed over and washed out the child's mouth.[34] In the words of Mrs. Lincoln's principal biographer, "she was a nervous, over anxious mother."[35] In short, she was an individual who had great difficulty in coping with many of life's smaller problems, and later, when faced with some great troubles, she broke entirely.

It cannot be denied, however, that living with Abraham Lincoln helped produce some of his wife's outbursts. Lincoln was a moody, somewhat absent-minded man given to melancholia. All of this was coupled with a tendency, at times, to ignore the niceties of polite society that were so important to Mary Lincoln. On many occasions he would be late to dinner, which would evoke mild criticism from his wife.[36] When the ladies of Springfield called at the front door, he had a habit of greeting them dressed in his shirtsleeves rather than properly attired in a coat.[37] Yet in spite of their personal shortcomings, all evidence indicates that Abraham and Mary Lincoln were extremely devoted to one another from the beginning of their relationship to the day of their deaths. They needed one another. Lincoln served as a re-

---

33 William H. Herndon, *Life of Lincoln*, 344.
34 Randall, *Mary Lincoln*, 118.
35 *Ibid.*
36 Helm, *Mary, Wife of Lincoln*, 112.
37 Herndon, *Life of Lincoln*, 345.

straining force on his flighty wife, while she, albeit by nagging at times, spurred him on. It seems clear that without a Mary Todd Lincoln in the house on Eighth Street, there would never have been an Abraham Lincoln in the White House.

Once settled into their permanent home in Springfield, the family settled into a routine. Usually the Lincolns had a servant girl, although in Illinois in the 1840's servants were difficult to hire, and more difficult to keep because of Mary's temper. One who was treated kindly by her mistress was Ruth Burns, a Negro girl, who worked for the Lincolns in 1849. On one occasion, though, she was scolded, and the story is worth retelling because of Mrs. Lincoln's southern background. Ruth and some other children were throwing stones at Negro children playing nearby. When her mistress upbraided her for it and demanded to know why she was acting in that manner toward others of her own race, the girl replied that she had always lived with whites and thought of herself as being of that group.[38] Of Robert, Ruth remembered that he wore patched blue jeans because of the relative poverty of the family.

The head of the household, in addition to his law practice, had chores to do around the house. He chopped the wood to keep the winter fires going, and little Robert worked alongside chopping the kindling wood.[39] Unlike many men of his period, Mr. Lincoln took a hand with the rearing of the children on occasion. In his role as parent, Lincoln anticipated more modern developments in child training. "Spare the rod and spoil the child," prevalent in that period, was not his motto; it was the more progressive, "Spare the rod for you may warp the child's personality." When he wrote to a friend concerning Robert who was about to enter college, "He promises well, considering we never controlled him much," he was giving an accurate description of himself as a parent.[40] The Lincoln children did as they pleased at all

[38] Typed copy of the recollections of Margaret Ruth Stanton, which appeared in the St. Louis *Post Dispatch*, Nov. 25, 1894, in files of the Illinois State Historical Library, Springfield (hereafter ISHL).

[39] Octavia Roberts, *Lincoln in Illinois*, 72.

[40] Lincoln to Anson G. Henry, July 4, 1860, *Collected Works*, IV, 81–82.

times. Not everyone in Springfield–probably almost no one—agreed with the Lincolns' methods of child rearing and undoubtedly there were raised eyebrows over the matter. Mr. Herndon, for one, took an extremely dim view of the upbringing of the little "brats." Yet Herndon was forced to admit that the flaws in the situation were not due to a lack of interest in the children and their welfare. Referring to Lincoln and his children, Herndon noted, "He loved what they loved and hated what they hated."[41] This same gentleman observed, "I have felt many and many a time that I wanted to wring their little necks and yet out of respect for Lincoln I kept my mouth shut."[42]

What bothered Mr. Herndon most of all was Lincoln's Sunday-morning habit of baby-sitting with the children at the law office while Mrs. Lincoln attended church. The office of Lincoln and Herndon was probably always far from tidy, but the Lincoln sons could make chaos out of confusion. Robert and his brothers could find many things with which to entertain themselves. There were books to pull from the shelves to the floor; papers and ink to mix in the proper proportion; and pen points that, when coupled with penholders, made excellent darts for throwing at a wall.[43] One can feel genuine sympathy with Herndon's desire to "wring the necks of these brats and pitch them out of the windows,"[44] and also understand his frustration when he noted "yet out of respect for Lincoln I kept my mouth shut."[45]

But all of Springfield came to know that Lincoln "worshipped his children."[46] James Gourley, a near neighbor, long afterward recalled, "Lincoln would take his children and would walk out on the railway out in the country, would talk to them, explain things carefully, particularly. He was kind, tender and affectionate to his children, very, very."[47] Once, when Robert and his father were out riding in a carriage, Lincoln, "who wanted to be

---

41 Herndon to Weik, Feb. 18, 1887, Herndon-Weik Mss.
42 Herndon to Weik, Nov. 19, 1885, *ibid.*
43 Herndon, *Life of Lincoln,* 344.
44 Herndon to Weik, Jan. 8, 1886, Herndon-Weik Mss.
45 Herndon to Weik, Nov. 19, 1885, *ibid.*
46 Herndon to Weik, Feb. 18, 1887, *ibid.*
47 Quoted in Hertz, *Hidden Lincoln,* 382–84.

known for a genius of accuracy,"[48] demonstrated his amazing memory, and probably hoped his son would learn a lesson, too.

Driving toward Springfield . . . he recalled he had surveyed the neighborhood they were driving through. He stopped the buggy several times, and each time, with a chuckle, asked Bob to go into the woods and at a certain distance find a blazed tree, which he had more than twenty years ago marked as a survey corner. "And he never made a mistake," said Bob.[49]

Willard L. King, the biographer of Justice David Davis, has observed: "Robert Lincoln had many characteristics of his father. He was scrupulously careful, a quality I have always attributed in his father to his early surveying experience. Robert Lincoln also had the same love of precision."[50] Apparently the son learned his lesson well. Abraham Lincoln once said to his wife, "It is my pleasure that my children are free, happy and unrestrained by parental tyranny. Love is the chain whereby to bind a child to its parents."[51] As in so many other matters, the wisdom and greatness of the man shows through in a relatively small and minor detail. Mr. Lincoln was not one of those who were so busy reforming the outside world that he neglected his own household.

Robert Lincoln was just past four years old when the family went to Washington, where his father in December of 1847, took his seat as a representative in Congress from Illinois. He had memories of that period, although they were limited and, in time, blurred. He wrote: "I followed the usual pursuits of infancy and childhood . . . until I was four years old, when I was taken by my parents to Washington, D.C. . . . Of my life in Washington my recollections are very faint."[52] The Lincolns' journey from Springfield to the national capital was made by way of Lexington, Kentucky, with a three-week stopover there for a visit with the Todds.[53] Their mode of travel included stagecoach, boat, and

---

48 Carl Sandburg, *Abraham Lincoln: The Prairie Years*, II, 249.
49 *Ibid.*
50 Letter to the author from Willard L. King, Chicago, June 6, 1958.
51 Randall, *Mary Lincoln*, 101.
52 "Autobiography of Robert T. Lincoln," ms. in Harvard University Archives.
53 Helm, *Mary, Wife of Lincoln*, 99–102.

railroad.[54] Young Bobbie may not have had any special recollections of the trip, but it produced an incident long remembered in the Todd family. Unknown to the Lincolns, a nephew of Mrs. Lincoln's stepmother traveled from Frankfort to Lexington on the same train with them. The gentleman got off the train when the Lincolns did but arrived at the Todd home first. Once there, he began to complain loudly about his train ride. The trouble, it seemed, was that "There were two lively youngsters on board who kept the whole train in a turmoil, and their long-legged father, instead of spanking the brats, looked pleased as Punch and aided and abetted the older one in mischief." Just then he looked out of the window and cried, "Good Lord, there they are now." Mrs. Todd's nephew made a quick exit and was not then introduced to the long-legged father who aided and abetted his son, Robert T. Lincoln, in mischief.[55] The visitors from Springfield after leaving Lexington journeyed on to Washington. There they lived at Mrs. Sprigg's boardinghouse just a short distance from the Capitol. The two lively children must have made life very interesting for the other boarders. A young physician then beginning his practice in Washington who was also a boarder at Mrs. Sprigg's remembered that Robert was "a bright boy" who "seemed to have his own way."[56]

Mrs. Lincoln, Robert, and Edward remained only three months in the national city, for by the spring of 1848 they were back in Lexington with the Todds.[57] There exist some letters that passed between Abraham and Mary Lincoln during this period of separation. In one dated April 16, 1848, Congressman Lincoln refers to a dream he has had about "Bobby." It must have been an unpleasant one for he says "I did not get rid of the impression of that foolish dream about dear Bobby till I got your letter written the same day. What did he and Eddy think of the little letters father sent them?" The conclusion of the correspondence

54 Wayne C. Temple, "Mary Todd Lincoln's Travels," *Journal of the Illinois State Historical Society*, Vol. LII (Spring, 1959), 180–81 (hereafter *JISHS*).

55 Helm, *Mary, Wife of Lincoln*, 101–102.

56 Samuel C. Busey, *Personal Reminiscences and Recollections*, 28.

57 Paul M. Angle and Earl S. Miers, eds., *The Living Lincoln*, 96.

is, "Don't let the blessed fellows forget father."[58] Mrs. Lincoln's reply contains much of the doings of the children. On the day she wrote her letter, Robert "in his wanderings" had found in the yard "a little kitten, your hobby."[59] The child brought the animal into the house, but his stepgrandmother, Mrs. Todd, disliked it and had it turned out of the home with "Ed-screaming & protesting loudly against the proceedings."[60] On June 12, Lincoln in another letter writes of how much he misses his family and also notes that "Every body here wants to see our dear Bobby."[61] Evidently the proud father had been telling "every body" he met about his son. In the last letter of the series, dated July 2, 1848, Lincoln, by now very lonely for his family, mentions that he had hoped to have them with him before then, but that Mary should stay at her father's as long as she pleases, and concludes with "Kiss and love the dear rascals. Affectionately, A. Lincoln."[62]

Sometime during the late summer or fall of 1848, the Lincolns went home to Springfield, but apparently they left Robert to spend the winter in Lexington. The only existing evidence of this is Robert's own statement, "I lived with my Grandfather at Lexington, Ky.," during the winter of 1848–49.[63] Ruth Painter Randall in her work *Lincoln's Sons* believes that the boy was profoundly influenced by his visit even though he was only five years old at the time.[64] She implies that he found a deep sense of kinship with his mother's family and that he took on Todd manners and ways to the extent of being out of sympathy with his father and his father's early struggles. However, the late Harry E. Pratt once severely criticized this line of reasoning as being based on a fragment of unsupported evidence.[65] Although the visit may have had some slight influence on the child in that he found himself

58 Abraham Lincoln to Mary Lincoln, Apr. 16, 1848, *Collected Works*, I, 465–66.
59 Referring to Lincoln's habit of bringing home stray animals. See Randall, *Mary Lincoln*, 111.
60 Mary Lincoln to Abraham Lincoln, May, 1848, quoted *ibid.*
61 Abraham Lincoln to Mary Lincoln, June 12, 1848, *Collected Works*, I, 477–78.
62 Abraham Lincoln to Mary Lincoln, July 2, 1848, *ibid.*, I, 495–96.
63 "Autobiography of Robert T. Lincoln."
64 Ruth Painter Randall, *Lincoln's Sons*, 26–28.
65 Pratt, Review of *Lincoln's Sons*, *Saturday Review*, Vol. XXXIX (Jan. 26, 1956), 26–27.

in a pleasant, affluent world, it was brief, for by the summer of 1849, Robert was back home.

On February 1, 1850, his brother died. Robert, by then an alert boy nearing seven, must have felt the loss keenly. The death of Eddie cut Robert off from sibling associations. One who has extensively studied the personalities of the Lincoln family members notes:

> Had it not been for the death of Edward at four years, the children would have been close enough in age to have made effective the education and social value of fraternal contacts and influences, without being so close as to overtax the mother's time and energy. As it was, Robert was too old to exercise much influence on the lives of Willie and Tad, nor did they help him much. In the grouping of the children in their activities, we find Willie and Tad in close and constant association, while Robert stood apart. Those men with whom I have talked of their Lincoln associations have referred to themselves as playmates of Robert or playmates of Willie and Tad, but never as playmates of Robert *and* the younger boys. Had Edward lived, he would have bridged this gap.[66]

Just before Christmas of the same year in which Edward died, the third Lincoln son, Willie was born. Partially to take the family's mind off the loss of one son and partially to show off the new arrival, as well as for business reasons, the Lincolns visited Lexington in the summer of 1851.[67] Robert again became acquainted with the host of Todd relatives.

The eldest Lincoln son had by then begun his formal education. By all accounts, he was a bright, even precocious, child; he knew what was going on in the world about him. David Davis reported to his wife that Lincoln had told him that Robert had heard discussion of a murder case in Boston and that the boy was aware of the fate of the convicted man. In fact, he was keeping count of the days "that Dr. Webster had to live & Thursday he said that Thursday was the last night he had to live. Rather singular that the event should so mark itself . . . on a child of

[66] Evans, *Mrs. Abraham Lincoln*, 137–38.
[67] Helm, *Mary, Wife of Lincoln*, 102–106.

seven years."[68] The facts of Robert's early schooling are somewhat obscure. He himself recalled, "I have a dim recollection of being under the slipper-guardianship of a School mistress until 1850," and then for the next three years he was in attendance at an academy operated by a Mr. Esterbrook.[69] There is a tradition that when Robert was learning Latin at this time, his father studied along with him and the two declined nouns together.[70]

It appears that at this time Robert was cross-eyed, a condition which was later corrected, but before it was, his schoolmates bestowed upon him the uncomplimentary name of "Cockeye." One who knew him slightly has said that he had sight in only one eye, the other having been injured as a result of an imperfect operation in childhood.[71]

Outside the classroom there were many things of interest to the growing child. Springfield abounded with animals, and the Lincolns had their share of family pets and visiting strays. On one occasion Bobbie was bitten by what was thought to be a mad dog, and the necessary medical precautions were taken. The possibility of hydrophobia could be alleviated, it was then believed, by the use of a madstone, an object which when applied to the wound was supposed to draw off the poison. Madstones were very rare; indeed, the nearest one was in Terre Haute, Indiana, but as Robert's aunt, Mrs. Frances Wallace, later recalled, father and son journeyed to Indiana where "Bobbie" was "cured."[72] This episode did not diminish Robert's interest in canines, for another story tells of the time when Robert and his friends decided to put on a trained dog show for the enjoyment of the neighborhood children. This involved teaching the dogs to stand on their hind legs and growl like lions. The animals refused to co-operate, so the boys tied their front legs up to the rafters of the shed in which the show was to be held. By then Mr. Lincoln had heard of the

68 Willard L. King, *Lincoln's Manager, David Davis*, 73.
69 "Autobiography of Robert T. Lincoln."
70 Randall, *Mary Lincoln*, 155.
71 Paper read by Harry J. Dunbaugh of Isham, Lincoln and Beale, to the Fortnightly, Chicago, May 2, 1962. Copy in the Chicago Historical Society (hereafter CHS).
72 Herndon, *Life of Lincoln*, 352.

situation—probably the animals themselves sounded the alarm—
and came to investigate. He arrived with a barrel stave in hand
and the boys fled.[73] On other occasions Robert and a friend would
harness a dog to what was probably a child's small wagon and let
the animal provide the motive power for the vehicle. There is
also some evidence of an attempt to use cats for the same purpose
but this did not work out very well.[74]

The Lincoln sons took turns attempting to get their father
away from the office when the dinner hour arrived. On one occasion Mr. Lincoln was playing chess with Judge Samuel H. Treat
in the offices of Lincoln and Herndon when his son—generally
identified as Robert—arrived to tell him dinner was ready. The
engrossed chess player promised to come at once. Time passed
and no Lincoln arrived. The boy went back and this time succeeded in getting his father home. He merely walked over to the
chessboard and kicked it into the air, thus effectively ending the
game. Judge Treat was surprised that his friend took no action
against the child but instead merely observed, "Well, Judge, I
reckon we'll have to finish this game some other time."[75] On
another occasion evidently it was Tad who had been sent to
bring father home, but when the two were walking past a hotel,
they encountered Lincoln's friend George T. M. Davis. The men
began to talk, and a few minutes later Robert Lincoln came down
the street and joined the group. Robert and Tad were discussing
something when Lincoln turned and said, "Tad, show Mr. Davis,
the knife I bought you yesterday." To Davis, Lincoln remarked
that it was Tad's first knife, quite an event in the youngster's life.
Tad looked embarrassed and his father asked, "You haven't lost
your knife, have you?" "No, but I ain't got any." "What has become of it?" said the by now suspicious father. Tad blurted out
the story. He had been induced by his older brother to trade the
knife for some candy. Lincoln pointed out the unfairness of the
trade since the knife was worth much more than the candy. How-

[73] Randall, *Lincoln's Sons*, 33–34.
[74] Hertz, *Hidden Lincoln*, 384.
[75] Sandburg, *Lincoln: The Prairie Years*, II, 280–81.

ever, since Tad had eaten the candy, it would not be possible to return it to Robert. Lincoln solved the problem by giving Tad money to buy more candy, and the two boys rushed off to a store.[76]

The Lincoln family of Springfield was very much a self-contained unit, although there were friends and relatives in abundance. Mary Lincoln's relatives were abundant in Springfield and there were also visitors from Kentucky. Lincoln's Coles County relatives were not generally in evidence, although the daughter of Dennis Hanks did stay with the Lincolns for a short time.[77] Of all these outside the immediate family circle, the person closest to Robert was the charming Emelie Todd. Abraham Lincoln called her "Little Sister," and Robert always addressed her as "Aunt Emelie," despite the fact that she was just seven years the boy's senior. Emelie first visited Springfield in the mid-1850's and was like an older sister to Robert. They passed hours together playing checkers. When they went out driving in the carriage, Robert was, "Aunt Emelie" recorded in her diary, very careful to help her in and out of the carriage.[78] Mary Lincoln was teaching her son to be mannerly, something that all those who met him in later life would note as a distinguishing characteristic of Robert T. Lincoln.

Mary Lincoln saw to it that her sons learned other social graces. Robert and his cousin John Stuart, Jr., were taught dancing by a local dancing master.[79] Mrs. Lincoln also introduced her children to good literature, which on at least one occasion Robert put to practical use in play. After a session with Sir Walter Scott's writings, Robert went out to play knight with another boy and Emelie Todd heard her nephew proclaim, "This rock shall fly from its

[76] George T. M. Davis, *Autobiography of the Late Colonel George T. M. Davis*, 362–64.

[77] Randall, *Mary Lincoln*, 134.

[78] Helm, *Mary, Wife of Lincoln*, 103. Emelie Todd Helm's name was variously written as Emelie, Emilie, Emile and Emily, the latter being the name conferred at birth. Here the form used by Robert T. Lincoln in his most florid mood is adopted throughout. In later years Mrs. Helm was simply "Aunt Emily."

[79] John T. Stuart to Elizabeth J. Stuart, Jan. 13, 1856, quoted in Pratt, *Personal Finances*, 97.

firm base as soon as I."[80] The boy was also learning to be useful around the house. He helped his father chop wood; he ran errands and went to the store. On occasion he was forced to be the baby-sitter for Willie and Tad.

At least once the planned sitting did not come off as expected. The Lincolns had been invited to an evening reception by Mr. Dubois, the state auditor of Illinois. While Mrs. Lincoln was dressing, the two younger boys came home from a candy pull "smeared with molasses candy from head to foot." They howled when told that they were to stay at home with their older brother, and Lincoln as usual could not bear to make the boys unhappy. He decreed that they could go along but must remain out of sight in the kitchen. Robert and a neighbor girl so hastily washed and dressed the two that Tad at first got his trousers on backwards. Not only did the pair go to the Dubois home, but, of course, they did not stay in the kitchen for long.[81]

In 1858, Robert Lincoln was fifteen, his childhood was over and he was ready for a serious formal education. His father was attracting more and more public attention and all members of the family were consequently drawn into public view. Robert was generally described as an alert, bright, and likable young man. A contemporary thought him "like his mother, a Todd, in appearance and disposition."[82] It was by then the eve of the Civil War and military matters were receiving public and private attention. A cadet group, with dark-blue uniforms similar to those worn in the regular army, had been organized in Springfield and Robert was fourth corporal. In October, during the Lincoln-Douglas debates, the cadets went to Alton to hear that important political discussion, and presumably the eldest son of the Republican candidate for senator went along.[83] Young Lincoln's horizon was being considerably widened by his father's new-found promi-

---

[80] Helm, *Mary, Wife of Lincoln*, 108.

[81] Philip W. Ayres, "Lincoln as a Neighbor," *Review of Reviews*, Vol. LVII, No. 2, (Feb., 1918), 183–85.

[82] Recollections of Fred T. Dubois, Jr., quoted in Rufus R. Wilson, *Lincoln Among His Friends*, 96–101.

[83] *Illinois State Journal* (Springfield), June 29 and Oct. 16, 1858.

nence. The Lincolns toured the line of the Illinois Central Railroad in July, 1859, as Mr. Lincoln had been retained by the company in litigation arising out of taxation by the state of Illinois.[84]

[84] Carlton J. Corliss, *Main Line of Mid America: The Story of the Illinois Central*, 118.

Chapter 2

Widening Horizons

THERE WAS LOCATED IN SPRINGFIELD in the 1850's an institution of higher learning that bore the lofty title Illinois State University. This private school had opened its doors in April, 1852, and was in no way connected with the University of Illinois. It later became Concordia College, a theological seminary. At the time, however, Illinois State University could hardly have been classified as a university or even a college; it was a preparatory school. To raise money, perpetual scholarships were offered for sale at $300 each. It was then possible for an unused scholarship to be rented out by the owner. On October 1, 1852, Abraham Lincoln paid the interest on the scholarship of P. C. Canedy, and for the years that Robert Lincoln attended it cost his father $95.50 a year in interest and $1.50 in incidental fees.[1] In the fall of 1854, Robert began attending classes as one of the youngest of the fifty-two students in the preparatory department.[2] All four faculty members were ministers and the curriculum was strictly classical. By attending summers young Lincoln forged ahead and entered the freshman class at the age of thirteen; he was the youngest of seven classmates.[3] The school itself prospered and within five years after its establishment, its building, an "elegant four story

[1] Harry Evjen, "Illinois State University, 1852–1868," *JISHS*, Vol. XXXI (Mar., 1938), 57.
[2] *Ibid.*, 62.
[3] *Ibid.*

ediface," was a prominent local landmark.[4] Grades were first recorded during Robert Lincoln's junior year, and his were 85 in Greek, 80 in mathematics, 75 in chemistry, and 60 in a subject not designated but probably "composition and declamation." His work there was called average.[5] Elected a member of the Philomathean Society in December, 1856, young Robert was once fined for not attending meetings, and even after being elected recording secretary in 1858, he showed little interest in the organization.[6] Concerning the all-important matter of the quality of instruction, Robert observed, "The government was very easy, and we did just what pleased us, study consuming only a very small portion of our time."[7] Eventually he came to realize that he was wasting his time and that he "could never get an education in that way."[8]

During the years at the Springfield school, Robert's friendship with John Hay began, a friendship that lasted until Hay's death in 1905.[9] Hay was Lincoln's private secretary, secretary of state under McKinley, and, like Robert, minister to England. It has been suggested that Hay, who was nearly five years older than Robert, fulfilled the role of older brother.[10]

After Robert and his family had realized the necessity of continuing his education elsewhere, the decision was made that he should do so at Harvard. The reason for the selection of this particular institution is not known, although it has been the subject of considerable speculation. In the fall of 1855, John Hay had gone east with the intention of entering Harvard, although he eventually chose Brown University instead.[11] Perhaps it was then that Robert Lincoln decided to aim for the Cambridge school. It has also been suggested that Abraham Lincoln's "determination to give his eldest son Robert the schooling he lacked" swung the

4 Paul M. Angle, *"Here I Have Lived,"* 202–203.
5 Evjen, "Illinois State University," *JISHS*, Vol. XXXI (Mar., 1938), 62.
6 *Ibid.*
7 "Autobiography of Robert T. Lincoln."
8 *Ibid.*
9 William R. Thayer, *The Life and Letters of John Hay*, I, 20.
10 Tyler Dennett, *John Hay, From Poetry to Politics*, 59–60.
11 Thayer, *John Hay*, I, 22–23.

decision to Harvard, then as always one of the better American colleges. As a result, "Lincoln decided to send Bob to Harvard."[12] Robert is supposed to have told attorney Frederick W. Lehmann that his father wanted him to attend Harvard.[13]

Accordingly, Robert Lincoln applied for admission to college at the beginning of the fall term in 1859 and set out for the East in August.[14] He carried with him a letter of introduction from Senator Stephen A. Douglas, who presented the young man as the son of his friend Abraham Lincoln "with whom I have lately been canvassing the State of Illinois."[15] In light of later history, it is ironical that the letter came from Douglas, but at that time the Senator's fame extended far and wide, while it is said that when Robert Lincoln presented himself in Cambridge, only one member of the Harvard faculty, James Russell Lowell, had ever heard the name Abraham Lincoln.[16]

When young Lincoln arrived at Harvard, he took the entrance examinations to gain admission. That the education he had received in Springfield was woefully deficient is indicated by his failure to pass the examinations. As he later recalled, "On being examined I had the honor to receive a fabulous number of conditions which precluded my admission."[17] The Harvard archives contain two sets of admission examinations used in 1859. One is dated July and the other September 1, and the prospective student from Illinois would have taken the latter. Several subjects were covered, with Greek and Latin emphasized. The test in the latter language included not only questions of grammar, but also several sentences to be translated from English into Latin. Typical was:

Let there be friendship for King Antiochus with the Roman people: let him depart from the cities on this side of Mount Taurus;

[12] Elwin L. Page, *Abraham Lincoln in New Hampshire*, 5–6.
[13] Walter B. Stevens, *A Reporter's Lincoln*, 72.
[14] Mary Todd Lincoln in a letter of Aug. 28, 1859, mentions that "Bob, left for college, in Boston, a few days since . . . ." Randall, *Lincoln's Sons*, 62.
[15] Quoted in J. Seymour Currey, *Chicago*, II, 82.
[16] Edward Everett Hale, *James Russell Lowell and His Friends*, 200–201.
[17] "Autobiography of Robert T. Lincoln."

let him carry forth no arms from those towns from which he may depart; if he has carried any forth, let him return them.

Geometry, algebra, and arithmetic were also covered in the examinations. Arithmetic questions ranged from the simple "Add together 23⅝, 28⁸⁄₁₂, 37³⁄₁₅, and 17½" to the more complicated "If 7 ounces of quicksilver cost 6 shillings, what is the cost of a pound, in shillings, pence, and farthings?" The history examination dealt with ancient matters and a typical question was "For what do you remember the year 218 BC?"

His failure to pass the Harvard entrance examinations was probably Robert Lincoln's first serious defeat. He must have been disheartened and, no doubt, very homesick. No known letter that passed then between the unhappy boy and his parents has survived, but it may be imagined that Abraham Lincoln consoled his own son even more sympathetically than he did Robert's friend, George Latham, when that young man failed the same set of examinations a year later. Then the busy Republican candidate for President took time to write:

I have scarcely felt greater pain in my life than on learning yesterday from Bob's letter, that you had failed to enter Harvard University. And yet there is very little in it, if you will allow no feeling of *discouragement* to seize, and prey upon you. It is a *certain* truth, that you *can* enter, and graduate in, Harvard University; and having made the attempt, you *must* succeed in it. "*Must*" is the word.

I know not how to aid you, save in the assurance of one of mature age, and much severe experience, that you *can* not fail, if you resolutely determine, that you *will* not.

The President of the institution can scarcely be other than a kind man; and doubtless would grant you an interview, and point out the readiest way to remove, or overcome, the obstacles which have thwarted you.

In your temporary failure there is no evidence that you may not yet be a better scholar, and a more successful man in the great struggle of life, than many others, who have entered college more easily.

25

Again I say let no feeling of discouragement prey upon you, and in the end you are sure to succeed.[18]

Robert Lincoln wrote of his own failure, "I was resolved not to retire beaten, and acting under the advice of President Walker [of Harvard], I entered the well-known Academy at Exeter, N.H."[19]

The "Academy at Exeter" was the famous preparatory school Phillips Exeter Academy. In Robert's words: "I went to Exeter, hoping to enter the Class preparing to enter college, the next July, as Sophomores. The worthy Principal, Dr. Soule, soon convinced me of the vanity of my aspirations and I was obliged to enter the Subfreshman Class."[20] Phillips Exeter had first opened its doors in April, 1783, and through the years had produced a number of distinguished alumni. Daniel Webster, Lewis Cass, Franklin Pierce, and George Bancroft were among its former students. The school had an excellent reputation and indeed could claim that it was "altogether the best-endowed institution of its class in the State of New Hampshire, if not in the country."[21]

The dominant figure of the Academy from 1838 to 1872 was the "worthy Principal," Gideon Lane Soule, Bowdoin graduate and, prior to assuming charge of the school, professor of ancient languages. Although it has been said that "as a teacher Dr. Soule was neither original nor progressive,"[22] he was well regarded by students and alumni.

When he entered his recitation room . . . , the class rose and remained standing until he bowed for it to sit. This was not mere form; it was genuine respect for the good doctor, whom all so loved and reverenced.[23]

[18] Abraham Lincoln to George C. Latham, July 22, 1860, *Collected Works*, IV, 87.

[19] "Autobiography of Robert T. Lincoln."

[20] *Ibid.* Lincoln means *subfreshman*, in the sense of the work not being on the college level.

[21] Professor Joseph G. Hoyt, quoted in Myron R. Williams, *The Story of Phillips Exeter*, 49. Robert Lincoln years later contributed to his school and thus further increased its endowment. Unidentified newspaper clipping dated 1921, Lincoln National Life Insurance Company, Fort Wayne, Indiana.

[22] Laurence M. Crosbie, *The Phillips Exeter Academy*, 94.

The principal, in addition to his administrative duties, taught Latin and placed equal stress on the language and on its literature. Students were constantly being called upon to recite in class, and many years afterward Robert Lincoln described Soule's selection method: "I shall never forget his lottery system of calling up a boy in recitation. The little tickets were carefully faced downward in a tin box, and delicately picked out, one by one, with the moistened tip of his finger, and laid aside until the name of the fellow he was after was reached."[24]

It seems likely that the principal was teaching more than his usual class in 1859, for the faculty was composed of only two other men. They became notable in their own right, but that year they were only commencing their careers. George Albert Wentworth had joined the staff as professor of mathematics in March, 1858, and Bradbury Longfellow Cilley became classics professor in February, 1859. Wentworth remained at the school until 1892; his colleague and Harvard classmate, Cilley, taught there until a month before his death in 1899.[25] Together with Dr. Soule they earned the name "The Great Triumvirate."[26] Robert Lincoln seems to have been instructed chiefly by Wentworth, of whom he later said, "He was, and still is, I suppose, a 'driver.' I shall always think him the most thorough instructor I ever saw."[27] This gentleman, "because of his burly frame and roaring habit in the classroom . . . was commonly known as 'Bull' "[28] Professor Cilley also seems to have been an interesting figure. He was described as "a gruff, warm-hearted veteran with a domelike head and piercing eyes, who hated affectation and sham, and . . . dismayed the timid with his roaring."[29]

Although the Academy was considered a good school, it gen-

23 Rev. A. P. Peabody, quoted in Frank H. Cunningham, *Familiar Sketches of the Phillips Exeter Academy and Surroundings*, 57.

24 Quoted *ibid.*, 57–58.

25 For material on Wentworth and Cilley, see Williams, *Phillips Exeter*, 64–65, and Crosbie, *Phillips Exeter*, 110–112.

26 Crosbie, *Phillips Exeter*, 110.

27 Quoted in Cunningham, *Sketches of Phillips Exeter*, 149.

28 Williams, *Phillips Exeter*, 64.

29 *Ibid.*, 65.

erally reflected an air of stagnant tradition. Reforms were on the way, but they were not realized until long after Robert Lincoln left. Just prior to his period of residence, the school had been fortunate in having on its staff Joseph Gibson Hoyt, who at Exeter was called the "Great Teacher." During his service there he endeavored to bring about some much-needed reform, but he left in 1858 to take another position.[30] The curriculum at Exeter in 1859 "was still characterized by devotion to the classics, Greek and Latin, with just a smattering of mathematics and a little history."[31] This situation was not changed until after Dr. Soule retired, for "changes in the course of study came slowly, and it is little exaggeration to say that with very few alterations, the curriculum in 1872 closely resembled that of 1818."[32]

When Robert Lincoln enrolled at Exeter, September 15, 1859, the school was small, with only 134 students during the academic year 1859–60.[33] Unfortunately there is no record of the subjects he took or the grades he made.[34] Most of the students lived in Abbot Hall, a dormitory in use after the mid-1850's, but, for one reason or another, Robert Lincoln did not live there. Perhaps the hall was filled or perhaps he desired to live elsewhere. For a time he visited at the Exeter home of Amos Tuck, a friend of his father's.[35] Then he took up permanent residence as a roomer in the home of Mr. and Mrs. Samuel B. Clarke, whose address was 7 Pleasant Street, not far from the campus.[36] There Lincoln shared a room with his friend George Latham. Abraham Lincoln paid his son's tuition, which amounted to $24 a year, plus room and board. If Robert had boarded on campus, the cost would have been approximately $1.30 to $1.50 a week, but it cost more to live in private homes—$2.25 and upwards.[37] Mr. Lincoln's financial

[30] Crosbie, *Phillips Exeter*, 96–102.
[31] *Ibid.*, 111.
[32] Williams, *Phillips Exeter*, 46.
[33] *Ibid.*, 209.
[34] All records prior to the year 1873 were destroyed by fire. Letter to the author from Gertrude E. Starks, alumni secretary, Phillips Exeter Academy, July 1, 1958.
[35] Page, *Lincoln in New Hampshire*, 98.
[36] Letter to the author from Gertrude E. Starks, July 1, 1958.
[37] Crosbie, *Phillips Exeter*, 202.

records indicate that from time to time he sent Robert checks or money orders to cover his expenses and to give him extra spending money.[38]

Students at the Academy in the 1850's were treated as children, not as young men. On the opening day of each year, Dr. Soule would announce to the assembled student body, "The Academy has no rules—until they are broken." Then he would usually continue, "But there is one rule I wish to make; whoever crosses the threshold of a billiard saloon, crosses the threshold of the Academy for the last time."[39] Without doubt, this caused countless students to go to the billiard parlor out of curiosity, although they would never have done so had the issue not been raised. One important change in the routine of Exeter had been made the year before Robert arrived. No longer did the students have to do their studying outside of class under the watchful eye of an instructor, but they could now work in their own rooms. However, they had to be in those rooms by seven in the evening.[40] It is not recorded whether the Clarkes made Lincoln and Latham adhere to this rule.

Robert Lincoln soon settled into the routine of academy life. He was now on his own and no longer under the family roof. He made new friends easily and was very well liked by his fellow students, as well as by the townspeople of Exeter. One of his classmates, Marshall S. Snow, later president of Washington University in St. Louis, recalled that he was a "very popular young fellow, a gentleman in every sense of the word," and very popular with the girls of the town.[41] For the most part, the year was as Robert himself once said, "devoid of excitement and full of hard work."[42] It was "characterized by little worth noting, except perhaps, a flight from Justice." The story of this "flight from Justice." has often been told, but all Robert said of it was that he fled from the pursuit by justice "in the shape of a policeman all over the

38 Pratt, *Personal Finances.*
39 Crosbie, *Phillips Exeter*, 95.
40 *Ibid.*, 98.
41 Quoted in Mearns, *Lincoln Papers*, I, 6.
42 Cunningham, *Sketches of Phillips Exeter*, 149.

flourishing village, for having, in company with others, committed sundry depredations on the property of various denizens. Filthy lucre, also the root of all evil, proved a great blessing in the present case," for they all got off by paying damages.[43] Presumably Robert and some friends had gone through the town of Exeter unhinging and carrying off fence gates. The group was apprehended and called to account. According to one version of the story, they were taken before the local justice of the peace, and according to another, before Dr. Soule. In both accounts it is said that young Lincoln's name was excluded from the list of culprits because of the prominence of his father, but that he refused such immunity and admitted his part in the prank.[44]

The highlight of Robert's year at Exeter was the visit of his father early in 1860. Without doubt his mother wished to make the trip too, but that was not possible. For a time financial considerations prevented Mr. Lincoln from making a visit, but late in 1859 he made his plans to go early the following year. He had received an offer to make a speech in New York for which he would be paid the sum of two hundred dollars plus expenses. This was to be the famous Cooper Union address, delivered February 27, 1860, which is said by many to have made Lincoln well enough known in the East that he was able to win the presidency later in the year. However, the speech was merely a by-product of Lincoln's desire to see his son. The trip "appealed to the father, not the politician."[45] According to Robert Lincoln, "It had not been his plan to do any speaking in New England, but as a result of the address in New York, he received requests from New England friends for speeches."[46] After the Cooper Union address, Mr. Lincoln traveled north toward Exeter. He arrived in the town from Providence, Rhode Island, on February 29, 1860, probably on the 4:27 P.M. train.[47] The day before, Robert Lincoln had re-

43 "Autobiography of Robert T. Lincoln."

44 New York *Tribune,* June 10, 1878.

45 Page, *Lincoln in New Hampshire,* 7.

46 Robert T. Lincoln to George H. Putnam, July, 1908, quoted in George H. Putnam, *Memories of My Youth,* 83–84.

47 Paul M. Angle, *Lincoln, 1854–1861,* 322.

ceived a letter from George W. Benn, a Republican leader of Dover, New Hampshire, inquiring about the possibility of Abraham Lincoln's speaking at Dover. Benn did not know Robert's first name so addressed him as "To ——— Lincoln, son of A. Lincoln."[48] How ironical this is in light of Robert's later life, for he was always destined to be Lincoln, son of A. Lincoln. Despite the limited address the letter was received, and Robert answered it as follows:

> EXETER, February 28
>
> DEAR SIR:—Your letter did not reach me until this evening. Mr. Lincoln is to speak in Providence, R.I., this evening, and will be here as soon as possible after that—probably to-morrow afternoon. I will give him your letter as soon as he arrives and he will answer it for himself, though I have no doubt he will be happy to comply with your kind invitation should his time permit.
>
> Yours truly,
>
> R. T. LINCOLN[49]

Robert must certainly have met his father at the station, and it is presumed that Mr. Lincoln spent the night with his son in the boys' quarters. Early the next morning, March 1, the father and son, together with George Latham, set out for Concord.[50] The trip was short, and when they arrived they were taken to their hotel, which was next door to the place where Lincoln was to speak.[51] The address was made at 1:45 P.M. as scheduled, and later the party went to the local courthouse where Judge Asa Fowler declared a recess in court proceedings so that Frederick Smyth, a local Republican leader, could introduce "Lincoln and his son to the judge and members of the bar who were present."[52] Following the Concord appearance, the party went on to Manchester, where the visitor from Illinois again spoke. The party then checked into the City Hotel and there they spent the night, returning to Exeter the next day. Mr. Lincoln went on to Dover

---

48 Page, *Lincoln in New Hampshire*, 26.
49 Robert T. Lincoln to George W. Benn, Feb. 28, 1860, quoted *ibid*.
50 Angle, *Lincoln, 1854–1861*, 322.
51 Page, *Lincoln in New Hampshire*, 30.
52 *Ibid*., 32.

to fulfill the engagement mentioned previously, but the boys did not accompany him.[53] The next day Robert's father was back in Exeter and it and the following day, Sunday, March 4, were about the only time he had free with his son.

Although it has been reported that "During his days in Exeter, Lincoln was seen much in Robert's company," still their schedule was so busy that it left little time for them to relax.[54] Sunday morning they attended the Second Church of the New Parish, of which the Reverend Orpheus T. Lamphear was the pastor. After the service father and son walked back to Robert's lodgings, and in the evening the latter had a group of friends in to meet his father. "Into the chatter Lincoln entered with true boy-like spirit."[55] In the course of the conversation, Robert remarked that one of the boys present, Henry Cluskey, played the banjo. "Does he?" asked Lincoln, and wanted to know where the instrument was. Soon the banjo was brought from Cluskey's quarters, the owner indicating that he would have brought it with him initially but he thought Mr. Lincoln would not care for it. Cluskey then gave an impromptu concert, after which Mr. Lincoln, indicating the banjo, said "with unaffected pleasure, 'Robert, you ought to have one.' "[56]

While the potential presidential nominee was in Exeter, he spoke on Saturday evening before an audience composed of townspeople and the faculty and students of the Academy. A local citizen, Judge Underwood, made a speech of introduction, but wrote one who was there, "I confess I heard none of it, nor did those of my friends who sat near me." Instead, the boys were intently watching Mr. Lincoln, "tall, lank, awkward; dressed in a loose, ill-fitting, black frock coat, with black trousers, ill fitting and somewhat baggy at the knees." They were much disappointed in the gentleman's appearance and whispered to one another, "Isn't it too bad Bob's father is so homely? Don't you feel sorry

[53] Abraham Lincoln to Mary Lincoln, Mar. 4, 1860, Abraham Lincoln Papers, Library of Congress.
[54] Page, *Lincoln in New Hampshire*, 112.
[55] *Ibid.*, 113.
[56] *Ibid.*

for him." The same observer continues to describe what happened after Underwood had finished:

He [Lincoln] rose slowly, untangled those long legs from their contact with the rounds of the chair, drew himself up to his full height of six feet, four inches, and began his speech. Not ten minutes had passed before his uncouth appearance was absolutely forgotten by us boys, and, I believe, by all of that large audience. . . . There was no more pity for our friend Bob; we were proud of his father. . . .[57]

All too soon the visit came to a close, and early Monday morning, Mr. Lincoln boarded the train for Hartford, Connecticut, and began the last week of his New England tour.[58] Robert now resumed his studies after an exciting few days. He did not see his father again until January of 1861, when he went home to Springfield.[59] No wonder people would later say he was ill informed on this eventful period in the Lincoln family's history for, except for the letters from home, he was far removed from the happenings of that time.

The year 1860 continued to be an eventful one for the Lincolns, and the family was drawn more and more into the public gaze. On May 16, 1860, the Republican National Convention met in Chicago and, on the third ballot, nominated Robert's father for the presidency. Hours later the news reached Exeter, and a friend of the younger Lincoln, Albert Blair, upon hearing it ran to find the one who would be most interested in it. Blair found Bob in a bowling alley "much frequented by him," where he was calmly engaged in a game. "Blair flourished the paper and yelled, 'Bob, your father got it!' 'Good!' said Bob, slapping his hip. 'I will have to write home for a check before he spends all of his money in the campaign.' "[60] Still, the nomination brought its serious consequences. Not only Mr. and Mrs. Lincoln but their sons as well were now considered by the citizenry to be at least semipublic

57 Recollections of Marshall S. Snow, quoted in Crosbie, *Phillips Exeter*, 257–58.
58 Page, *Lincoln in New Hampshire*, 114; Angle, *Lincoln 1854–1861*, 322.
59 Robert T. Lincoln to Truman H. Bartlett, Dec. 26, 1916, Boston University Library.
60 Page, *Lincoln in New Hampshire*, 134.

property. It marked a turning point in Robert's life, for the public gaze focused on him in 1860 never ceased during the next sixty-six years of his life. Members of the family reacted differently to the publicity. Outwardly, Robert was living up to expectations. Amos Tuck wrote David Davis that young Lincoln "has behaved himself as the son of Abraham Lincoln might be expected to do. He stands at the top of the ladder as a scholar, and is a singularly discreet, well behaved, brilliant and promising young man." Not only was he all of this, but he had joined a group of "Wide Awakes" in Exeter and had taken part in the raising of a Lincoln and Hamlin banner.[61] Privately, Robert Lincoln was not at all fond of what was happening.

On the Fourth of July in that crucial year of 1860, the good citizens of New Hampshire held the customary celebrations. At Stratham Hill, halfway between Portsmouth and Exeter, there was scheduled a fine gathering. There would be singing, music, oratory, and strawberries for refreshments. Posters were put up to announce the gathering, the highlight of which would be the reading of the Declaration of Independence by the son of the Republican nominee for President. A hitch in the proceedings developed when Robert refused to perform unless his father gave his permission. One suspects that getting parental permission was a dodge to avoid the matter altogether. However, Mr. Lincoln is supposed to have telegraphed, "Tell Bob to read that immortal document every chance he has, and the bigger the crowd, the louder he must holler."[62] This Robert did with all his might and "entered into the spirit of the occasion with all the fervor of youth."[63]

When the election was over, Mr. Lincoln was the President-elect and the publicity became even more intense. Early in December, Robert inquired of his mother in a joking manner, "Aint you beginning to get a little tired of this constant uproar?"[64]

[61] Amos Tuck to David Davis, Aug. 24, 1860, quoted in Randall, *Lincoln's Sons*, 70.

[62] Frank Fuller, *A Day With the Lincoln Family*, rare booklet in ISHL.

[63] *Ibid.*

Writing while on a visit to Exeter, for he was now a resident of Cambridge, Massachusetts, he reported that he and his friend Dick Meconkey had "been in a constant round of dissipation since we came." "Dissipation" included "dinner at Miss Gale's" and a large party given by Amos Tuck. However, Robert had something about which to complain; he had already written his father about an individual who had apparently been trying to gain political influence with the President-elect through his son:

> He capped the climax lately. There was a Republican levee and supper at Cambridge, to which I was invited—I did not go for I anticipated what really happened.
>
> I was sitting in my room about 9½ when two boys came up and handed me an admission ticket in the back of which this fellow had written, asking me to come over as they were calling for me.—I wrote him a note excusing myself. He must be the biggest fool in the world not to know that I did not want to go over, when if I did, I would be expected to make a speech! Just phancy my phelinks mounted on the rostrum, holding "a vast sea of human faces" & c. I stop overwhelmed. Yours affectionately.
>
> R. T. LINCOLN[65]

Robert Lincoln's visit to Exeter, late in 1860, took place some weeks after he entered Harvard. This was an important, as well as exciting, period in the life of the young man. He was, at last, safely in the college of his choice; his father was President-elect; the Civil War was almost at hand; and the Lincolns were preparing to embark early in 1861 for Washington and their new life. There were many preparations to be made. Mrs. Lincoln decided to go to New York on a shopping expedition, and Robert joined her there.[66] It was reported that while in the metropolis young Lincoln visited "the Stock Exchange, Treasurer's office and other public places, where he was kindly received and shown the various objects of interest which might please the young

[64] Robert T. Lincoln to Mary Lincoln, Dec. 2, 1860, quoted in Page, *Lincoln in New Hampshire*, 22–23.

[65] *Ibid.*

[66] New York *Herald*, Jan. 23, 1861.

gentleman from the Far West."[67] Mother and son left New York for home on January 23, 1861,[68] and arrived in Springfield the evening of the next day, where they were met by the President-elect.[69] The Springfield press now reported, " 'Bob' who is out on vacation furlough from Cambridge, is in robust health, and meets with a cordial welcome home, from his old associates and friends."[70]

By February the family's plans were complete, and they were ready to start for their new home. On the evening of the sixth of the month, they gave a final reception for their friends. One who was present described it as the biggest crowd she had ever seen assembled in a private home. That same guest noted that Robert Lincoln was very much in evidence, and "While I was standing near Mr. L. he came up, and in his humorous style, gave his hand to his father saying: 'Good evening *Mr. Lincoln!*' In reply his father gave him a gentle slap in the face."[71] On the morning of February 11, nearly all of Springfield was gathered at the Great Western Railroad depot. A special train waited to take the President-elect and his party to Washington. Slowly Abraham Lincoln, accompanied by his eldest son and a group of friends, walked through the crowd and boarded the train. As he stood on the back platform of the last car, Mr. Lincoln turned and looked out over the assembled crowd. A few words of farewell were uttered, and in one of his most touching speeches, he spoke of his past life and of the uncertain future that lay ahead. The train jerked forward and the journey had begun. Mrs. Lincoln and the two younger boys left Springfield later in the same day and were reunited with the others at Indianapolis the next day.

The trip was a serious affair, but Robert has been described as "probably the happiest and most carefree member of the party."[72] However, there was one aspect of the situation that pleased him

[67] *Ibid.*

[68] *Ibid.*, Jan. 24, 1861.

[69] Angle, *Lincoln, 1854–1861*, 369.

[70] *Illinois State Journal*, Jan. 28, 1861.

[71] Mrs. James Conkling to her son, Clinton, Feb. 12, 1861, quoted in Randall, *Mary Lincoln*, 195.

[72] Helen Nicolay, *Lincoln's Secretary*, 63.

not at all. He was frequently called upon, as were the other members of the family, to say a word or two to the assembled crowds that lined the railroad tracks. By this time the eldest Lincoln son had acquired a nickname, "The Prince of Rails."[73] Only the year before, the Prince of Wales, later Edward VII of England, had visited the United States, and it was inevitable that the eldest son of the "rail-splitter" should be nicknamed by the press. At Indianapolis the crowd called for the "Prince," but Robert only responded with a wave of the hand. Mr. Lincoln wanted to relieve the boy's embarrassment and so told the crowd that "his boy, Bob, hadn't got in the way of making speeches."[74] When the party reached Cincinnati, Robert Lincoln was honored at a banquet given him by fifty young men of the city. It was held the evening of February 12, and the food was plentiful and good. "The volley of corks that flew for a time reminded one of hostile operations." Yet, when there came the inevitable call for a speech, the guest of honor politely declined.[75] On through Ohio went the special train, and then into western Pennsylvania. From that state the party went north into New York. At Albany the President-elect made another of his countless speeches, and when the Lincoln's reboarded the train to go to New York City, Robert rode part of the distance in the locomotive cab.[76]

Somewhere along the trip an event of potentially great calamity took place. Throughout most of the trip, Mr. Lincoln had been constantly in possession of a gripsack containing his inaugural address. However, at one point, he turned it over to Robert for safekeeping, but neglected to tell the young man the precious contents of the case.[77] Later, when the President-elect

73 Harry W. Gourley to Robert T. Lincoln, Feb. 22, 1861, Abraham Lincoln Papers. The letter is addressed, "To His Royal Highness, the Prince of Rails."

74 Cincinnati *Daily Commercial*, quoted in Randall, *Mary Lincoln*, 201.

75 Cincinnati *Gazette*, quoted in Carl Sandburg, *Abraham Lincoln: The War Years*, I, 43.

76 Sandburg, *Lincoln: The War Years*, I, 54.

77 There is not complete agreement about where the incident took place. *Ibid.*, I, 74, indicates that it was at Harrisburg, Ben: Perley Poore, *Perley's Reminiscences*, 65–67, concurs, as do other sources. Nicolay, *Lincoln's Secretary*, 63–64, implies that it was at Indianapolis. Miss Nicolay got her information from Robert T. Lincoln.

asked for its return, his son casually reported that he had given it to a porter and let him take it to the hotel. Accounts of Mr. Lincoln's reaction to this vary. One witness, Ward H. Lamon, who later came to have an intense dislike for Robert T. Lincoln, claimed that the President-elect lost his temper for the first time on the trip.[78] However, one who was told of the incident by Robert Lincoln himself, wrote quoting her source, "Father did not scold."[79] Abraham Lincoln immediately went to the hotel baggage room and began searching for the lost article, undoubtedly thinking of the results of the address' falling into the wrong hands. Any newspaper would have given much to have an advance copy of the speech. At last the gripsack was found, unopened, and the owner "carried the bag back to his room, handed it once more to his son, told him this time what it contained, and added, 'Now you keep it!' "[80]

As the travelers went south, the reception they received changed. There were rumors of a plot to assassinate Mr. Lincoln in Baltimore, and those in charge of his safety removed him from the train and sped him into Washington by another special train.[81] When Lincoln was separated from his family, Mrs. Lincoln became very alarmed and fearful for her husband's safety. To Robert fell the task of calming his mother as much as it was possible to do so, and he also took over the task of attempting to keep up the spirits of the remainder of the party. "To counteract the depression, Bob Lincoln had led the party in a rendition of 'The Star-Spangled Banner' as the cars crossed the Maryland line."[82] The brief stay in Baltimore had been trying for all members of the party. Groups of "plug-uglies" hurled epithets at Mrs. Lincoln, and John Hay slammed the door in the face of one man who tried to force his way into her carriage.[83] At the same time, "a rough pressed his face against a window, leered at Robert Lin-

[78] Sandburg, *Lincoln: The War Years*, I, 74–75.

[79] Nicolay, *Lincoln's Secretary*, 65.

[80] *Ibid.*

[81] Norma B. Cuthbert, *Lincoln and the Baltimore Plot, 1861* is a good account of the incident.

[82] Margaret Leech, *Reveille in Washington*, 37.

[83] Robert S. Harper, *Lincoln and the Press*, 88.

coln, and asked 'How's your old man?' Robert, who was calmly smoking a cigar at the time, declined to answer."[84]

The Lincolns were safely reunited on the afternoon of February 23 and were soon settled in their hotel. The following days were busy ones for the head of the family, but the rest of the Lincolns had some free time to themselves. One can only guess that Robert was probably busy becoming acquainted with the capital, for it was his first visit there since he was a small boy. He had, at least, one close friend with him, John Hay, who was to be the President's assistant secretary throughout the next four years.

March 4 brought the inauguration, with Mrs. Lincoln and the boys in attendance. It was the first of many such scenes that Robert Lincoln watched. He was now the son of President Lincoln, a title that would remain with him to the day of his death. During the years 1861 to 1865, Robert Lincoln was not only a student, he was a public figure as well. The young man was subjected to almost constant attention from the press and the population in general. This was a difficult position for him, especially as he came more and more to dislike the publicity. Even at this early date a familiar popular notion of this presidential son was beginning to form. If he held himself aloof from the prying gaze of the public, he was haughty and snobbish; if he gave any appearance of capitalizing on his position as the son of the Chief Executive, he was damned for that. Steadfastly he adhered, as he would for the next six decades, to the former position, and while "some people inevitably called him proud and affected," yet "he conducted himself sensibly during a prolonged ordeal of popular attention and flattery."[85] Rumors of one sort or another were circulating about him almost constantly. Even before the inauguration unfavorable stories about him were invented, and a friendly segment of the press felt it necessary to comment:

> He is a young man of fine abilities and much dignity of character. The reports in various papers intimating that his course of life is what is popularly denominated "fast," are strictly erroneous, and

84 *Ibid.*
85 Leech, *Reveille in Washington,* 41.

39

no less painful to him than to his excellent parents, to whom he has ever been a dutiful and affectionate son.[86]

Another account contrasted the son with the father, something that would not be unknown in the future: "The effect of a residence within the improving influence of genteel, well dressed and well behaved Boston is plainly noticeable in his outward appearance, the comparative elegance of which presents a striking contrast to the loose, careless, awkward rigging of his Presidential father."[87]

[86] Harper, *Lincoln and the Press*, 86, quoting the New York *Tribune*, Feb. 22, 1861.
[87] Henry Villard, *Lincoln on the Eve of '61*, 54.

Chapter 3

College Years

Robert T. Lincoln entered Harvard as a member of the Class of 1864. Since it was necessary to have his college bond signed by a citizen of Massachusetts, his father got David Davis to have it done by the Judge's brother-in-law, Julius Rockwell.[1] Harvard was probably the best college then existing in the United States, but by later standards it was inadequate in many ways. Perhaps no one better characterized the school of this period than Henry Adams when he observed that it "taught little, and that little ill."[2] Still it did have the saving grace of leaving "the mind open, free from bias, ignorant of facts, but docile."[3] The Harvard of 1860 was more than a decade away from the revolution brought to it by Charles W. Eliot. The then prevailing philosophy was that college men were children, and as such, they were more in need of discipline than education.

A member of Robert Lincoln's own class of 1864, Professor George H. Palmer, some fifty years after their graduation, looked back at the college they had known and characterized it thus:

> Harvard University, when our Class entered it, was an advanced high school, with only 896 students and forty teachers in all its departments. Excepting a single study in the Junior and another in

1 King, *Lincoln's Manager*, 149–50.
2 Henry Adams, *The Education of Henry Adams*, 55.
3 *Ibid.*

the Senior year, all our work was prescribed and, therefore, elementary. Greek and Latin were required for three years, Mathematics for two. There was no instruction in English literature, nor could any modern language count for a degree, although a year's work on Anglo-Saxon was demanded of us all. There was but one course in History, one in Philosophy, three in text-book Science, and half a course in Economics. The opportunities for writing English were about the same as those for writing Latin. Few lectures were given, and to only two or three of our instructors did it occur that it was possible to interest us in our studies.[4]

The elective system being yet some years in the future, Robert Lincoln settled down to work on the required courses. In his first year, 1860–61, he studied composition, Greek, Latin, mathematics, elocution, and, in the first term, religious instruction, replaced in the second by history. In his Sophomore year, 1861–62, the subjects taken were Greek, Latin, mathematics, rhetoric and themes, chemistry, and elocution in the first term but replaced by botany in the second. The Junior year, 1862–63, brought with it the privilege of taking one elective, which was French, studied both terms. The regular courses were Greek, Latin, physics, chemistry (first term only), declamations (first term only), themes (first term only), and rhetoric (second term only). The course of study for Lincoln's final year, 1863–64, was history, physics, forensics, philosophy, political economy, and one elective, which was, this time, Italian.[5]

Then, as always, Harvard could boast of a distinguished faculty, including such men as Louis Agassiz, Oliver Wendell Holmes, James Russell Lowell, and Asa Gray.[6] So far as is known, Robert Lincoln formed a lifelong association with only one of his instructors, James Russell Lowell, then Smith professor of French and Spanish languages and literatures and professor of belles-lettres. Many years later the former student wrote that he

4 Harvard College, *Class of 1864, Secretary's Report*, No. 8, 180.

5 From the records of Harvard College. Letter to the author from Kimball C. Elkins, senior assistant in the Harvard University Archives, July 28, 1958.

6 *A Catalogue of the Officers and Students of Harvard University for the Academical Year, 1860–1861*, 6.

had studied Dante under the poet and man of letters and "when now I take up my Dante, Mr. Lowell seems to be with me."[7] He remembered the Professor for "his erudition, humor and kindness," which made the association with him memorable beyond any other college experience.[8] Many years after the Harvard days, when Robert Lincoln was minister to England—a post Lowell himself had once held–the former teacher wrote to Henry White:

> I do not wonder that you like Mr. Lincoln. I have known him since he was a boy and always thought well of him. He was in one of my classes at Harvard. I don't think he distinguished himself as a scholar—perhaps that may have been my fault as much as his— but he was always an honest fellow with no harm in him and I was sure he would turn out well.[9]

In the 1860's the grading system in the College was an elaborate point method based on both scholarship and deportment. A student could earn points by good classroom performance, only to have them taken away by some minor infringement of the established rules of conduct.[10] The Class of 1864 contained ninety-nine men who were graduated. In his Senior year Robert Lincoln was tied with two others for thirtieth position in the class, with a merit ranking of seventy-nine based on a scale of one hundred. For the entire four years of study, he was tied with one other man for thirty-second position, with a mark of sixty-nine, also on a scale of one hundred. Hence, it may be concluded that Robert Lincoln as a student was somewhat above the average, but by no means the most successful in his class.

The academic year at Harvard was organized so as to provide several periods of vacation. Students often arranged other vacations less formally sanctioned. The fall semester started in late August or early September and ran until mid-January, with a brief vacation at Thanksgiving. There was a six-weeks vacation between terms and another brief one late in May. By special ar-

7 Hale, *Lowell and His Friends*, 142–43.
8 *Ibid.*
9 James Russell Lowell to Henry White, Oct. 11, 1890, quoted in Allan Nevins, *Henry White*, 69.
10 Mark DeWolfe Howe, *Justice Oliver Wendell Holmes*, 36–37.

rangement it was possible for students to be absent up to thirteen weeks in the first term for the purpose of "keeping school." Commencement was held toward the end of July.[11]

Upon arriving in Cambridge in 1860, Robert took rooms at "Pasco's, corner of Main & Linden Sts.," where he resided during his Freshman year. Then, for the next two years, he lived in Room 22 of Stoughton, a campus dormitory, and finally, in his Senior year, he roomed in Hollis 25, also on campus.[12] During these years the young man from Springfield was a celebrity, but this fact probably counted for less in Cambridge than it would have in many places. Harvard was accustomed to educating the sons of important men. One newspaper writer said that "of course his parentage gave him celebrity . . . but it was a very insignificant factor in determining his essential importance."[13]

It was the custom at Harvard in the 1860's for the Sophomores to haze the Freshmen. Early in the fall after Lincoln arrived, members of the Class of 1863 descended upon the new arrivals one night and, in the process, hauled Robert Lincoln from his bed. "Tell us," they demanded as he stood before them in his nightshirt, "are you the son of the Mr. Lincoln who is named by the Republicans for the presidency?" The young man admitted that he was. The next question was, "What manner of man is this father of yours?" Robert's reply was simple and straightforward. "Father is the queerest old cuss you ever saw." The author of this anecdote recalled that "Bob" Lincoln promptly became a great favorite around the campus.[14]

Another friend said that one of his "most vivid recollections" was of "young Lincoln, as he hied with nimble and elastic step across the college campus, the shrewd, good-natured glance of his eye, the quick and abrupt nod to right and left as he greeted passing friends, his cheery voice as he hailed some crony or another

11 Harvard University catalogues, 1860–64.
12 "Autobiography of Robert T. Lincoln."
13 Unidentified newspaper clipping, "The New War Secretary," Harvard University Archives.
14 H. S. Wardner to the "Editor of the Bulletin," n.d., copy in the Vermont Historical Society. Charles S. Fairchild, a Harvard graduate of 1863, told the story to Wardner.

with some odd nick-name of his own fresh coinage."[15] Still another remembered that he "was a sturdy, whole-souled, modest fellow, of strong affections and friendships, and to his closer friends he was without reserve and delightfully entertaining."[16]

While at Harvard, Robert T. Lincoln was a member of the famed Hasty Pudding Club. "On Friday nights during junior and senior years Bob was one of the choicest spirits at the meetings."[17] He took part in the plays put on by this group, "and to this day tradition speaketh loud under the Cambridge elm of how Lincoln used to enact the villainy of 'Old Daddy Wylie' in Hardwicke's 'Bachelor of Arts' or illustrated the swinging passion of that cruel parient [parent] 'Russett,' in the 'Jealous Wife.' "[18]

For all of their frivolity, Harvard students of the period 1861 to 1864 could hardly forget that there was a bitter war in progress. Although many joined the service, many more remained in school until they had finished their studies.[19] For Robert Lincoln the question of military service had peculiar overtones and presented problems. Those who were yet civilians participated in military activities of a sort:

> The lawns of Harvard College became drill grounds. Officers of the Cadet Corps of Boston took charge of the United States Arsenal, with undergraduates for enlisted men. A competent French drillmaster, named Salignac . . . , had his school, and between recitations in physic [*sic*] and astronomy, Professor——took a hand at military instruction with more spirit than would be evidenced by the command he once gave: "G-e-n-t-l-e-m-e-n, would you please A-D-V-A-N-C-E!"[20]

While college was his major activity, the comings and goings of Robert Lincoln were always news. Under the date line of March 4, 1861, it was reported, "Bob, the Prince of Rails, starts

15 "The New War Secretary."
16 Henry S. Huidekoper, *Personal Notes and Reminiscences of Lincoln*, 5.
17 "The New War Secretary."
18 *Ibid.*
19 The war affected Harvard's enrollment only slightly. According to the catalogues, total enrollment in the entire university was 896 in 1860–61; 833 in 1861–62; 814 in 1862–63; and 822 in 1863–64.
20 Huidekoper, *Personal Notes*, 7.

for Cambridge to-morrow. He is sick of Washington and glad to get back to his college."[21]

Once back in school, Robert was writing the news of the day to John Hay. He reported, "The Star of Boston and vicinity, particularly Cambridge, has gone, alas, to remain a month or two in New York." Being a normal young man, he had girls on his mind. He reported receiving a letter from Indiana, "stating that the writer had a baby, she had named after me (!) and requesting me to send said baby a dress or a pair of boots (size not stated)." The letter had commenced, "Sir, you have a baby here," which nearly caused Robert to faint from "an excess of supposed paternal dignity." The matter, however, he noted was cleared up later when his correspondent identified the youngster as only "a namesake of yours."[22]

In the middle of May, Mrs. Lincoln came for a visit. Then beginning the sometimes aimless wandering that was to mark her later life, she arrived in Boston on the morning of May 18. She was honored in the city by a reception arranged by Senator Charles Sumner and held in the Revere House.[23] Robert was, of course, present. The First Lady's visit was a short one; two days later she returned to New York.[24] By the end of May, Robert himself was back in Washington.

On the afternoon of May 31, he, John G. Nicolay, and John Hay, went for a horseback ride into Virginia. Their destination was Arlington House recently abandoned by the Robert E. Lee family. Nicolay recorded:

> in the garden we found an old negro at work, who was born at Mt. Vernon before General Washington's death. We asked him many questions—delighted him with introducing Bob, the President's son, in whom the old darkey expressed a lively interest—and further pleased him with a gift of small change.[25]

21 New York *Herald*, Mar. 5, 1861.
22 Robert T. Lincoln to John Hay, Mar. 21, 1861, John Hay Papers, Brown University Library.
23 Temple, "Mary Todd Lincoln's Travels," *JISHS*, Vol. LII (Spring, 1959), 184–85.
24 *Ibid.*

In July, Robert was briefly ill—with the mumps, but he reported to his father by telegraph from Cambridge that he would be home "in a few days" and that he was "not sick at all."[26] When, on the evening of August 3, a formal state dinner was given for visiting Prince Napoleon of France, Robert Lincoln was among the twenty-seven guests at what was described as a most brilliant affair.[27] By then, of course, the hostilities of the Civil War had begun, but Washington social life continued as though no such events were happening.

A few days later, "The Prince of Rails" was off again to New York, where it was reported that he arrived at the Metropolitan Hotel. On the same day, August 13, Senator Charles Sumner arrived at that same hotel from Washington, so perhaps the two made the trip together.[28] Robert's trip may well have been made for the purpose of arranging a vacation for his mother at Long Branch, New Jersey, as she came north a few days after Robert arrived in New York.[29]

Included in the First Lady's party was her cousin, Mrs. Elizabeth Todd Grimsley, who had been a guest at the White House for some months. When, in late summer, Mrs. Grimsley started home to Springfield, Mrs. Lincoln and Robert accompanied her as far as Niagara Falls, New York.[30] The Springfield visitor regarded Robert as "a manly, dignified youth, unspoiled by petting and adulation, and giving promise of the man into which he was to develop."[31]

With the approach of fall, young Lincoln returned to Harvard and his studies, although early in November, Mrs. Lincoln again visited him in Boston.[32] At Christmas, Robert was home again to

[25] John G. Nicolay to Therene Bates, later Mrs. Nicolay, May 31, 1861, quoted in Nicolay, *Lincoln's Secretary*, 106.

[26] Robert T. Lincoln to Abraham Lincoln (telegram), July 17, 1861, ISHL.

[27] New York *Herald*, Aug. 5, 1861.

[28] New York *Tribune*, Aug. 14, 1861.

[29] Randall, *Mary Lincoln*, 244–45.

[30] Elizabeth Todd Grimsley, "Six Months in the White House," *JISHS*, Vol. XIX (Oct., 1926; Jan., 1927), 72.

[31] *Ibid.*, 48.

[32] New York *Herald*, Nov. 5, 1861.

spend the holidays with his parents in the Executive Mansion.[33]

About this time the young man may have tried his hand at some pressure politics. The story is that a citizen of Cambridge, Massachusetts, talked Robert into writing to his father a letter of recommendation for the man who desired a city postmastership. The reply Robert received from his father is supposed to have been "somewhat" as follows: "If you do not attend to your studies and let matters such as you write about alone, I will take you away from college." Furthermore, it is said that " 'Bob' carried this letter in his pocket, and on many occasions afterward, when other aspirants to office importuned him for assistance, it served him a good turn."[34] If such a letter was ever written, it is not impossible to imagine that Robert might have had his father write it just to avoid such pleadings.

The story sounds less plausible, though, in the light of other happenings, for when Robert wanted to really help someone, he could get action. Robert had a friend, Henry M. Rogers, who was interested in seeing military service after he had graduated from Harvard. The actual letter to the President is not known to exist, but Lincoln sent a note to the secretary of the navy, October 27, 1862, in which he said he was enclosing "Bob's" letter on behalf of his friend. Rogers was appointed an assistant paymaster in the Navy.[35] An interesting sidelight to this is that Rogers reported that Robert Lincoln called his father "The Great Tycoon," a nickname also used by the two presidential secretaries, Nicolay and Hay.[36]

Robert was besieged by those wanting help in obtaining jobs. Occasionally the letter writer would report that he or a friend for whom he was writing had been fired from his old job for supporting President Lincoln.[37] Robert sometimes became involved with the pleas of soldiers for one kind of assistance or another. Pre-

33 Randall, *Lincoln's Sons*, 126.
34 Huidekoper, *Personal Notes*, 5. No such letter is known to exist.
35 Henry M. Rogers, *Memories of Ninety Years*, 69; *Collected Works*, V, 480.
36 Rogers, *Memories*, 69.
37 Prescoe Wright to Robert T. Lincoln, Feb. 22, 1861; Harry W. Gourley to Robert T. Lincoln, Feb. 22, 1861, Abraham Lincoln Papers.

48

sumably, in December, 1864, Robert wrote his father asking the release of a seventeen-year-old boy from the service. Lincoln wrote, "Let this boy be discharged on refunding any bounty received," and sent the letter to the proper authorities.[38]

The year 1862 was one of trial both for the Union and for the Lincoln family personally. In February, Robert's brother Willie became ill. Robert came down from Cambridge and, like his parents, waited at the bedside of the lovable boy. All medical efforts were to no avail, and the child died February 20, 1862.

> They buried Willie Lincoln on a day of great wind, that tore the roofs off houses and slashed the flags to ribbons. The father drove, unseeing, through the wreckage in a carriage with Robert and the two Illinois Senators, Trumbull and Browning. Mrs. Lincoln was too ill to attend the funeral services.[39]

Indeed, Mary Lincoln was prostrate with grief, and while the President bore his sadness with more calm, the sense of the loss was no less keen. The funeral over, Robert had to return to his studies, but before he left he wrote his aunt, Elizabeth Todd Edwards, imploring her to come to Washington to stay with his mother, which she did.[40] Either at this time or at some later date, an entry was made in the Lincoln family Bible recording the death of William Wallace Lincoln. It was in the hand of Robert Lincoln.[41]

When the summer of 1862 arrived, Robert's vacation at home was understandably welcomed with more than usual eagerness, for by then, only the eldest and youngest of the four Lincoln sons were living. Late in May, Mrs. Lincoln reported to an old Springfield neighbor, "Robert will be home from Cambridge in about 6 weeks and will spend his vacation with us. He has grown and improved more than anyone you ever saw—."[42] Evidently, the

[38] *Collected Works*, VIII, 571.

[39] Leech, *Reveille in Washington*, 129–30.

[40] Randall, *Mary Lincoln*, 286.

[41] Sandburg, *Lincoln: The War Years*, II, 218–19.

[42] Mary Lincoln to Mrs. Julia Sprigg, May 29, 1862, quoted in Carlos W. Goltz, *Incidents in the Life of Mary Todd Lincoln*, 34–37.

First Lady felt that Harvard had had a civilizing influence on her first-born.

Early in July, to escape the turmoil and heat of Washington, the President left the White House and took up residence in the Anderson Cottage at the Soldiers' Home near the capital, where he and his family passed most of the summer. On July 8, Abraham Lincoln telegraphed to Washington asking John G. Nicolay to borrow $280 for him and to then send it to Robert, noting "I forgot to send it before leaving."[43] Probably, not all of this money was intended for his son, for on July 9, Mrs. Lincoln, accompanied by Tad and servants, arrived in New York and stopped at the Metropolitan Hotel. "Robert Lincoln joined her there on the evening of July 10."[44]

The main purpose of this trip was to see the tourist attractions of the city and was designed, no doubt, to help the family forget its recent grief. At noon on July 14, the three boarded the revenue cutter *J. C. Winants* and sailed for Flushing Bay. "There they were received aboard the *Great Eastern* by Captain Walter Paton of the Royal Navy; they later paid a call on the steamer *City of New York* where they had lunch."[45] The next day Mrs. Lincoln again boarded the *J. C. Winants* for another tour, but this time Robert did not accompany her. Instead he remained the guest of Colonel Frank E. Howe on Staten Island.[46] Early on the morning of July 16, the touring over, the family entered a private railroad car attached to the regular train between Washington and Jersey City, New Jersey, and started back home.[47]

The President on July 28, 1862, wrote a note to Secretary of War Stanton saying, "Please put Bob in the way to find where John Reed of Co. C., 11 Mass. may be found."[48] On the back of the communication, Stanton wrote that Robert should be furnished with the needed information. Therefore, the implication

43 Abraham Lincoln to John G. Nicolay, July 8, 1862, *Collected Works*, V, 309.
44 Temple, "Mary Todd Lincoln's Travels," *JISHS*, Vol. LII (Spring, 1959), 185.
45 *Ibid.*
46 *Ibid.*, 186.
47 *Ibid.*
48 Abraham Lincoln to Edwin M. Stanton, July 28, 1862, *Collected Works*, V, 347.

is strong that Robert found Private Reed, but his purpose in seeking him is unexplained. What makes this incident worthy of comment is that exactly three months from the date of the President's letter, John Reed deserted from the service, a year after he had enlisted from Cambridge, Massachusetts.[49]

Robert Lincoln did not long remain in Washington that summer of 1862. By the evening of August 18, he was back in New York and registered at the Metropolitan Hotel, where he was joined by his mother two days later.[50] As fall approached, the young man returned to his studies and his mother continued her wanderings with Tad.[51]

During the winter of 1862–63, the Harvard student made at least one visit to Washington. He was reported as staying at the Metropolitan in New York on January 16, 1863, and he then went on to the White House.[52] While he was there, a reception was given for the famous midget "General" Tom Thumb and his recent bride, but Robert apparently declined to attend. It is said that Mrs. Lincoln suggested that her eldest son might come downstairs and see the visitors, provided he had nothing better to do than remain in his room. His reply was, "No, mother, I do not propose to assist in entertaining Tom Thumb. My notions of duty, perhaps, are somewhat different from yours."[53] The First Lady's biographer notes that "the superior young man from Harvard missed a unique and unforgettable scene" by not being in attendance when the tall Chief Executive received the two little people.[54]

When the summer of 1863 arrived, the Lincolns moved again to the Soldiers' Home. Robert, as was his custom, planned to join them there as soon as his vacation began. However, before he arrived, his mother on the morning of July 2 was hurt in a carriage accident. The President, knowing that the papers would

49 *Ibid.*
50 New York *Herald*, Aug. 20, 1862.
51 Temple, "Mary Todd Lincoln's Travels," *JISHS*, Vol. LII (Spring, 1959), 187.
52 New York *Herald*, Jan. 16, 1863.
53 Elizabeth Keckley, *Behind the Scenes*, 121.
54 Randall, *Mary Lincoln*, 320.

report the incident and wanting his son to know the truth regarding it, telegraphed: "Dont be uneasy. Your mother very slightly hurt by her fall."[55] This may have described Mrs. Lincoln's condition as it was first understood, but within a few days it became evident that her injuries were far more serious. To New York City, where Robert was stopping for the moment, the President sent the simple message, "Come to Washington."[56] When no immediate reply was received, another telegram, more anxious in tone, was sent: "Why do I hear no more of you?"[57] The harassed Chief Executive was under the greatest possible pressure at this time. His beloved wife was ill, the crucial battle of Gettysburg had just been fought, and there were serious draft riots in New York where his son was.

Robert Lincoln arrived in Washington either on the fourteenth or the fifteenth of July to find his mother somewhat better,[58] but his father deep in despair. Following the Gettysburg campaign, Lee and the Confederate forces were blocked in their retreat into Virginia by the flooded Potomac River. The President ordered General Meade to attack, but Meade inexcusably procrastinated, the water subsided, and Lee escaped on July 13. Robert, upon going to his father's room, found him "in tears with head bowed upon his arms resting on the table at which he sat." When Robert asked, "Why, what is the matter, father?" the great man replied, "My boy, I have just learned that at a council of war of Meade and his Generals it has been determined not to pursue Lee, and now the opportune chance of ending this bitter struggle is lost."[59] Robert told John Hay about it, and the presidential secretary noted in his diary that the Chief Executive was "grieved silently but deeply" about the escape. Of his own feel-

---

55 Abraham Lincoln to Robert T. Lincoln, July 3, 1863, *Collected Works*, VI, 314.

56 Abraham Lincoln to Robert T. Lincoln, July 11, 1863, *Collected Works*, VI, 323.

57 Abraham Lincoln to Robert T. Lincoln, July 14, 1863, *Collected Works*, VI, 327.

58 However, even two years later Robert would tell his Aunt Emelie Helm that his mother had not yet fully recovered from her injuries. Helm, *Mary, Wife of Lincoln*, 250.

59 Sandburg, *Lincoln: The War Years*, II, 354.

ings Hay wrote, "If I had gone up there I could have whipped them myself."[60]

A question which logically presents itself at this point is, to what extent was Robert Lincoln involved in the affairs of government during the war period? Did his father confide in him regarding matters of state? Young Lincoln once wrote of the war years, "I was a boy occupied by my studies at Harvard College, very seldom in Washington, and having no exceptional opportunity of knowing what was going on."[61] He may frequently have had access to information of a confidential nature, but he took little active part in the affairs of government.

Occasionally he acted as a messenger to his father. For example, when in February, 1861, William H. Seward sent his son Frederick to warn the President-elect of an assassination plot, the younger Seward arrived in Philadelphia and found Lincoln surrounded at his hotel by well-wishers. The messenger then sought out Robert Lincoln to tell him of his mission. Frederick Seward was greeted by Robert with courteous warmth, but he turned the visitor over to Ward H. Lamon, the bodyguard and friend of Lincoln, who arranged for him to see the President-elect.[62] Another example occurred later, just after that, when the Lincolns arrived in Washington. William E. Dodge, prominent New York merchant, gave up his suite in Willard's Hotel to the party. Robert later came to Dodge's room and took him to Lincoln for a greeting and thanks.[63]

Sometimes Robert was the confidant of his father. At one point during Lincoln's administration, several senators bore ill will toward Secretary Seward. Lincoln suspected that Secretary of the Treasury Chase was at the bottom of the antagonism. The feelings led to action when some senators, including Trumbull of Illinois, came to the President and claimed that in a cabinet meet-

---

[60] Clara Hay, ed., *Letters of John Hay and Extracts from His Diary*, I, 86.

[61] Robert T. Lincoln to Alexander K. McClure, Jan., 10, 1877, Pennsylvania Historical Society.

[62] Frederick W. Seward, *Reminiscences of a War-Time Statesman and Diplomat*, 135–36.

[63] Sandburg, *Lincoln: The War Years*, I, 89.

ing Seward had made remarks to the effect that secessionists and extreme anti-slavery men had both worked in the same direction; namely, to bring on war. Lincoln called an evening cabinet meeting and, with the senators present, asked each administration official to recount what had actually been said by Seward. Chase was forced to back down. This secret session was known to Robert Lincoln, for he later recounted it to Helen Nicolay, the daughter of John G. Nicolay.[64]

In the case of the famous Pomeroy Circular, Robert Lincoln was directly involved. The President had refused to read the contents of this document, but his son was fully aware of its intent and meaning. After the item was made public, Secretary Chase offered to resign, but the President drafted a note to him in which he stated that political considerations were not involved in whether or not Chase should resign, and that the Secretary should consider only the public welfare in the matter. Mr. Lincoln showed this letter to his son before he sent it, and Robert "asked in surprise if he had not seen the circular. Mr. Lincoln stopped him almost sternly, saying that a good many people had tried to tell him something he did not wish to hear."[65] Robert later recalled, "Thereupon, I called a messenger and the note was sent."[66] There are various other examples of situations in which the President's eldest son was privy to affairs of state or, at least, had what might be called inside information.[67]

During the summer of 1863, while the Harvard student was at home, he accompanied his father to see a demonstration of a new rifle. The inventor, Christopher M. Spencer had brought the device, a repeating model, to Washington, and one afternoon the President, Spencer, Robert Lincoln, and a War Department expert went off to test the weapon near the Washington Monument. After they had started, the Chief Executive sent his son to get

---

[64] Nicolay, *Lincoln's Secretary*, 158–59.

[65] *Ibid.*, 188–89.

[66] *Ibid.*

[67] For example, Robert T. Lincoln talked to George H. Putnam regarding his father's comments on matters pertaining to the election of 1864. Putnam, *Memories of My Youth*, 396.

Secretary of War Stanton. In a few minutes Bob was back to report that Stanton was too busy to go and, therefore, the party of four continued on its way and conducted the tests.[68]

On July 26, 1863, Robert T. Lincoln traveled by gunboat to Fortress Monroe in Virginia with a party including the Seward family,[69] but three days later he started back to New York to be with his mother who had recovered enough to make her first trip after the accident.[70] The oppressive heat of Washington greatly bothered the First Lady, and her destination was the White Mountains in New Hampshire, then very much in vogue as a summer resort.

John Hay confided to his friend Nicolay that Robert was bothered by quite another matter. Indeed, Bob was so shattered by a wedding which had taken place "that he rushed madly off to sympathise with nature in her sternest aspects."[71] During this sojourn the presidential family—minus the head of the household who remained at his desk in Washington—visited various places including, late in August, Manchester, Vermont, where they stayed at the Equinox House.[72] This was Robert Lincoln's first visit to a place where decades later he would acquire land, build an estate, and eventually die.[73]

By the latter part of September, Mrs. Lincoln was back in New York and Robert had gone back to Harvard.[74] Shortly thereafter, the First Lady returned to the White House. In January, 1864, Robert Lincoln took time to write a typical college boy's letter home for money. His father's reply was: "I sent your draft to-day. How are you now? Answer by telegraph at once."[75] A week later another message from the President advised Bob, "There is a

[68] Sandburg, *Lincoln: The War Years*, I, 294.

[69] New York *Herald*, July 29, 1863.

[70] Abraham Lincoln to Mary Lincoln, July 28, 1863, *Collected Works*, VI, 353.

[71] John Hay to John G. Nicolay, Aug. 7, 1863, Hay, *Letters and Diary*, I, 89–90.

[72] Temple, "Mary Todd Lincoln's Travels," *JISHS*, Vol. LII (Spring, 1959), 189.

[73] Henry Edwards Scott, "Hon. Robert Todd Lincoln, L.L.D.," *New England Historical and Genealogical Register*, Vol. LXXXI (July, 1927), 246.

[74] Abraham Lincoln to Mary Lincoln, Sept. 20, 1863, *Collected Works*, VI, 469.

[75] Abraham Lincoln to Robert T. Lincoln, Jan. 11, 1864, *Collected Works*, VII, 121.

good deal of small-pox here. Your friends must judge for themselves whether they ought to come or not."[76] Evidently the young
man planned to bring friends for a White House visit. It appears
that he went to Washington and then wired his friend Fred P.
Anderson at the Astor House in New York: "Bring Robeson
along with you—Come tomorrow."[77]

The academic year 1863–64, was Robert Lincoln's Senior year
at Harvard and an exciting time for him. He spent his usual vacations at the White House and was in Washington in January,
1864, for Senator Browning recorded in his diary for Sunday,
January 31, that the First Lady and her son Robert had driven
him home from church.[78] In June he joined his mother in New
York and the two went to Washington on the morning of July 2.
They proceeded directly to the Soldiers' Home, where they occupied, for the first time that season, the presidential apartments.[79]
That same evening Robert Lincoln accompanied his father to
the Capitol, where the President signed bills during a night session of Congress.[80]

No sooner had the Lincolns moved to their summer home than
a wave of fear swept the area regarding a possible Confederate
invasion. At first the War Department seemed unconcerned
about the threat, but on the evening of July 4, "Mr. Stanton sent
a carriage out to the Soldiers' Home, with positive orders that the
President and his family should return to the White House."[81]
They arrived at the mansion well after midnight, for John Hay
was awakened by Robert going to his room.[82]

On July 20, 1864, Robert Lincoln was graduated from Har-

---

76 Abraham Lincoln to Robert T. Lincoln, Jan. 19, 1864, *Collected Works*, VII,
137.
77 Robert T. Lincoln to Fred P. Anderson, Jan. 24, 1864, Indiana University Library. Robert Lincoln dates his message 1863, but the telegraph office stamp correctly reads 1864. At the bottom of the message there is the phrase "Charge to me
A. Lincoln," written in a well-known hand.
78 Theodore C. Pease and James G. Randall, eds., *The Diary of Orville Hickman
Browning*, I, 657.
79 New York *Herald*, July 3, 1864.
80 *Ibid.*
81 Leech, *Reveille in Washington*, 337.
82 *Ibid.*

vard. It was not possible for the weary President to go to Cambridge to see the ceremonies, although there were those who hoped he might attend. Robert dashed those ideas by writing from the Executive Mansion, "The President will not be at Commencement."[83] Commencement Day was described as "very warm," and the crowd assembled on the college grounds, including the First Lady, heard the great orator Edward Everett give the principal address.[84]

The Class of 1864 was by no means the most distinguished group ever to go forth from that institution. In fact, few of the ninety-nine graduates of that year became well known, and undoubtedly the name of Robert T. Lincoln was the most famous of the group. His class had held its organizational meeting in the Music Hall on campus, January 14, 1864, at seven in the evening.[85] The following morning the group elected class officers and Robert T. Lincoln was one of three making up the Class Day Committee.[86] After graduation the group held yearly meetings, but due to Lincoln's residence in Chicago, he was able to attend only a few of the annual reunions. He was present at the conclave held in the Music Hall, Cambridge, in July of 1867 and attended the two hundred and fiftieth anniversary celebration of Harvard in 1887. Other than that, he attended the class meeting held in the latter part of June, 1904, and presided over the session.[87]

Few American universities have a stronger tradition of alumni support than does Harvard. As early as 1866 the Class of 1864 was asked to begin its contributions to the University; in this instance, the class fund was for the purpose of erecting an alumni hall. Robert Lincoln was among those giving to that project.[88] It is known that he frequently contributed to many worthy causes, as well as supported friends and relatives without funds, but he usually managed to remain an anonymous donor. However, late

[83] Robert T. Lincoln to H. P. Sprague, July 18, 1864, ISHL.
[84] New York *Herald*, July 21, 1864.
[85] Harvard College, *Class of 1864, Secretary's Report*, No. 6, 175.
[86] *Ibid.*
[87] Harvard College, *Class of 1864, Secretary's Report*, 8, 168–69.
[88] Harvard College, *Class of 1864, Secretary's Report*, No. 2, 55.

in his life one of his generous contributions became known. In 1918, it was reported that he had given to Harvard, then engaged in an attempt to raise its endowment substantially, the sum of twenty thousand dollars in securities. Curiously the story was headlined, " 'Tad' Lincoln Gives Harvard $20,000."[89]

89 Unidentified newspaper clipping dated Mar. 25, 1918, Harvard University Archives.

Chapter 4

Changing Roles

IMMEDIATELY FOLLOWING the Harvard commencement in July of 1864, Robert Lincoln and his friend John Hay went to the seaside resort of Long Branch, New Jersey, for a vacation. There Mrs. Lincoln joined them. As usual, the press was much interested in the President's eldest son and a contemporary estimate of him ran as follows:

> He does everything very well, but avoids doing anything extraordinary. He doesn't talk much; he doesn't dance differently from the other people; he isn't odd, outré nor strange in any way. . . . In short, he is only Mr. Robert Lincoln. . . . He does nothing whatever to attract attention, and shows by every gentlemanly way how much he dislikes this fulsome sort of admiration, but it comes all the same. . . . Mr. Robert is happier when . . . doing his share in a good laugh than among all the doings of the Branch.[1]

In August, Mrs. Lincoln traveled to Manchester, Vermont. It was reported that the First Lady, Robert, and Tad left New York on August 15 "for Saratoga,"[2] and yet, three days later, Robert was staying at the Astor House in New York City.[3] On August 31 the President telegraphed his wife, "Bob not here yet," but there was no indication where he might be.[4] At any rate, the young man

[1] New York *Herald*, quoted in Leech, *Reveille in Washington*, 292.
[2] New York *Herald*, Aug. 16, 1864.
[3] *Ibid.*, Aug. 18, 1864.
[4] Abraham Lincoln to Mary Lincoln, Aug. 31, 1864, *Collected Works*, VII, 526.

was in Washington early in September, for on the eighth Mr. Lincoln reported, "Bob left Sunday afternoon. Said he did not know whether he would see you."[5] The assumption is strong that Bob was on his way back to Harvard where he was to enter the Law School.

For some time there had been considerable discussion by the public of the fact that while other men's sons were engaged in fighting this most terrible of wars, the President's son remained in college. Robert's trips here and there, which were always reported, did little to silence the gossipers. It was then generally believed that when Robert graduated he would immediately enter the service. Indeed, the Chicago *Journal* in July reported, "It is rumored that Mr. Robert Todd Lincoln, the President's son, on graduation from Harvard College, will immediately enter the army as a private."[6] Sometime during the summer Robert had a talk with his father concerning his future, for he told a friend:

> I returned from college in 1864 and one day I saw my father for a few minutes. He said, "Son, what are you going to do now?" I said, "As long as you object to my joining the army, I am going back to Harvard to study law." "If you do," said my father, "you should learn more than I ever did but you will never have so good a time."[7]

Robert added, "That is the only advice I had from my father as to my career."[8]

The question "Why did the President object to his son's joining the army?" has no final answers. Almost everyone agrees that Robert Lincoln was no coward or shirker; he wanted to do his duty and get into the war.[9] Abraham Lincoln apparently had no unusually strong feelings about the matter, for he had once enjoyed the role of citizen-soldier in the Black Hawk War. But his wife did have. Visiting the White House in 1863, Emelie Todd

5 Abraham Lincoln to Mary Lincoln, Sept. 8, 1864, *Collected Works*, VII, 544.

6 Chicago *Journal*, July 15, 1864, quoted in Sandburg, *Lincoln: The War Years*, III, 417.

7 *Ibid.*, III, 416–17.

8 *Ibid.*, III, 417.

9 Typical evidence on this point is Keckley, *Behind the Scenes*, 119. Mrs. Keckley indicates that Robert had wanted to enter the service for some time.

Helm, the recently widowed half-sister of Mrs. Lincoln, confided in her diary the subject of the First Lady's current fears, "She is frightened about Robert going into the Army."[10] Almost daily the President was reminded of the situation, and sometimes not in the most gentle fashion. For example, the super-sleuth Pinkerton was using his son, Billy, as a part of the spy system, but Lincoln objected to sending the boy on a dangerous mission. The none-too-diplomatic agent told the President, "I can use no other man's boy when I have one of my own."[11] The reference to Robert's status went unanswered. When the Chief Executive did attempt to discuss the matter with his wife, her reply was "of course, Mr. Lincoln, I know that Robert's plan to go into the Army is manly and noble and I want him to go, but oh! I am so frightened he may never come back to us."[12] It seems logical, therefore, to infer that Mrs. Lincoln's attitude and fears played no small part in the problem.

When the occasion warranted, Mary Lincoln did not hesitate to take full responsibility for her son's continued status as a civilian. While Mrs. Helm was visiting at the White House, a clash occurred between Mrs. Lincoln and Senator Harris of New York and General Sickles. The two men called, and upon encountering the First Lady, the Senator rudely demanded, "Why isn't Robert in the Army? He is old enough and strong enough to serve his country. He should have gone to the front some time ago." Mrs. Lincoln worked hard to maintain her self-control and to her credit she did.

> Robert is making his preparations now to enter the Army, Senator Harris; he is not a shirker as you seem to imply for he has been anxious to go for a long time. If fault there be, it is mine. I have insisted that he should stay in college a little longer as I think an educated man can serve his country with more intelligent purpose than an ignoramus.[13]

10 Helm, *Mary, Wife of Lincoln*, 227.
11 Lloyd Lewis, "Lincoln and Pinkerton," *JISHS*, Vol. XXXXI (1948), 367.
12 Helm, *Mary, Wife of Lincoln*, 227.
13 *Ibid.*, 229–30.

After making some remarks about the presence of Mrs. Helm, "a rebel," Senator Harris dropped the subject and departed.

Yet another line of reasoning on this subject is possible. In 1915, Robert Lincoln wrote:

> At the end of the vacation after my graduation from Harvard, I said to him that as he did not wish me to go into the Army (his reason having been that something might happen to me that would cause him more official embarrassment than could be offset by any possible value of my military service), I was going back to Cambridge and enter Law School. He said he thought I was right.[14]

It must be remembered that 1864 was an election year, and a bitter one at that. The hostile press had often stooped to using the President's family and its activities against the Chief Executive, and it is entirely possible to imagine situations in which Robert's military role would be a point of controversy. It is perhaps stretching a point to suggest, as has been done, that the President feared the consequences if Robert were to fall into enemy hands,[15] but it is not impossible to imagine the difficulties that would be caused by his falling into politicians' hands.

Robert Lincoln enrolled at Harvard Law School on September 7, 1864.[16] At that time no marks were kept and no record was made of the courses attended by students.[17] Once again it was Lincoln's fate to be in a situation where change and modernization were long overdue. The Law School was in a rather unfortunate condition in the middle 1860's; it was several years before Christopher C. Langdell arrived to head the school and to revolutionize legal training not only at Harvard, but throughout the nation. At this point in its development, the Law School was still operated as it had been since its founding. Not only was there no record made of a student's participation in class, but there was no system of written examinations for candidates for law degrees.

14 Robert T. Lincoln to Winfield M. Thompson, Mar. 2, 1915, quoted in *Lincoln Lore*, Apr. 16, 1956.
15 "Robert Todd Lincoln," *National Cyclopedia of American Biography*.
16 Letter to the author from George A. Strait, assistant librarian, Harvard University, May 11, 1959.
17 *Ibid.*

The *American Law Review* in October, 1870, openly criticized the system by stating, "For a long time, the condition of the Harvard Law School has been almost a disgrace to the Commonwealth of Massachusetts."[18]

The Harvard Law faculty in 1864 and 1865, consisted of three men, Theophilus Parsons, Joel Parker, and Emory Washburn.[19] Each was in his own right an able teacher, but teaching methods were considered outmoded. A student went, or did not go to classes, as he saw fit. "Lectures began at eleven and ended at one."[20] Assignments were made but there was no way for the professor to determine if they had been prepared. Perhaps most useful to the students were the moot courts organized either by the faculty or by the students themselves.[21] It is said that Robert Lincoln took part in the proceedings of the Marshall Club, one of the important student organizations, and that there he argued cases with Oliver Wendell Holmes, Jr.[22] In January, 1865, Professor Parker, a man who held strong strict-constructionist views of the Constitution, denounced President Lincoln's use of his war powers, while Robert sat in the classroom listening to the lecture. One assumes that the Professor must have been aware of the presence of the Chief Executive's son.[23]

Robert Lincoln spent only a short time at the Harvard Law School, and little information regarding his stay there is available. Evidently in October, 1864, he was ill, for the President wired him: "Your letter makes us a little uneasy about your health. . . . If you think it would help you, make us a visit."[24] Perhaps the young man was not happy with the school, for although he left to enter the army, there was little to prevent him from returning

---

[18] Quoted in Howe, *Justice Holmes*, 205.

[19] For a general history of the law school, see *The Centennial History of the Harvard Law School.*

[20] Samuel F. Batchelder, "Old Times at the Law School," *Atlantic Monthly*, Vol. XC (Nov., 1902), 651.

[21] Howe, *Justice Holmes*, 189–90.

[22] Catherine Drinker Bowen, *Yankee from Olympus*, 206.

[23] Howe, *Justice Holmes*, 186.

[24] Abraham Lincoln to Robert T. Lincoln, Oct. 11, 1864, *Collected Works*, VIII, 44.

there after the war. In later years Robert Lincoln did occasionally take an interest in the affairs of the Law School. In November of 1886, he was elected a vice-president of the Harvard Law School Alumni Association, along with Rutherford B. Hayes and William M. Evarts.[25]

On New Year's Day, 1865, the President's eldest son was present at the reception held in the White House, which no fewer than 5,000 attended.[26] He was also present at the First Lady's reception held January 14.[27]

A few days later Abraham Lincoln wrote a letter to his general, Ulysses S. Grant:

> Please read and answer this letter as though I was not President, but only a friend. My son, now in his twenty second year, having graduated at Harvard, wishes to see something of the war before it ends. I do not wish to put him in the ranks, not yet to give him a commission, to which those who have already served long, are better entitled, and better qualified to hold. Could he, without embarrassment to you, or detriment to the service, go into your Military family with some nominal rank, I, and not the public, furnishing his necessary means? If no, say so without the least hesitation, because I am anxious, and as deeply interested, that you shall not be encumbered as you can be yourself.[28]

Two days later the General replied as follows:

> Your favor of this date in relation to your son serving in some Military capacity is received. I will be most happy to have him in my Military family in the manner you propose. The nominal rank given him is immaterial, but I would suggest that of Capt. as I have three staff officers now, of considerable service, in no higher grade. Indeed I have one officer with only the rank of Lieut. who has been in the service from the beginning of the war. This however will make no difference and I would still say give the rank of Capt. Please excuse my writing on a half sheet. I had no resource but to take the blank half of your letter.[29]

25 Chicago *Tribune*, Nov. 6, 1886.
26 Esther Singleton, *The Story of the White House*, II, 92.
27 New York *Herald*, Jan. 15, 1865.
28 Abraham Lincoln to Ulysses S. Grant, Jan. 19, 1865, *Collected Works*, VIII, 223.

At last, on February 11, 1865, Robert T. Lincoln was appointed captain and assistant adjutant general of volunteers.[30] A week later his commission was signed by his father and Secretary Stanton. On the twentieth he wrote to Major S. F. Chalfin:

Sir:

I hereby accept my commission of assistant adjutant General. I have the honor to state that I am twenty-one years of age, was born and reside in the State of Illinois and that my full name is Robert Todd Lincoln. I am, Sir, very respectfully,

Your obedient servant,
R. T. LINCOLN[31]

General Grant had persuaded his commander in chief to abandon his idea that Robert should be paid by the President himself, "saying that it was due to the young man that he should be regularly commissioned, and put on an equal footing with other officers of the same grade."[32] It goes without saying that Robert Lincoln owed his place to his father's position, but his use of influence was not unique. There were twenty-one members of the Harvard class of 1864 who served in the Union Army. One was a major, while Robert Lincoln and three others were captains.[33]

Before leaving home Robert purchased a riding horse. The seller brought the animal to the White House and at first demanded $200, although the President thought it was worth only $150. The sale was eventually made at the lower figure, while an observer listened "to the comments of the quiet, businesslike father and the more enthusiastic son."[34] After young Lincoln left Washington to join Grant, the President became concerned about not hearing that he had safely arrived. "I have not heard of

29 Ulysses S. Grant to Abraham Lincoln, Jan. 21, 1865, *Collected Works*, VIII, 223–24.

30 *Ibid.*, VIII, 224.

31 Robert T. Lincoln to Maj. S. F. Chalfin, Feb. 20, 1865, National Archives, Washington. A notation on the letter reads, "oath of office herewith enclosed; properly filled up."

32 Horace Porter, *Campaigning With Grant*, 388.

33 Harvard College, *Class of 1864, Secretary's Report*, No. 2, 46.

34 John M. Bullock, "President Lincoln's Visiting-Card," *Century Magazine*, Vol. LV (Feb., 1898), 567.

my son's reaching you," telegraphed the President,[35] but the next day he was told, "Capt. Lincoln reported on the 22nd and was assigned to duty at my Head Quarters."[36] Robert T. Lincoln's war record was no more distinguished than had been that of his father many years before in the Black Hawk War. A member of Grant's staff remembered:

> The new acquisition to the company at headquarters soon became exceedingly popular. He had inherited many of the genial traits of his father, and entered heartily into all the social pastimes at head-quarters. He was always ready to perform his share of hard work, and never expected to be treated differently from any other officer on account of his being the son of the Chief Executive of the nation.[37]

Captain Lincoln's work as an army officer seems to have consisted primarily of escorting visitors here and there. In March, 1865, the financier Jay Cooke and his family visited General Grant at his headquarters. Robert T. Lincoln was assigned the task of ac-companying Mr. Cooke on a tour of the front.[38] Later in the month General Ord, who was a high-ranking member of the Grant staff, assigned Robert to escort two ladies on a flag-of-truce boat to the Confederate lines near Petersburg. The Captain, upon boarding the ship, exclaimed in astonishment, "Well, if it isn't my Aunt Emelie!" Mrs. Helm, the widow of a Confederate general was most happy to see her nephew and the two caught up on recent family news.[39]

On Saturday, March 4, 1865, Abraham Lincoln was inaugu-rated President of the United States for a second time. All of his immediate family were present to witness the ceremony, as his son the Captain was on leave. The inaugural ceremonies were considered a great success, at least by all but the President, who

[35] Abraham Lincoln to Ulysses S. Grant, Feb. 24, 1865, *Collected Works*, VIII, 314.
[36] Ulysses S. Grant to Abraham Lincoln, Feb. 25, 1865, *Collected Works*, VIII, 314.
[37] Porter, *Campaigning With Grant*, 388–89.
[38] Ellis P. Oberholtzer, *Jay Cooke, Financier of the Civil War*, I, 495.
[39] Helm, *Mary, Wife of Lincoln*, 250.

was worn out by the tiring proceedings.[40] With the end of the war in sight, Washington was beginning to shed its cloak of somberness and to shine once more as a great nation's capital. Monday evening the inaugural ball was held in the Patent Office Building, and it was a grand affair. At half past ten the military band struck up "Hail to the Chief," and President and Mrs. Lincoln appeared.

Robert Lincoln was already there, "in uniform" and with the daughter of Senator James Harlan of Iowa.[41] On his arm was Mary Eunice Harlan, three years younger than Robert and a most attractive and charming young lady. Educated at Madame Smith's French School in Washington, she was poised and gracious and, it was said, "played the harp divinely."[42] Exactly when the couple first met is not known, but it could have been at any time after the Lincolns came to Washington, for the Harlans had been there since 1855. Robert Lincoln and Mary Harlan were not married until 1868, but as early as the summer of 1865, rumors that they would wed appeared in the newspapers.[43]

The inaugural festivities over, Captain Lincoln returned to duty. A week later he wrote to John Hay late one night while he was on watch. He reported that he had been out under a flag of truce and the "rebels" were, he found, looking well and in fine condition. The letter concluded, "There have been lots of pretty girls down here lately—If you want to do a favor, send some more."[44] Later in the month of March, the Captain inquired of his father: "Will you visit the Army this week? Answer at City Point."[45] The President replied: "We now think of starting to you about One P.M. Thursday. Don't make public."[46] Robert Lincoln participated in the engagement that prompted the evacu-

[40] Leech, *Reveille in Washington*, 370–73.
[41] An extended account of the ceremonies appears in the New York *Herald*, Mar. 5, 1865.
[42] Julia Taft Bayne, *Tad Lincoln's Father*, 64.
[43] Chicago *Times*, Aug. 19, 1865.
[44] Robert T. Lincoln to John Hay, Mar. 14, 1865, Hay Papers.
[45] Robert T. Lincoln to Abraham Lincoln, Mar. 21, 1865, ISHL.
[46] Abraham Lincoln to Robert T. Lincoln, Mar. 21, 1865, *Collected Works*, VIII, 369.

ation of Petersburg, Virginia, by the Confederates the night of April 2–3. The next day Robert informed his father, "I am awaiting you at Hancock Station."[47] Accompanying Mr. Lincoln were Mrs. Lincoln, Tad Lincoln, and the family of Senator Harlan, including his daughter.[48] By then the war was almost over, and the visit was social as well as official.

The Harlans and the Lincolns, the Captain excepted, returned to Washington on April 9.

On that same day Lee surrendered at Appomattox, and Robert T. Lincoln was there to witness the event. The young captain was personally presented to the great Confederate leader.[49] After the ceremonies Grant, with Robert Lincoln in his party, started for Washington, where they arrived early on April 14, in time for Grant to attend a cabinet meeting.[50] Robert Lincoln immediately went to the White House, where he was early enough to have breakfast with his father. They chatted about the war. It is said that the son had with him a recent picture of General Robert E. Lee and the President upon looking at it mused: "It is a good face; it is the face of a noble, noble, brave man. I am glad that the war is over at last."[51] Thereupon the conversation turned to the future, and Mr. Lincoln commented:

> Well, my son, you have returned safely from the front. The war is now closed and we will soon live in peace with the brave men who have been fighting against us. I trust, that an era of good feeling has returned and that henceforth we shall live in harmony together.[52]

It seems highly likely that at this breakfast meeting Robert Lincoln was invited to accompany his parents to the theater that evening. However, he did not go.

47 Robert T. Lincoln to Abraham Lincoln, Apr. 3, 1865, Abraham Lincoln Papers.
48 Lloyd Lewis, *Myths After Lincoln*, 13.
49 Robert T. Lincoln to Judd Stewart, June 1, 1918, Huntington Library.
50 New York *Herald*, Apr. 17, 1865; Robert T. Lincoln to Judd Stewart, May 14, 1919, Huntington Library.
51 Keckley, *Behind the Scenes*, 135.
52 Francis Fisher Browne, *The Every-Day Life of Abraham Lincoln*, 582.

One wonders why he did not accompany his parents to see *Our American Cousin*. Perhaps he was tired. Long afterwards he wrote, "Personally I never attended a play with my father, but that was a purely accidental matter, as I was very little in Washington while he was there."[53] What might have happened if he had gone that fatal night? After Robert Lincoln died, Nicholas Murray Butler, who probably never knew Robert as well as he pretended to, stated that Robert could never forgive himself for not going with his father and mother. Butler said:

> Robert's argument was that had he gone to the theatre with his father and mother, he, being the youngest member of the party would have been in the back of the box and, therefore, Booth would have had to deal with him before he could have shot the President. On this rather fantastic ground Robert Lincoln based his sad reflection that had he gone to see Our American Cousin, his great father's life would not have come to so tragic an end.[54]

If this statement of Butler's is true, it does not matter whether or not Robert Lincoln could have prevented the assassination, but the fact that he believed he could have is important. One wonders how many times in his long life this man pondered his decision to remain at the White House that Good Friday evening.

Robert Lincoln and John Hay had spent the spring evening talking (some suggest they were studying Spanish[55]), but they had gone to their rooms when the news reached the White House. Thomas F. Pendel, a guard at the mansion, heard the news of the shooting and, according to his account, was the one who told Robert Lincoln. Pendel reported that when he reached Robert's room the young man did not seem to be feeling well. He had a vial of medicine and a spoon in his hand. The informant said simply, "Captain, there has something happened to the President; you had better go down to the theatre and see what it is." Robert Lincoln sent Pendel to get John Hay and the two started

---

53 Robert T. Lincoln to Edward Freiberger, Mar. 10, 1910, Lincoln National Life Insurance Company.

54 Nicholas M. Butler, "Lincoln and Son," *Saturday Evening Post* (Feb. 11, 1939), 64.

55 Dennett, *John Hay*, 36.

for the murder scene.[56] At one point, when their way was blocked by soldiers, the President's son in anguish cried: "It's my father! My father! I'm Robert Lincoln."[57]

When Hay and Lincoln entered the little room where the President lay, they saw one of the truly tragic scenes in United States history. On the bed lay the dying Abraham Lincoln, surrounded by officials of government and his friends. Throughout the long night, as life ebbed, Robert Lincoln stood at the bedside; at intervals he wept upon the shoulder of Senator Charles Sumner.[58] Recalled a physician in attendance, "at first his terrible grief overpowered him but soon recovering himself. . . . [he] remained in silent grief during the long, terrible night."[59] Mary Todd Lincoln was by then near a state of collapse. Robert sent a carriage to bring Mrs. Elizabeth L. Dixon, wife of a Connecticut senator, to be with his mother.[60] At one point, when the First Lady's grief became almost too much for her, Robert knelt and "crouched before her, rubbing her hand in his and murmuring: 'Mother, please put your trust in God and all will be well.' "[61] However, nothing that either Robert or Tad could do gave her comfort. When Secretary Stanton finally ordered the First Lady out of the room, Robert Lincoln went with his mother.[62] At 7:22 A.M., April 15, 1865, the end came. Robert T. Lincoln was no longer the son of the President of the United States.

Of all the coincidences and ironies surrounding the assassination of Abraham Lincoln by John Wilkes Booth, none is more dramatic than the contrast of another Lincoln-Booth encounter: Edwin Booth's rescue of Robert T. Lincoln. The incident, which Robert Lincoln placed as having occurred in 1863 or 1864,[63]

---

56 Thomas F. Pendel, *Thirty-Six Years in the White House*, 42–43.

57 Jim Bishop, *The Day Lincoln Was Shot*, 225.

58 John T. Morse, Jr., ed. *The Diary of Gideon Welles*, II, 288.

59 Recollections of Dr. Charles Sabin Taft, quoted in Wilson, *Lincoln Among His Friends*, 396.

60 *New York Times*, Feb. 12, 1950, quoting a letter written by Mrs. Dixon, May 1, 1865.

61 Bishop, *The Day Lincoln Was Shot*, 237.

62 Charles A. Leale, *Lincoln's Last Hours*, 11. Leale was a physician in attendance that night.

while he was in Jersey City on his way from New York to Washington, he described in 1909:

> The incident occurred while a group of passengers were late at
> night purchasing their sleeping car places from the conductor who
> stood on the station platform at the entrance of the car. The plat-
> form was about the height of the car floor, and there was of course
> a narrow space between the platform and the car body. There was
> some crowding, and I happened to be pressed by it against the car
> body while waiting my turn. In this situation the train began to
> move, and by the motion I was twisted off my feet, and had dropped
> somewhat, with feet downward, into the open space, and was
> personally helpless, when my coat collar was vigorously seized and
> I was quickly pulled up and out to a secure footing on the plat-
> form. Upon turning to thank my rescuer I saw it was Edwin Booth,
> whose face was of course well known to me, and I expressed my
> gratitude to him, and in doing so, called him by name.[64]

It was said that this rescue gave the great Edwin Booth some comfort in the troubled time that followed his brother's insane
action.[65]

With the President dead Robert Lincoln became the head of
his family.[66] The hours immediately following the murder of
Abraham Lincoln were terrible ones for his eldest son. A President of the United States who dies in office remains the property
of the public until he is accorded the last rites, and his family is
forced to share their dead with the nation. In this instance, the
poor widow was nearly out of her mind with grief and so it became the responsibility of her sons to handle necessary matters.

On the same day the Chief Executive died, John Hay suggested that someone should go and see the new President, Andrew
Johnson, and ask him to tell the widow that she need be in no
hurry to leave the Executive Mansion. Edward D. Neill, another

[63] Robert T. Lincoln to Emelie Todd Helm, quoted in Helm, *Mary, Wife of
Lincoln*, 251–52. However, Eleanor Ruggles, *Prince of Players, Edwin Booth*, 171,
favors the year 1865.

[64] Robert T. Lincoln to Richard Watson Gilder, Feb. 6, 1909, ISHL.

[65] Ruggles, *Prince of Players*, 201.

[66] Hereinafter when the name Lincoln alone is used, it is referring to the son
and not the father.

of the presidential secretaries, went to Senator Ramsey of Minnesota to ask him to discuss the matter with the President. The Senator saw Johnson, and about eleven the next morning, Sunday, he arrived at the Mansion with Senator Norton. A brief meeting was held with Robert Lincoln, standing by the table where his father had conducted business, and Senator Ramsey spoke of the new President's wish that the Lincolns not move until the widowed First Lady had taken all the time she needed to make arrangements for her new life. Of Robert Lincoln, Secretary Neill, who was a Presbyterian minister, said, "his manly bearing on that trying occasion made me feel that he was a worthy son of a worthy father."[67] That day Lincoln also saw Orville H. Browning and told him that his mother did not wish to return to Springfield, or even to have her husband buried there.[68]

Many helping hands were extended to the grieved son. A few years later, Robert Lincoln recalled his feelings of that time when he attempted to comfort his friend Edwin Stanton upon the death of his own father, the great war secretary: "I know that it is useless to say anything . . . and yet when I recall the kindness of your father to me, when my father was lying dead and I felt utterly desperate, hardly able to realize the truth, I am as little able to keep my eyes from filling with tears as he was then."[69] One of those to whom Lincoln turned was David Davis, the man of whom he later wrote, "Upon my father's death I went to Judge Davis as a second father, and this he was to me until his death."[70] Lincoln's request of Davis was: "Please come at once to Washington & take charge of my father's affairs. Answer."[71] When the Justice indicated his willingness to undertake the task, Lincoln wired: "Many thanks. Please come as soon as possible. R. T. Lincoln."[72]

67 Paper by Edward D. Neill, read at an 1885 meeting of the Loyal Legion, in Rufus R. Wilson, *Intimate Memories of Lincoln*, 613.

68 Pease and Randall, *Diary of Orville H. Browning*, II, 20.

69 Robert T. Lincoln to Edwin L. Stanton, Dec. 24, 1869, Benjamin P. Thomas and Harold M. Hyman, *Stanton*, 638.

70 Robert T. Lincoln to Thomas Dent, Sept. 12, 1919, quoted in Pratt, *Personal Finances*, 141.

71 Robert T. Lincoln to David Davis, Apr. 15, 1865, ISHL.

72 Lincoln to Davis, Apr. 16, 1865, *ibid.*

The President died on Saturday, and the following Wednesday the state funeral took place in the great East Room of the Executive Mansion. At the appointed hour the mourners took their assigned places: President Andrew Johnson stood facing the middle of the coffin; General Grant was seated alone at the head; Robert Lincoln, with a few relatives, sat at the foot.[73] Following the services, the casket was taken to the Capitol to wait until Friday when the journey to Springfield began. The long, tedious trip lasted from April 21 to May 3.[74]

Mrs. Lincoln at first insisted that the President be buried in Chicago, not in Springfield, as Robert, Justice Davis, and others thought proper.[75] After she was persuaded to agree to burial in Springfield, there was disagreement about the exact location. On May 1 her son wrote to Governor Oglesby of Illinois: "There seems to be a disposition at Springfield to disregard my mother's wishes in regard to the interment. Both the temporary and final interment must take place in Oakridge [*sic*] Cemetery."[76]

The same day, he left Washington for Springfield to attend the final services.[77] After the funeral the key to the burial vault was given to Captain Lincoln.[78] Lincoln then boarded a train for Washington, where he arrived the evening of May 8. He at once wrote John T. Stuart, whose house guest he had been in Springfield,[79] that he found his mother feeling much better; and, when he had shown her a map of the cemetery, she was pleased with the burial place.[80]

During the period following his father's death, many matters demanded Robert T. Lincoln's presence and attention. On April 21, he wrote to the Adjutant General: "I have the honor to tender to you the resignation of my Commission as Captain and

---

[73] Leech, *Reveille in Washington*, 400–403.
[74] Victor Searcher, *The Farewell to Lincoln*.
[75] King, *Lincoln's Manager*, 227.
[76] Lincoln to Richard J. Oglesby, May 1, 1865, ISHL.
[77] Lincoln to David Davis, May 1, 1865, ISHL.
[78] E. D. Townshend to Edwin M. Stanton, May 4, 1865, U.S. War Dept., *The War of the Rebellion*, Ser. I, Vol. XLVI, Pt. 3, 1090.
[79] *Illinois State Journal*, May 4, 1865.
[80] Lincoln to John T. Stuart, May 8, 1865, ISHL.

Assistant Adjutant General of Volunteers, and respectfully request that it be accepted."[81] On the back of the letter is written:

> Hd. Qtrs. Armies of the U. States, Washington, D.C., Apl. 30, 1865. In approving the resignation of Capt. Lincoln it affords me pleasure to testify to the uniform good conduct of this young officer and to say that by his course in the performance of his duties, and in his social intercourse, he has won the esteem and lasting friendship of all with whom he has come in contact.
>
> U. S. GRANT, *Lt. Gen.*[82]

It was not until June 10, 1865, however, that the resignation took effect.[83]

Most of the time in the weeks that followed his father's death, Lincoln was at the White House vainly trying to console his mother, not to mention his brother Tad who was also disconsolate. Occasionally there were visitors; Orville Browning reported spending an hour with Robert Lincoln on Sunday evening May 14.[84] Four days later, however, Lincoln wrote Mrs. Elizabeth Grimsley, "I leave this P.M. for Springfield and will be your guest while in town."[85]

The new head of the Lincoln family may have been concerned over their continued residence in the Executive Mansion, for on April 25, Lincoln addressed the new President: "My mother and myself are aware of the great inconvenience to which you are subject, but my mother is so prostrate that I must beg your indulgence. . . . Mother tells me that she cannot possibly be ready to leave here for 2½ weeks."[86] There was much discussion about where the widow would live, although as early as May 9, Robert wrote, "Mrs. Lincoln will certainly live in Chicago."[87] At last, on May 22, a "feeble, black-clad Mary Lincoln walked for the last time down the White House stairs of stately memories and was

81 Lincoln to the Adjutant General, Apr. 21, 1865, ISHL.
82 *Ibid.*
83 Extract of Special Orders, No. 294, United States Army, National Archives.
84 Pease and Randall, *Diary of Orville H. Browning*, II, 27.
85 Lincoln to Elizabeth Grimsley, May 18, 1865, ISHL.
86 George F. Milton, *Age of Hate*, 228–29.
87 Lincoln to Charles L. Wilson, May 9, 1865, ISHL.

driven to the station to take the train to Chicago."[88] The family took the 6:00 P.M. train and arrived at their destination at noon May 24, where they took rooms at the Tremont House.[89]

Before long the family moved to less expensive quarters in Hyde Park, where, according to Mrs. Keckley, who was a part of the household, Robert Lincoln was most unhappy.[90] Lincoln had good reason to be unhappy. Aside from the recent tragedy, there was the matter of his mother's mental state. Mary Lincoln was clearly beginning to show signs of the emotional instability that would eventually lead to the insanity trial. At about this time her son confided to Mary Harlan, "it is very hard to deal with one who is sane on all subjects but one."[91] That one subject, of course, was money.

[88] Randall, *Mary Lincoln*, 389.
[89] New York *Herald*, May 23, 1865; Chicago *Times*, May 25, 1865.
[90] Keckley, *Behind the Scenes*, 211.
[91] Lincoln to Mary Harlan, quoted in Carl Sandburg and Paul M. Angle, *Mary Lincoln, Wife and Widow*, 133.

Chapter 5

Family Matters

Wᴵᴛʜᴏᴜᴛ ᴅᴏᴜʙᴛ, except for the tragic circumstances under which the three remaining Lincolns left the White House, Robert Lincoln was not unhappy with no longer being a White House resident. Never in his long life did he come to appreciate the glare of publicity. At least for the time being he could escape the nation's frequently prying if not hostile press, which had in the past four years called him a coward, a shirker, and a war profiteer. In the election of 1864, for instance, Robert Lincoln had figured as a minor campaign issue. A pamphlet entitled "The Lincoln Catechism: A Guide to the Presidential Election of 1864: wherein the Eccentricities and Beauties of Despotism are Fully Set Forth," published in New York, set forth a series of questions and answers. To the question "Who is Master Bob Lincoln?," the answer given was, "A lucky boy, yet in his teens, who has been so happy as to obtain shares in Government contracts by which he has realized $300,000."[1] The antiadministration journals, such as the Chicago *Times*, would print items like this one: "The President's son, 'Bob,' as he is called, a lad of some twenty summers, has made half a million dollars in government contracts."[2] As Carl Sandburg observed:

That was the item entire. How or where the President's son spent

1 Quoted in Sandburg, *Lincoln: The War Years*, III, 267–68.
2 Chicago *Times*, quoted *ibid.*, II, 132–34.

76

his time or his money, or in what particular field of contracts he might have made $500,000 could not be told without at once confusing any political reader whose sympathies already inclined him to believe that the President was corrupt as well as despotic. . . . Surrounding one viciously false item with strictly correct facts about fire, murder, hog and corn shipments, disasters at sea, they could snare the careless reader into accepting the false item and spreading it by word of mouth.[3]

Perhaps the bitterest newspaper item of them all appeared first in the *Philadelphia Age* and was then reprinted in the Columbus (Ohio) *Crisis*. It was an editorial entitled "Cheap Sympathy" and dealt with the famous Bixby letter:

Our readers will remember the letter of President Lincoln to Mrs. Bixby, condoling with her on the loss of her five sons in this war. He speaks of the "solemn pride that must be hers, at having laid so costly a sacrifice upon the altar of freedom." This kind of sympathy is cheap, and easily manufactured; and when one reflects that the man who is ostentatiously shedding his tears over the remains of Mrs. Bixby's sons, has two sons who are old enough to be laid upon the "altar," but whom he keeps at home in luxury, we can easily understand the hypocrisy of all this sympathy for the poor bereaved widow. Why is it, we ask, that Mr. Lincoln's sons should be kept from the dangers of the field, while the sons of the laboring man are to be hurried into the harvest of death at the front? Are the sons of the rail-splitter, porcelain, and these others common clay? Or is it that Mr. Robert Lincoln, the young gentleman whose face is so familiar at watering places and billiard rooms in the metropolis, has taken his younger brother into the speculation of cultivating cotton on Island Number Ten, through the agency of slave labor, and they can't be spared from their businesses?[4]

Obviously Robert was being used by persons who lost no opportunity to hit at the President by any means possible. The other son referred to in the editorial was, of course, Tad, then eleven

[3] *Ibid.*
[4] Columbus (Ohio) *Crisis*, Dec. 16, 1864, quoted *ibid.*, III, 667–68.

years old, and perhaps not quite as advanced in years as the writer imagined.

As soon as the White House years were over, Robert Lincoln was subjected to another form of criticism, more subtle perhaps, but constant and unending, even after his death. It seems to be an article of faith among those who admire Abraham Lincoln that his eldest son is to be criticized at every possible point. The Todd middle name is always emphasized, as if to imply only a remote relationship to the Great Emancipator. Questions have often been raised about the relationship between Abraham and Robert Lincoln. A typical analysis is:

> There were undoubtedly times when father and son found a congenial topic to talk about, but true sustained companionship between them apparently could not be achieved. This sometimes happens between a father and son of marked personalities—it is not necessarily the fault of either. There may also be inherent in the relation of father and son certain possibilities of antagonism. In spite of Mr. Lincoln's parental pride and affection and Robert's sense of filial obligation, they seem to have been too different in make-up for either to feel essential kinship with the other. There are cases of incompatibility where the chemistries of two personalities simply will not mix.[5]

It is most difficult to chronicle correctly the relationship between a father and son. However, it is said that "Lincoln's remarks about Robert are characterized by a curious restraint which seems strange coming from one who gave out an all-embracing parental affection to young people in general."[6] Evidence to support this theory includes such matters as the father's statement that Robert "promises very well, considering we never controlled him much."[7] It ought not to be forgotten also that Robert Lincoln left home at the age of sixteen, and that his father was murdered prior to the son's twenty-second birthday. Perhaps the companionship between them might have developed

[5] Randall, *Lincoln's Sons,* 152–53.

[6] Randall, *Mary Lincoln,* 269–70.

[7] Abraham Lincoln to Anson G. Henry, July 4, 1860, *Collected Works,* IV, 81–82.

more fully after the President's retirement, if indeed it did not already exist before his death.

There are those who regard Robert's noncommittal response to questions about his father as evidence of ill feeling between them. Until his death in 1926, Robert Lincoln was asked questions about his father, often ones concerning minor matters and details. Some have concluded that he "did not know his father well."[8] The son's answer to this charge always was to point out that he was away at school just as his father was beginning the public phase of his life.

Of course there is evidence of an occasional disagreement within the Lincoln household involving father and son. The artist Carpenter, while staying at the White House in 1862, related that Robert burst into John Hay's room and exclaimed, "Well I have just had a great row with the President of the United States."[9] This "row" involved Tad, who, as usual, had gotten away with something for which he should have been punished. What could be more natural than an older brother being frustrated because a doting parent would not correct a younger child? On the other hand, there are examples of Abraham Lincoln's fondness for his eldest son. Noah Brooks recalled that the President once, in referring to Tad's rearing, said: "Let him run, there's time enough yet for him to learn his letters and get poky. Bob was just such a little rascal, and now he is a very decent boy."[10] It would seem best to conclude that between Abraham Lincoln and Robert T. Lincoln there existed a reasonably normal father and son relationship, and to attempt to prove the contrary is difficult if not impossible.

It was Robert Lincoln's sad duty to assist in the settlement of his father's estate. The President left no will, so his eldest son and his widow wrote to the judge of the Sangamon County Court at

---

[8] Randall, *Mary Lincoln*, 270. David C. Mearns is also among those who feel that Robert Lincoln was very poorly informed on his father's career. Conversation with Mr. Mearns, June, 1962.

[9] F. B. Carpenter, *Six Months at the White House with Abraham Lincoln*, 300.

[10] Randall, *Lincoln's Sons*, 123.

Springfield, requesting that David Davis be appointed administrator of the estate. On June 16, 1865, the court so ordered.[11]
Shortly afterwards Robert, after consulting with his mother,
wrote to Judge Davis that he could use his discretion in giving
out the value of the late President's estate. Wryly Lincoln noted
that the papers were crediting Tad and himself with "private
fortunes," and that he had cleared large amounts in government
contracts.[12] The myth is still abroad that Abraham Lincoln died
a poor man; he did not. After all claims on the estate had been
paid and the residue was settled on the three heirs, each received
$36,991.54.[13] Much credit is due Justice Davis for his able
handling of the estate; under his administration it grew from
$83,343.70 left by the President to $110,974.62, the amount finally distributed.[14] In addition, this good man handled all matters
connected with the administration of the estate at his own ex-
pense and no fees whatsoever were incurred.

At twenty-two Robert inherited nearly $37,000.00. Upon the
death of his brother in 1871, he received half of the $35,750.00
which Tad had. Upon the death of Mary Lincoln in 1882, her
only surviving son was administrator of her estate, as well as sole
heir. She left $84,035.00.[15] Thus, Lincoln received three inher-
itances worth a total of $138,901.54, an amount that was small
by comparison with the total estate left by Robert Lincoln at
his death.

In the years that followed 1865, Lincoln was often in close
contact with his "second father." Frequently he, too, made trips
in connection with matters dealing with the estate. In June following the assassination, Lincoln was in Springfield "on business
connected with his father's estate."[16] Early in August, Lincoln
made another trip to Springfield, this time for the purpose of
bringing back his father's papers that were in the office of Lincoln

11 Pratt, *Personal Finances*, 133–34.
12 Lincoln to David Davis, June 24, 1865, ISHL.
13 Pratt, *Personal Finances*, 140.
14 *Ibid.*, 141.
15 *Ibid.*, 184–85.
16 Chicago *Times*, June 15, 1865. See also the *Illinois State Journal*, June 15, 1865.

and Herndon. He reported to Judge Davis that he had collected everything he could find except for some law briefs.[17] Sometime during this period the question of ownership of the office arose. Although Lincoln admitted the "pecuniary" value was small, he regretted that Herndon had the items. Long afterward he wrote that his father left his furniture with Herndon because he planned to return to his law practice after he retired from the presidency. However, when Davis asked about it, Herndon replied, "falsely as we both believed," that the items had been given to him. "Judge Davis shrugged his shoulders and with my assent dropped the matter."[18]

When, in December, 1865, the remains of the President were transferred to a new vault, his widow and eldest son were present. They made the melancholy trip during the midst of the Christmas holidays arriving from Chicago at four in the morning. They took rooms at the Chenery House but returned to Chicago that same night.[19]

A short time later Robert Lincoln moved; he informed the judge, "I have taken a pair of rooms here so as to be a little more comfortable." He added that he needed money and requested eight hundred dollars from his father's estate.[20] Evidently Davis was a bit slow in responding, for shortly there was another letter with a plaintive plea: "I wrote you some time ago, saying that I was getting out of funds and from you silence. I fear that you may not have received my letter." The eight hundred dollars he requested would do him for the next six months but it had better arrive soon as he had bills due on the first of the month.[21] Lincoln's next letter to Davis announced that he had an opportunity to buy 150 acres of land, located ten miles from Chicago, at twenty dollars an acre. "I have no doubt I could realize a handsome profit on it in a short time." The main question, of course,

---

[17] Lincoln to Davis, Aug. 8, 1865, ISHL.
[18] Lincoln to Frederic Geiger, Jan. 16, 1919, *ibid.*
[19] *Illinois State Journal*, Dec. 22, 1865. See also Lincoln to Davis, Dec. 22, 1865, ISHL.
[20] Lincoln to Davis, Jan. 3, 1866, *ibid.*
[21] Lincoln to Davis, Jan. 15, 1866, *ibid.*

was whether the needed capital could be obtained from the President's estate. On the back of the letter is the Judge's decision in his own hand, "Wants $3,000 to buy land—advised against it and he abandoned it."[22] Lincoln cheerfully accepted the decision and wrote not long afterwards that other friends in Chicago had felt the same way the Justice did.[23]

Throughout this period Robert Lincoln was gaining in knowledge about business matters. His letters to Davis show the abilities that he displayed in accumulating a substantial fortune. Lincoln was responsible for advising not only his mother, but Tad as well. As it was necessary to draw money for the youngster from the estate in January, 1866, Robert raised the question of being declared Tad's guardian for the time being.[24] This, he made clear, was to be only temporary, until the Judge had time to handle the matter himself. Although Lincoln said it would not be difficult to manage his brother's estate, "I would prefer that when he needed advice or restraint some older person should have authority to give it to him. You doubtless know that both my Mother and I would prefer that you, of all persons we know, would be willing to assume the task." He added, with ominous overtones for the future, "My Mother thinks Tad should pay his own expenses as he is perfectly well able to do so, and better than she is to do it for him."[25] When the estate was finally closed, Davis became Tad's legal guardian.[26]

Not long after the death of the President, his son began to be besieged by would-be biographers of Abraham Lincoln. Evidently the first person to bring up the subject of a Lincoln biography was Professor Francis James Child of Harvard, who was interested not in the project for himself, but on behalf of Charles Eliot Norton. In late April, 1865, Lincoln wrote in reply to Child's letter that, while he had great respect for Norton, who is "well known to me as a cultivated scholar and gentleman"

22 Lincoln to Davis, Feb. 3, 1866, *ibid.*
23 Lincoln to Davis, Feb. 21, 1866, *ibid.*
24 Lincoln to Davis, Jan. 25, 1866, *ibid.*
25 Lincoln to Davis, Feb. 21, 1866, *ibid.*
26 King, *Lincoln's Manager*, 243.

(although he did not know him personally very well), still the important fact was:

> It will be impossible, however, for the complete work which Mr. Norton contemplates to be written for a number of years, exactly how long it is impossible to say because there are no doubt many documents (I myself know several) which are necessary to the history but which would be damaging to men now living.[27]

Although this letter stopped Norton in his projected writing, it did not stop others. There were countless items being written about President Lincoln and the bulk of them were worthless. When, however, Robert Lincoln read something he liked he told the author about it. He wrote Senator Charles Sumner how "deeply gratified" he was by the Massachusetts stateman's eulogy of the late Chief Executive.[28] Nor did Lincoln fail to be helpful on several occasions to those who were working on studies of his father. Although he side-stepped the issue of the personal papers, he wrote J. G. Holland that there were various persons who could supply him with personal information about his father. Lincoln mentioned Dr. A. G. Henry, Joshua F. Speed, and William H. Herndon.[29]

At about this same time Mr. Herndon became interested in historical research and writing. It has been said that the death of Abraham Lincoln "was the most important event in Herndon's life."[30] He at once began to collect material concerning his former partner, whom he had known only as a Springfield lawyer, not as the President of the United States. Herndon's methods were, to say the least, questionable; yet, a debt of gratitude is owed to this man, for without his efforts much concerning Lincoln would have been lost. Tirelessly Herndon traveled here and there interviewing persons who had known Abraham Lincoln. He, of course, appealed to Robert Lincoln for aid in his projects, and at

---

27 Lincoln to Francis James Child, Apr. 27, 1865, quoted in Mearns, *The Lincoln Papers*, I, 45.

28 Lincoln to Charles Sumner, July 5, 1865, Harvard College Library.

29 Lincoln to J. G. Holland, June 6, 1865, Robert T. Lincoln Misc. Papers, University of Chicago Library.

30 David Donald, *Lincoln's Herndon*, 167.

first Lincoln was co-operative. In August, 1866, he wrote Judge Davis that Herndon wanted to look through a group of papers left by the President with C. M. Smith which dealt with the senatorial campaigns of 1854 and 1858. Lincoln said that if the Judge had no objection, Herndon could go through the collection after Lincoln had looked them over himself.[31]

However, in late 1866, Herndon also began to lecture in public. In November he first raised the specter of Ann Rutledge, Abraham Lincoln's alleged lost love.[32] Some months after the lecture was first given, Mrs. Lincoln learned of it and was understandably unhappy with the entire business. Robert T. Lincoln, who heard of it at once, did not take the matter with much good grace either. "Mr. William H. Herndon is making an ass of himself" was his opening comment to Justice Davis. He continued by noting that he was getting "seriously annoyed at his way of doing things":

> I have no doubt you will feel the impropriety of such a publication even if it were, which I much doubt, all true. His reflections, which make up a large portion, would be very ludicrous if I did not feel strongly that he speaks with a certain amount of authority from having known my father so long. Do you think it would be advisable to write to him? He is such a singular character that I am afraid of making matters worse, but I think something ought to be done to stop his present course.[33]

The Justice replied that he would attempt to stop Herndon from spreading the story,[34] but his efforts were to no avail.

In order to understand the unpleasant relationship between Robert Lincoln and Herndon, it is necessary to go back to Lincoln's college days at Harvard. During that time Herndon had written to the student "absurd pseudophilosophical letters," which the latter thought insane.[35] Long afterward Lincoln ob-

---

[31] Lincoln to David Davis, Aug. 21, 1866, ISHL.

[32] This was done in a lecture titled "A. Lincoln–Miss Ann Rutledge, New Salem–Pioneering" and the poem called "Immortality—or Why should the Spirit of Mortal be Proud," first delivered Nov. 16, 1866.

[33] Lincoln to David Davis, Nov. 19, 1866, ISHL.

[34] King, *Lincoln's Manager*, 239.

served to a boyhood friend: "I confess to you that it is one of my puzzles to understand how it was my father stuck to Herndon as long as he did. Personally, I regarded him as insane."[36]

In September of 1866, Mary Lincoln met Herndon in Springfield and they discussed several matters relative to Herndon's work. The interview got off to a bad start, for Herndon had been drinking and this revolted and upset Mrs. Lincoln.[37] A few weeks later, Robert Lincoln made reference to this meeting when he wrote Herndon, "I spoke to my mother . . . and she says she had a talk with you on the subject when at Springfield and that her letters are of too private a nature to go out of her hands."[38]

After the specter of Ann Rutledge was raised, Lincoln himself went to Springfield in December of 1866 to talk personally with the one who had conjured up the story. In recalling the meeting some two decades afterward, Herndon said, "I think Bob wanted to fight, but I kept my temper and he couldn't fight, because he had no one to fight with."[39] Of course, nothing was accomplished by discussing the matter. Belatedly Lincoln's oldest son appealed to Herndon's better nature. "All I ask," he wrote after returning to Chicago from his fruitless mission, "is that nothing may be published by you, which after careful consideration will seem apt to cause pain to my father's family, which I am sure you do not wish to do. I hope you will consider this matter, carefully, my dear Mr. Herndon," he entreated, "for once done there is no undoing."[40] By then it was obvious that Herndon could expect no help from the Lincolns in his work, but he continued his collecting, writing, and lecturing nonetheless.

There was also the question of the custody of the Abraham Lincoln papers, letters, and other manuscripts that Justice Davis

35 Lincoln to Clinton L. Conkling, Dec. 17, 1917, ISHL.
36 *Ibid.*
37 Randall, *Mary Lincoln*, 395.
38 Lincoln to William H. Herndon, Oct. 1, 1866, quoted in Mearns, *The Lincoln Papers*, I, 49–50.
39 William H. Herndon to Jesse W. Weik, n.d. but about 1888, quoted in Donald, *Lincoln's Herndon*, 230.
40 Donald, *Lincoln's Herndon*, 231, quoting in part Lincoln to Herndon, Dec. 13 and 24, 1866.

brought from Washington and held "under seal" at his home in Bloomington, Illinois. Over the years Robert, always acting in consultation with the Judge, refused to give them to several different people. Davis' biographer feels that posterity gained by these refusals for none of the early would-be writers had the capacity to use adequately the great collection of papers.

During the summer of 1867, Lincoln wrote that he knew of no need to go through the papers, and besides "It would be a great advantage to have Nicolay by when they are opened as he would know the purport of all of them."[41] In 1869, when Ward H. Lamon started his literary work, Lincoln wrote that he had just learned that Lamon had paid Herndon four thousand dollars for his Lincoln materials but that as yet Lamon had not contacted him personally. Wryly the Chicago attorney noted that he did not know what type of book Lamon planned, but it "will have to be sensational to get his money back."[42] A short while later, however, Lincoln was writing to Lamon that a mutual friend had mentioned that the would-be author wanted a certain diary from the Lincoln papers. Once more Lincoln reiterated his feeling that the time was not yet right to embark upon such a project, but if Lamon would say specifically what he wanted, Lincoln would judge the individual item requested, and if it seemed proper, he would allow it to be used. As to the question of a diary, "I never understood that my father kept a diary."[43]

In future years many persons became angry because Lincoln regarded his father's personal papers as his personal property, but that they were and that they would remain until he saw fit to place them before the public. As late as the middle part of 1873, Judge Davis could still write, "President Lincoln's papers have never been opened since they were hurriedly packed at the time of his death."[44] However, early the next year Lincoln wrote Davis that Nicolay and Hay were anxious to get to work on their project, and that they would need the papers stored at Bloomington. Lincoln

41 Lincoln to David Davis, Aug. 13, 1867, ISHL.
42 Lincoln to Davis, Nov. 26, 1869, *ibid.*
43 Lincoln to Ward H. Lamon, Dec. 30, 1869, Huntington Library.
44 David Davis to J. W. Schuckers, June 27, 1873, ISHL.

requested that the Judge have them sent by express to his office in Chicago where he had a vault and where he could first make a quick examination so as to remove "anything purely private," and then he would turn them over to his two friends.[45]

Although Mrs. Lincoln and her sons chose not to live in Springfield, they still owned their family home, which was generally rented out to one tenant or another. When, in 1867, Mrs. Lincoln's sister's husband, Dr. Wallace, died, his family was left almost destitute. Robert Lincoln proposed that Mrs. Wallace live in their old home and he would pay his brother Tad money to compensate for the loss of his share of the yearly rental. Arrangements were accordingly made, but Mrs. Wallace finally declined the offer.[46]

Taking all matters into consideration, "Robert Lincoln could hardly have shown himself to better advantage than in his correspondence regarding his father's estate."[47] Not only was he kindly and considerate of others, but he was starting to demonstrate those executive and administrative abilities that would contribute to his eventual success in his profession, in business, and in politics. Although in future years he would manage matters much more complicated than the Abraham Lincoln estate, still this was his first important experience in that type of work, and his success in that first instance was such that it was possible for the busy Justice Davis, who had his own affairs and career to handle, to be concerned with only major matters and issues. Robert Lincoln handled the details and did the chores.

During these years Lincoln's mind was not entirely on either his legal career, the estate, Lincoln biographers, or his mother's problems. He continued to live in Chicago, sometimes alone and sometimes with his mother and brother. Mrs. Lincoln bought a house at 375 West Washington in Chicago, where she and her sons lived until about May 1, 1867. When she moved from there, Robert took up residence alone at the Tremont House.[48] At

---

45 Lincoln to Davis, Feb. 18, 1874, *ibid.*
46 Lincoln to Davis, Nov. 18 and Dec. 6, 1867, *ibid.*
47 King, *Lincoln's Manager*, 242.
48 Evans, *Mrs. Abraham Lincoln*, 189.

least twice he took trips out west, once in the fall of 1866 and again in late 1867, when he went to Cheyenne, Wyoming, with a "pleasant party" and "enjoyed the trip very much."[49] During the summer of 1867, he was in Washington and, accompanied by Congressman Judd of Illinois, sat in on the Surratt trial then in progress.[50]

There was also the problem of Mary Harlan. Lincoln's name had been linked with other young ladies. It is said that he was once interested in the daughter of Senator John P. Hale of New Hampshire; another admirer of hers was an actor named John Wilkes Booth.[51] After April, 1865, Robert Lincoln only occasionally saw Mary Harlan, for she continued to live in Washington. However, they must have had some understanding between them that they would wed; possibly the wedding would have taken place sooner had not the tragedy of the spring of 1865 taken place. The parents of the young couple favored the match. Mary Todd Lincoln wrote of her future daughter-in-law as a "young lady, who is so charming and whom I love so much."[52]

According to the Washington *Evening Star* of September 21, 1868, "Robert Lincoln, son of the late President, it is rumored, will be married this fall to a daughter of Senator Harlan."[53] Three days later the same paper reported that the groom, his mother and brother had arrived the night before and that the marriage would take place immediately.[54]

On the evening of September 24, 1868, Robert Todd Lincoln and Mary Eunice Harlan were married at the home of the bride's parents, 304 H Street, with Bishop Matthew Simpson, of the Methodist Episcopal Church, officiating. An account of the event reported:

> Owing to the sad circumstances connected with the death of

[49] Lincoln to Davis, Oct. 30, 1866, and Dec. 6, 1867, ISHL.
[50] Chicago *Times*, June 26, 1867.
[51] Lewis, *Myths After Lincoln*, 168.
[52] Mary Lincoln to Mrs. White, Aug. 19, 1868, quoted in Sandburg and Angle, *Mary Lincoln*, 285.
[53] Washington *Evening Star*, September 21, 1868.
[54] Washington *Evening Star*, Sept. 24, 1868.

President Lincoln in this city, now nearly four years ago, it was determined by the families of both the bride and groom that the ostentatious displays customary on such occasions should be avoided.[55]

The approximately thirty-five invited guests began to arrive at the Harlan home at about half-past seven in the evening. They included: Secretary of the Treasury and Mrs. Hugh McCulloch with their daughter; Secretary of the Navy and Mrs. Gideon Welles and their son, Edgar T. Welles, the latter a close friend of the groom; Mrs. Edwin M. Stanton and her son Edwin, Jr.[56]; and Senator Alexander Ramsey of Minnesota.[57] Shortly after eight o'clock, the bridal couple entered the parlor, which was described as "tastefully decorated with rare flowers," and took their places before Bishop Simpson in the center of the room. Mary Harlan was gowned in white silk and satin, "plain," but "exceedingly tasteful and rich." By contrast, nearby stood Mrs. Abraham Lincoln in deep mourning attire. After the ceremony was concluded, the party was served a supper and for an hour and a half they chatted before leaving the Harlan home.

The next day Mr. and Mrs. Lincoln left Washington for New York in a car attached to the 12:30 P.M. train. Mrs. Abraham Lincoln and Tad went with them as far as Baltimore, where they sailed for Europe on October 1. Edgar Welles and Edwin M. Stanton, Jr., went with them to New York. "Mr. J. H. Wormley, Jr., accompanied the party to New York as caterer."[58] The young couple spent at least part of their honeymoon at the Hoffman House in New York City, where they were reported to be staying early in October.[59] After two weeks there they returned to Washington to stay a few days with the Harlans.[60] Then, on October

55 *Ibid.*, Sept. 26, 1868.

56 Edwin M. Stanton was absent from Washington and speaking in Ohio, or presumably he would have been in attendance. *Ibid.*, Oct. 6, 1868.

57 For a full description of the guests, their attire, and the like, see *ibid.*, Sept. 26, 1868.

58 *Ibid.*, Sept. 25, 1868.

59 *Ibid.*, Oct. 3, 1868.

60 *Ibid.*, Oct. 20, 1868.

19, they left "for Chicago, where Mr. Lincoln is permanently and successfully engaged in the legal profession."[61]

One of the guests at the wedding, Gideon Welles, recorded his impressions of the groom, who had often been his house guest during the years he had visited Washington to see Mary Harlan:

> Regard for his father made him always a welcome guest, and I also highly esteem and respect Robert himself and have done so from our first acquaintance in 1861, when he was here with his father at the inauguration. His deportment and character, then and always, impressed me favorably.[62]

Robert and Mary Lincoln lived together as husband and wife for nearly fifty-eight years. They had three children: Mary, born October 15, 1869; Abraham, born August 14, 1873; and Jessie Harlan, born November 6, 1875.

[61] *Ibid.*
[62] Morse, *Diary of Gideon Welles*, III, 444.

Chapter 6

Chicago Attorney at Law

IT HAS BEEN SAID that had Abraham Lincoln lived to retire from the presidency, he and his son Robert would have become law partners in Springfield or, if not there, perhaps Chicago where Mrs. Mary Lincoln would have preferred to live.[1] Instead, Robert Lincoln entered the law office of Scammon, McCagg and Fuller, located on Lake Street in Chicago. Jonathan Young Scammon, a distinguished attorney was head of the firm;[2] his partners were E. B. McCagg and Samuel W. Fuller.[3] Lincoln studied for over a year learning his chosen profession, and, in addition, he took law courses at the "old" University of Chicago in 1865 and 1866.[4]

Early in 1867, Lincoln was ready to commence his practice. In January he wrote Judge Davis that Mr. Fuller was making a trip to Washington, and although he was inclined to join him because Mary Harlan was there, he would stay in Chicago and look after his interests. Something important might turn up, for "You

---

[1] Albert A. Woldman, *Lawyer Lincoln,* 337.

[2] For a sketch of Scammon and the firm, see John Moses and Joseph Kirkland, eds., *History of Chicago,* II, 58–59.

[3] Fuller is sometimes confused with Melville Weston Fuller, later Lincoln's friend and chief justice of the United States. However, Melville Fuller was not associated with this firm.

[4] Records in the Archives Library, University of Chicago. Letter to the author from Elizabeth V. Benyon, assistant law librarian, University of Chicago, Mar. 7, 1960.

know men are sometimes struck by lightning."[5] On February 25 he was admitted to the Illinois bar.[6] Lincoln then formed a partnership with Charles T. Scammon, the son of Jonathan Young Scammon. However, it was not long before trouble appeared. In July, 1867, Lincoln reported to David Davis that his partner had been on "a successsion of 'sprees' since early in May and is now I believe under treatment in the East." Mr. Fuller felt that Robert should "cut loose from him regardless of the pecuniary consequences," and this Lincoln was inclined to do. He felt that his partner was "utterly worthless and I cannot tell to what extent his debauches damage me personally." Turning philosophical, he added, "I suppose my experience is that of most men— sometimes smooth and sometimes rough sailing—though I think I have too much of the rough."[7] Shortly thereafter Lincoln learned that young Scammon would not return for "some time if at all again." When the older Scammon returned from a business trip, Lincoln told him of his intention to dissolve the partnership, which he did although it was not formally ended until several months later.[8]

Without doubt the magic name of Lincoln opened many doors for the young attorney, but it may be said with equal certainty that he had considerable ability and soon won for himself a place in the legal profession. The story was told that just after Lincoln started his business, he was sitting alone in his office when a messenger brought a note from the Chicago agent of a respected insurance company. The agent asked the young lawyer to look up the title of a piece of property, which he did in about half an hour. Then, the messenger returned with a request that Lincoln present his bill. At first the young man was tempted to charge nothing since he hoped more business from the company might come his way. But then he remembered what he had been taught about the value of a lawyer's time, so he finally hit upon twenty-five

---

[5] Lincoln to David Davis, Jan. 19, 1867, ISHL.

[6] Mr. James T. Hickey of the Illinois State Historical Library now owns the original law license.

[7] Lincoln to Davis, July 29, 1867, ISHL.

[8] Lincoln to Davis, Aug. 1, 1867, *ibid.*

dollars as what he thought was a rather high fee. Just then an older attorney arrived on the scene. (In the account of the incident he is identified as "old Judge Logan," under whom Lincoln was supposed to have studied.) When told of the situation, he tore up the bill, which led Lincoln to assume he had charged too much. The Judge then wrote out a new statement in the amount of $250! The bill was paid and Lincoln was told more work would come his way. Commented his more experienced friend, "You don't want to be a d——d eleemosynary institution for insurance companies, do you?"[9]

While his partner was away, Lincoln wrote Judge Davis, "I am doing the work to the best of my ability and know of no cause of dissatisfaction with me."[10] By the fall of 1867, Lincoln could report to his "second father," "My business as it is running now, does not fall very far short of supporting me." At this time the young man had collected a note due to his father and sent the money along to the Judge with the suggestion that it be invested in United States securities. He added that he was not yet ready to start speculating so had no particular need for the money.[11] In December of that same year, Lincoln took some time off and went to Ottawa, Illinois, for the wedding of his friend Norman Williams to the daughter of Judge Caton.[12] The guest observed, "Judge Caton made a very large entertainment of the affair and kept us all there for the rest of the week."[13]

In the years immediately following his marriage, Lincoln was busy with his practice. Often he traveled on business, and sometimes, too, he and his wife visited the Harlans in Washington. In December, 1868, the week after Christmas, he wrote that he was a bachelor again for his wife had remained with her family.[14] These were months of comparative calm and happiness. After the ar-

---

9 Newspaper clipping, "From the Washington Post," dated in pencil 1889, Lincoln National Life Insurance Company. Robert Lincoln had no known connection with a "Judge Logan," though his father had been a partner of Stephen T. Logan.
10 Lincoln to Davis, Aug. 1, 1867, ISHL.
11 Lincoln to Davis, Sept. 4, 1867, *ibid.*
12 Lincoln to Davis, Dec. 18, 1867, *ibid.*
13 *Ibid.*
14 Lincoln to Davis, Dec. 31, 1868, ISHL.

rival of their first child, Lincoln reported to Judge Davis that the baby was "as fat and healthy as one could wish. My wife has progressed towards her complete recovery very rapidly." The family had established a home on Wabash Avenue and they hoped "to be able to welcome" the Judge "before long."[15] Almost a year later he informed Davis that he had been so busy in court he had not yet had an opportunity to go to Springfield, which evidently was necessary for one reason or another.[16]

Robert Lincoln also felt responsible for his mother and brother. On January 17, 1868, he wrote Judge Davis of Tad's trials:

> I have put Tad into a very good school where he appears to be learning very fast. While I was away in Washington, mother took him to a dentist—a very good one—who said that his teeth should be gradually forced into a proper position by means of a spring frame set in his mouth. He had already made it and it was annoying Tad very much. He could hardly speak so as to be understood and to keep him talking in that way for a year I thought, with his present bad habits of speech, to be risking too much. I got the advice of another dentist, who said that such an apparatus was not at all necessary. I have stopped his using it and I have put him in charge of a man named McCoy of whom you may have heard, who teaches Elocution telling him to make him pronounce correctly— I think he is improving under McCoy's efforts.[17]

At that time Tad was enrolled at the Chicago Academy,[18] but the latter part of 1868 he and his mother went to Europe and stayed until the spring of 1871.

On May 10, 1871, Robert wrote Judge Davis that he expected his mother and Tad to return at any time. As to the future, "I have not thought much as to what I shall advise Tad to do. He is now past eighteen and entitled to be consulted. I have no fears about him if he is as good a boy as I am told."[19] The joy of their

15 Lincoln to Davis, Nov. 4, 1869, *ibid.*
16 Lincoln to Davis, Nov. 10, 1870, *ibid.*
17 Lincoln to Davis, Jan. 17, 1868, *ibid.* According to the Chicago city directory for 1868, Amasa McCoy was a professor of vocal culture and elocution.
18 Randall, *Lincoln's Sons*, 237.
19 Lincoln to Davis, May 10, 1871, *ibid.*

arrival soon turned to grief. Tad had caught cold on the ocean voyage and by the end of May he was seriously ill. At first there was hope for his recovery, but, as the weeks passed, that hope vanished. Thomas Lincoln died in Chicago, July 15, 1871.[20] A decade later Robert Lincoln, in a letter to Isaac N. Arnold, said of his brother: "Poor Tad was a good boy and extra ordinarily affectionate and firm in his friendships. . . . He was only eighteen when he died but he was so manly and self reliant that I had the brightest hopes for his future."[21] Weeks after Tad's funeral and burial in Springfield,[22] which Robert had taken charge of, the sole surviving son of Abraham Lincoln confided, "There is no use trying to disguise the fact that things are very gloomy here."[23] Work proved to be the restorer and at the end of November, Lincoln said he was pressed with so much insurance work so as hardly to have any time to himself.[24]

ROBERT T. LINCOLN was a resident of Chicago from 1865 to 1911. Chicago of the post-Civil War era was the ever-growing, bustling, hard-working city so celebrated in story and song. The population was increasing rapidly, partly as a result of the arrival of large numbers of immigrants. It was during this period that many of Chicago's great fortunes began and that some of its cultural organizations and institutions were established. One of these was the Chicago Club, established in 1869.[25] This organization was formed by the younger, rising generation of men in the city. Lincoln was a charter member and in later years served as its president.[26] In 1874 the Chicago Literary Club was formed, and in February, 1876, Lincoln joined this group and remained a member for many years.[27] When the Chicago Bar Association was formed on May 27, 1874, he took an active part in its organiza-

---

[20] See especially Helm, *Mary, Wife of Lincoln*, 293–95.
[21] Lincoln to Isaac N. Arnold, Mar. 28, 1881, CHS.
[22] Randall, *Mary Lincoln*, 425.
[23] Lincoln to Davis, Oct. 30, 1871, ISHL.
[24] Lincoln to Davis, Nov. 30, 1871, *ibid.*
[25] Caroline Kirkland, *Chicago Yesterdays*, 201–15.
[26] *Ibid.*, 203, 211.
[27] Frederick William Gookin, *The Chicago Literary Club*, 224.

tion.[28] In 1876 and 1877, Lincoln served as vice-president of the Chicago Historical Society.[29] An active church member, he was an elder and trustee of the Second Presbyterian Church from 1879 until 1889.[30]

In a sense, Robert Lincoln belonged to the new Chicago, for not too long after he took up residence in the city, the old town was destroyed by the great fire of October, 1871. This conflagration made possible the great new metropolis that later came into existence. Lincoln was in the city at the time of the fire, but there is no record of what, if anything, he lost in the destruction, other than certain of his father's papers which perished.[31] John Hay was visiting Lincoln at the time and together they did what they could to help their friends. Jonathan Young Scammon was away from his home at the time and Lincoln and Hay called on Mrs. Scammon to offer their help. At that moment it looked as though the Scammon residence was not in great danger, and Lincoln advised the lady of the house to remain calm and not to remove any of the household goods, since in the event they were damaged, their removal would cause possible complications with the company that insured them. Mrs. Scammon eventually disregarded this advice and fled with what she could take with her, leaving the home and the remainder of the furnishings to be consumed.[32]

Sometime in 1872, Robert T. Lincoln formed a new law partnership. The exact date of the beginning of this new firm, Isham and Lincoln, is not known. February, 1872, has been suggested, but there is some possibility that it might have been started later in the year, as during the summer Lincoln and his family took a tour of Europe and were away from Chicago for several months.[33] The senior partner of the new firm was Edward Swift Isham

28 Currey, *Chicago*, II, 319–20.

29 A. T. Andreas, *History of Chicago*, III, 413.

30 Letter to the author from Eleanor J. Stiles, Church secretary, Oct. 7, 1960.

31 Lincoln to H. S. Horne, Jan. 4, 1873, Historical Society of Pennsylvania. Fortunately the bulk of the Lincoln manuscripts was in Bloomington with Justice Davis.

32 Kirkland, *Chicago Yesterdays*, 219–20.

33 John M. Palmer, ed., *The Bench and Bar of Illinois*, II, 390, gives the February date. Harry J. Dunbaugh of Isham, Lincoln and Beale, in a conversation, Chicago, July, 1959, said the date is in doubt. In May, Lincoln wrote to David Davis,

Robert T. Lincoln as a college student.

At the Caton wedding, 1867. Robert T. Lincoln, center, standing.

Young Robert T. Lincoln as shown in a photograph in the possession of the Lincoln National Life Foundation, Fort Wayne, Indiana.

Mary Harlan Lincoln, 1868.

Mary, Abraham II (Jack), and Jessie, the children
of Mary and Robert Lincoln.

Robert T. Lincoln's beloved "Hildene."
Reproduced, with permission, from Bigelow and Otis,
Manchester, Vermont, a Pleasant Land Among the Mountains.

The Lincoln home on Lake Shore Drive in Chicago.

Left to right: Edgar T. Welles, Robert T. Lincoln,
and Edwin M. Stanton, Jr., at Brady's Studio, *circa* 1876.
Reproduced from the collections of the Library of Congress.

Robert T. Lincoln, 1889.

(1836–1902), a native of Bennington, Vermont, and graduate of Williams College.[34] It was natural that the two men should become acquainted for Lincoln lived at 653 Wabash Avenue while Isham lived at 554. Since Isham was somewhat older and more experienced in the legal profession, he logically was the head of the firm. Lincoln looked up to him. When, in 1874, John Hay tried to get his friend to write something for a fraternity group, Lincoln protested that he had "long passed the follies of youth"; furthermore "Recall that I have to set an example to a daughter and a son, to say nothing of Isham."[35] Lincoln and his partner were very congenial and always maintained excellent relations. Isham had a summer home in Manchester, Vermont, and his partner frequently spent time there until finally he built a home of his own. From time to time several other attorneys were associated with the firm, but fifteen years after its founding the partnership became Isham, Lincoln and Beale, which it remains today. The third partner was William Gerrish Beale (1854–1923), a native of Winthrop, Maine, and a graduate of Bowdoin College.[36] The offices of Lincoln and his associates were located in several places before being moved to 72 West Adams Street, the permanent headquarters of the firm. In 1879 their building burned, but the loss to the firm was small—one thousand dollars —for their law library was saved almost intact.[37]

Both Isham and Lincoln brought to their new firm an already established practice, and from the beginning the pair prospered. Much of the business came from Chicago and Cook County, but as early as 1874, Isham and Lincoln were doing business out of state.[38] As time passed, the partnership took on more and more

"I am hoping to get off next month for a few months across the water with my family." (Lincoln to Davis, May 17, 1872, ISHL.) Lincoln was in Paris in September, as confirmed by a letter to Elihu B. Washburne, Sept. 7, 1872, Washburne Papers, Library of Congress.

34 For a sketch of Isham, see *History of the City of Chicago, Its Men and Institutions*, 363–64.

35 Lincoln to John Hay, Jan. 17, 1874, Hay Papers.

36 For a sketch of Beale, see the *National Cyclopedia of American Biography*.

37 *Illinois State Journal*, Jan. 6, 1879.

38 Lincoln to Darwin W. Esmond, Jan. 22, 1874, regarding land matters in New York. Letter in possession of the writer.

the aspect of a counseling firm, but in the early period, they did mostly trial work.[39] Robert Lincoln was an able practitioner, who always did his full share of the work. Isham was more often concerned with the actual presentation of the case, but Lincoln usually did the preparation.[40] So long as the latter remained a member of the firm, he put in long hours at his desk. In time, Isham and Lincoln had cases that ranged from local matters to cases before the Supreme Court of the United States. The firm represented a number of important clients including the Pullman Company, Commonwealth Edison Company, Chicago Elevated Railways, and Marshall Field and Company. It also drew the wills of Walter L. Newberry, Marshall Field, and Joseph Medill of the Chicago *Tribune*. Lincoln was himself responsible for the Newberry will and also personally handled the litigation that followed in the courts when the will was contested. This estate involved some five million dollars, and the legal involvements were quite complicated. It was said that Lincoln's handling of the matter was "a marvel of ingenuity."[41] In 1872, Lincoln obtained for General Horace Porter the job of New York representative for the Pullman Company.[42] The young man's position was such that he received free passes on the railroads.[43]

By the early 1870's Robert T. Lincoln was an important and influential member of the legal and business community. Said a contemporary in discussing his abilities:

> He inspires one immediately with perfect faith in his uprightness and honesty. The result of this is seen in the perfect confidence placed in him by his clients, and also in the great consideration and weight given to his statements by the courts. He is not only scrupulously accurate and just in all his doings and statements, but

[39] Conversation with Harry J. Dunbaugh, Chicago, July 13, 1959.

[40] *Ibid.*

[41] Hulburd Dunlevy, "Robert Todd Lincoln," *Green Bag*, Vol. I, No. 8 (Aug., 1889), 322.

[42] Elsie Porter Mende, *An American Soldier and Diplomat*, 123.

[43] Acknowledging receipt of his annual pass, Lincoln to S. H. Melvin, president of the Gilman, Clinton and Springfield Railroad, Jan. 18, 1873, ISHL.

his whole moral sense is so keen that the slightest irregularity on the part of others meets with the severest condemnation.[44]

Almost inevitably, Lincoln's abilities as a lawyer were compared to those of his father and it was noted that he had much of the same humor that had characterized the elder Lincoln.

> Not very long ago in trying a suit, Mr. Lincoln addressed the defendant, Mr. Windet,—a man who was hopelessly insolvent, but given to great schemes about which he did a great deal of talking. Mr. Lincoln pronounced the defendant's name with the accent on the first syllable. The gentleman corrected him saying, "Mr. Windét, if you please, sir, Mr. Windét" accenting the last syllable. Mr. Lincoln replied very quietly: "I beg your pardon, sir; but I think that I am to be excused for not knowing whether to associate more of wind or debt with you."[45]

Although Lincoln was achieving considerable success in his public life, personal problems were crowding in to mar an otherwise happy existence. Following the death of her youngest son, Tad, Mrs. Abraham Lincoln was almost totally unable to cope with life's problems. As early as 1867 the Chicago *Tribune* carried a story implying that she was insane.[46] Never emotionally sound, she had been shattered by the tragic loss of her husband and three of her sons. For some time her eccentricities had been common knowledge, presented before the general public by the newspapers. There had been the celebrated incident when the former First Lady, believing herself poverty stricken, put her old clothes on sale in New York.[47] This incident alone caused Robert Lincoln to behave "like a maniac," and made him almost threaten to take his own life.[48] For some time the question of his mother's future had been a matter of concern. Lincoln, writing to Mary Harlan before their marriage, had said, "I have no doubt that a great many good and amiable people wonder why I do not take

[44] Dunlevy, "Robert Todd Lincoln," *Green Bag*, Vol. I, No. 8 (Aug., 1889), 322.
[45] *Ibid.*
[46] Chicago *Tribune*, Oct. 9, 1867.
[47] Randall, *Mary Lincoln*, 408–22.
[48] Mary Lincoln to Elizabeth Keckley, quoted in Sandburg and Angle, *Mary Lincoln*, 131.

charge of her affairs and keep them straight." At the same time he predicted, "I am likely to have a good deal of trouble in the future."[49] Mrs. Lincoln's troubles were now complicated by the fact that she was engaged in a running feud, this time supported by her son, with William H. Herndon, self-appointed authority on Abraham Lincoln. Among other issues that Herndon was then raising was the question whether or not Abraham Lincoln's parents had ever been married. Mrs. Lincoln, proper southern lady that she was, was horrified at the thought that her husband might have been illegitimate. Even when evidence to the contrary was found, Herndon continued his accusations and would not be silenced. Then, too, the Ann Rutledge story did not help Mrs. Lincoln's emotional stability.

After the death of Tad, Mrs. Lincoln continued the wanderings that had so characterized her life after 1861. The year 1875 brought a crisis. In March she was in Florida, when she was seized by the hallucination that her only surviving son was dying. She at once telegraphed Robert's physician, Dr. Ralph N. Isham, in Chicago: "My belief is that my son is ill; telegraph. I start for Chicago tomorrow."[50] Dr. Isham, who was the uncle of Lincoln's law partner, immediately upon receipt of this strange message contacted Lincoln, who wired his mother that he was in perfect health. Mrs. Lincoln before receiving his message sent the following to her son: "My dearly beloved son, Robert T. Lincoln— Rouse yourself and live for your mother; you are all I have; from this hour all I have is yours. I pray every night that you may be spared to your mother."[51] It is not difficult to understand that a mentally ill woman, who had lost three sons already, could imagine that her surviving child was also dying. She arrived in Chicago, March 15, 1875, and, refusing to stay at Lincoln's home, went instead to the Grand Pacific Hotel.[52] Her son must have instantly recognized her state of mind, and he watched over the poor woman as best he could. On one occasion she attempted to

49 Lincoln to Mary Harlan, quoted *ibid.*, 133.
50 Mary Lincoln to Dr. Ralph N. Isham, Mar. 12, 1875, quoted *ibid.*, 307.
51 Mary Lincoln to Lincoln, quoted *ibid.*, 307.
52 Sandburg and Angle, *Mary Lincoln*, 308.

leave her room without being properly dressed, and when Robert attempted to restrain her, she screamed, "You are going to murder me." At other times her hallucinations returned. She predicted that fire would destroy Chicago, as it had four years earlier, but this time her son's home would be the only house in the city untouched by the flames.[53]

Mary Todd Lincoln's problems were made more serious by her carrying on her person, fifty-seven thousand dollars in cash and securities. Her long standing mania for buying things was worse than ever. Her shopping expeditions resulted in the purchase of items for which she had no need or even any use.[54] It goes without saying that a mentally disturbed woman given to wanderings about a large city with large sums of money in her possession was in danger. For temporary protection Robert Lincoln hired a man to guard his mother, without her knowledge, when she went out. For her permanent safety some other solution would have to be found.

Lincoln consulted David Davis and his mother's favorite cousin, John Todd Stuart. Several years before, he had mentioned to the judge the problem of his mother's spending money. Lincoln then said, "I am in constant hot water with her about the matter."[55] Both Davis and Stuart gave advice, but clearly the decision was with her son. "Robert Lincoln took the only possible course," he requested an insanity hearing.[56] This was the only method whereby Mrs. Lincoln could be restrained from possible self-injury, and more important, the only method whereby she could receive medical treatment. However, one can well imagine the effect that such a decision had on Robert Lincoln. To his friend John Hay he wrote at that time of the distress and anxiety of his mind: "I knew that the next day after my action the whole country would be flooded with criticisms, kind or unkind as might happen, but all based on a short press dispatch, which

53 *Ibid.*, 309.
54 *Ibid.* See also the papers relating to the insanity of Mary Lincoln collected by William E. Barton, University of Chicago.
55 King, *Lincoln's Manager*, 244. Lincoln to Davis, Nov. 10, 1870, ISHL.
56 Sandburg and Angle, *Mary Lincoln*, 305–308; see also the Barton Collection.

could not sufficiently give the facts. Yet I could not wait any longer." If he had waited, Lincoln wrote, he was leaving himself "responsible for a probable tragedy of some kind."[57]

To most people of that day, mental illness was something to be hidden and never discussed. Lincoln, always sensitive to the public gaze, had to go through a trial involving a figure in which the public was much interested—the widow of the sixteenth President of the United States.

On May 18, 1875, Dr. Isham wrote, "I hereby certify that I have examined Mrs. Mary Lincoln—widow—and that I am of the opinion she is insane and a fit subject for hospital treatment."[58] The following day Ayer and Coles, attorneys for Robert T. Lincoln, filed with the Cook County Court a petition for an insanity hearing. It was held the same afternoon and a series of witnesses told of Mrs. Lincoln's strange behavior, as she sat and listened and watched.

> Robert T. Lincoln, the petitioner then took the witness stand. His face was pale; his eyes bore evidence that he had been weeping, and his whole manner was such as to affect all present. His mother looked upon him benignly.[59]

He told his story, beginning with the day his mother first imagined that he was ill when he had not been sick in a decade. He recounted the later trouble he had with his mother, and mentioned that she had told someone he had attempted to poison her. Twice he broke down and cried in court. When Lincoln finished his testimony, the jury deliberated only a few minutes and returned a verdict of insanity. The court then ordered Mrs. Lincoln committed to an institution and appointed her son conservator of her estate. Mary Todd Lincoln in disbelief turned to her only living child and said, "O, Robert, to think that my son would have ever done this." To her tortured mind he had betrayed her, and that night she attempted suicide, only to be

57 Lincoln to John Hay, June 6, 1875, Hay Papers.
58 Barton Collection.
59 Sandburg and Angle, *Mary Lincoln*, 307.

frustrated in the attempt. Then she was taken to a private sanitarium where she received excellent care and treatment.[60]

The nation had watched with interest these proceedings. While many doubtless remembered Mrs. Lincoln's sometimes strange behavior during the White House years, others probably saw the trial as Robert Lincoln's method of getting his mother "put away" so that he could obtain her estate. Such tactics were, after all, not unknown. Even some relatives of the Lincolns disagreed with what Robert did. Through it all, however, Lincoln kept silent except to a few close friends. Mrs. Sally Orne, a good friend of Mary Lincoln's, wrote to him to inquire about her. Robert replied that he and his mother were "on the best of terms"—which was certainly stretching the truth—and went on to describe the care she was now receiving. He concluded that he had had no alternative but to take the action he had.[61]

Mary Todd Lincoln, confined to an institution, now had a purpose in life—to obtain her freedom. After four months in the sanitarium, she was released and was taken to the Edwards' home in Springfield where she lived quietly. Thirteen months after the first trial had found her insane, a second proceeding found her sane and the court ordered her estate restored to her. A physician who carefully studied her case, concluded that she had the same degree of irrationality at the second trial that she had had at the first.[62] Eight months after the first trial Robert Lincoln wrote to Judge Davis that he still regarded her "as unsound in mind."[63] Immediately after her second appearance in court, Mrs. Lincoln directed a bitter letter to "Robert T. Lincoln," which ordered the return of her possessions in these terms, "Send me all that I have written for, you have tried your game of robbery long enough."[64]

Lincoln had, of course, kept a detailed account of the management of his mother's estate, but he and his mother were completely separated and remained so for several years. It was not

---

[60] Randall, *Mary Lincoln*, 432–35.
[61] Lincoln to Mrs. J. H. Orne, as found in Helm, *Mary, Wife of Lincoln*, 295.
[62] Evans, *Mrs. Abraham Lincoln*, 226.
[63] Lincoln to David Davis, Nov. 16, 1875, ISHL.
[64] Mary Lincoln to Lincoln, quoted in Randall, *Mary Lincoln*, 434.

until May of 1881, that they were, at least to a limited degree, reconciled. One Sunday, Lincoln accompanied by his daughter Mary, namesake of her grandmother, called at the Edwards' home.[65] Lincoln in his capacity as secretary of war had been on an official visit to Fort Leavenworth and, accompanied by Adjutant General Drum and Judge Advocate Barr, had arrived in Springfield May 28 for a short visit.[66] Upon his return to Washington, Lincoln wrote Mrs. Orne that the reports in the press about his mother were "exaggerated very much. She is undoubtedly far from well and has not been out of her room for more than six months and she thinks she is very ill. My own judgment is that some part of her trouble is imaginary."[67] A little over a year later, on July 16, 1882, Mrs. Abraham Lincoln died; she had at last found rest.

The mental troubles of Mary Lincoln without doubt had an effect upon her eldest son. To Lincoln this was another of the personal tragedies that plagued him throughout his long life. David C. Mearns has written that Robert Lincoln had "the instincts of a recluse and the destiny of an exhibitionist."[68] He never liked publicity and his mother's troubles brought him a peculiar brand of attention. By 1870 he was already camera shy. When asked for a photograph, he replied, "I have not had a likeness of myself taken in a good many years."[69] How much his mother contributed to his attitude toward publicity is impossible to say with certainty. He did try to erase the record of "the distressing mental disorder" of his mother.[70] Part of that record was in the letters she had written. He had tried to destroy them, but he finally realized the futility of such a venture.

> Hundreds of them have been kindly sent to me for destruction and I am quite sure that there exist still other hundreds. All that I have known are of the same tenor; many have been printed in

65 *Ibid.*, 440.
66 *Illinois State Journal*, May 30, 1881.
67 Lincoln to Mrs. J. H. Orne, June 2, 1881, ISHL.
68 Mearns, *The Lincoln Papers*, I, 72.
69 Lincoln to M. D. Phillips, Sept. 10, 1870, ISHL.
70 Lincoln to LeGrand Van Valkenburgh, May 26, 1913, *ibid.*

newspapers and catalogues; and I long ago came to the conclusion that one could not imagine a more hopeless work than an effort to collect them or even a large fraction of them.[71]

Lincoln could well be described as overly sensitive, but considering the age in which he lived, his reaction was fairly normal. Of some comfort to him, if he read it, was the *Illinois State Journal*'s summation in November, 1881:

> The whole business is a most painful one, but justice to Secretary Lincoln and other friends of Mrs. Lincoln demands that the truth should now be told. The fact is, that while Mrs. Lincoln is, undoubtedly, physically and mentally ill, she is a hypochondriac as to her health and a monomaniac on the subject of money.[72]

Later, Adam Badeau perhaps summed up the situation better than anyone else when he wrote regarding the first insanity trial:

> It was a great relief to me to learn it, and doubtless the disclosure of the secret which her son must have long suspected—though, like the Spartan boy, he cloaked his pain—was to him a sort of terrible satisfaction. It vindicated his conduct; it proved him a worthy son of that great father who also bore his fate so heroically. The revelation . . . redeemed the unfortunate woman herself from the odium for which she was not responsible.[73]

[71] *Ibid.*
[72] *Illinois State Journal*, Nov. 26, 1881.
[73] Adam Badeau in the Chicago *Tribune*, Jan. 17, 1887.

Chapter 7

An Entry into Politics

Nothing could be more logical than for the son of Abraham Lincoln to be drawn into politics, willing or not. From the very start of his residence in Chicago, Lincoln, if yet unwilling to take part in politics himself, was still very much aware of events that were taking place around him. In the summer and fall of 1866, Chicago witnessed a bitter campaign for the federal House of Representatives. As Lincoln wrote to Justice Davis:

> There is a great deal of political excitement here and I hope Mr. J[ohnson] will not give any room for trouble by a stirrup speech. The fight between Wentworth and Judd is occupying the wire pullers and is somewhat bitter. The Tribune is going so far in its denunciation of Wentworth that it will have hard work if he is nominated.[1]

Writing to Davis in early 1867, he referred to a hot senatorial contest which indicated that Lyman Trumbull would "be elected without however any great enthusiasm on the part of his adherents."[2] That September, Lincoln was interviewed by a visiting Englishman who noted, "No one seemed to regard him as possessing any rank, by reason of his father having been President, nor did he so regard himself."[3] One wonders when Lincoln

1 Lincoln to David Davis, Sept. 4, 1866, ISHL.
2 Lincoln to Davis, Jan. 8, 1867, *ibid.*
3 The Reverend Newman Hall, "My Impressions of America," *The Broadway:*

first gave thought to the fact that he would inevitably be drawn into politics. About 1868, John G. Nicolay in writing to John Hay commented on the situation:

> I send back Bob's letter, which is certainly characteristic and shows the latent power of observation and comparison which is evidently in the blood. He still looks at politics through a reflecting medium—perhaps I should say an opaque one,—either making him incapable of arriving at a true estimate. Politics is a thing *à laisser ou à prendre*, but by no means to be despised, either in its nobler or baser relations to the times we live in. Nobody had a clearer perception of that point than his father. A little more age and experience will probably enable Bob to see it as well.[4]

The time in which Lincoln was then living was the Reconstruction period—the triumph of the radical Republicans over all that for which his father had stood. There followed the Grant regime with its corruption, which was merely typical of what was going on over the nation. Throughout his life Lincoln was a strong Republican and, indeed, never once waivered in his support of the party and its fortunes.[5] Yet, on actual issues his views are frequently not recorded. Where did he stand on the Reconstruction question? It is generally presumed that Lincoln was a loyal supporter of President Grant, yet in November, 1874, he wrote Gideon Welles:

> I wish that I could be as satisfied with the elections as you are. I am not interested in Grant and if I were satisfied the result was merely his overthrow there would be little cause for grief. You and I will yet pay taxes to compensate for the loss of slaves—I am afraid. If the effect of the elections shall be to divorce the Republican party from Grant and name a patriotic Union man President in '76 there will none rejoice more than I.[6]

A London Magazine (Mar.–Aug., 1869), reprinted in *JISHS*, Vol. XXXVII (1944), 184–85.

[4] John G. Nicolay to John Hay, about 1868, as found in Nicolay, *Lincoln's Secretary*, 253.

[5] For example, see the sketch of Lincoln in the Chicago *Tribune*, Jan. 11, 1887.

[6] Lincoln to Gideon Welles, Nov. 24, 1874, files of Isham, Lincoln and Beale, and used through the courtesy of Harry J. Dunbaugh.

Of course, he was far from willing to support the opposing group. On the views of Grant's 1872 opponent Horace Greeley, Lincoln commented, "of course, his opinions had ceased to be very important to sensible men."[7]

In 1876 the Republicans nominated "a patriotic Union man," Rutherford B. Hayes, and Lincoln did some campaigning on his behalf. He was one of the speakers at a mass meeting held at the Tippecanoe Battleground, near Lafayette, Indiana, in September,[8] for by then Lincoln was much in demand as a speaker at all sorts of functions.[9] After that most unusual of presidential elections, Hayes was declared duly chosen and inaugurated. The new Chief Executive thought well enough of Lincoln to write across one of his letters, "From a son worthy of his illustrious father, Abraham Lincoln."[10] Lincoln was also offered an appointment as assistant secretary of state. The President's friend and confidant, William Henry Smith, wrote Hayes regarding Lincoln's reaction to the offer:

> He is greatly delighted with your letter as well as the one written him by Mr. Evarts. He was already a warm friend of the administration but these letters have touched him deeply. The impulse at first was to write accepting, but he waited to consult his wife, business partner and a few other friends, nearly all of whom have presented to him the material interest side. He is building up a lucrative practice, and to go away now for any considerable length of time would be to sacrifice it.

Smith closed by noting that the friends of President Lincoln who knew of the offer were most pleased.[11] On October 10, 1877, Lincoln replied to the Chief Executive:

7 Lincoln to Judd Stewart, July 17, 1918, Huntington Library.

8 *Illinois State Journal*, Sept. 28, 1876.

9 Lincoln was so much in demand that he could not accept all the invitations. A request for him to speak at the Decoration Day observance in New York in 1875 received a not uncommon reply. Writing on May 20, Lincoln regretted that his engagements were such and his duties so great that it would be impossible for him to attend. *New York Times*, June 1, 1875.

10 President Hayes's notation on Lincoln to Rutherford B. Hayes, Oct. 10, 1877, Hayes Library, Fremont, Ohio.

11 William Henry Smith to Rutherford B. Hayes, Oct. 10, 1877, *ibid.*

It is with great regret therefore that I find myself, after grave consideration, compelled by the necessity of devoting myself to my profession for at least some years yet to come, to refrain from accepting the position.[12]

Not long after, John Hay wrote his friend: "I saw the President in Washington. The only thing of any importance he talked about was you. You evidently made a great impression on His Excellency."[13] Lincoln was still ripe for political preferment, but when Hayes was in search of a district attorney his friend Smith wrote: "Robert Lincoln would not accept because he could not afford to. Ditto with the other estimable men of that class."[14] Ultimately, John Hay became the assistant secretary of state and to him Lincoln wrote on one occasion, "I don't want to be minister to England or anywhere else," but he did wish to recommend a friend to office.[15] Suggesting and endorsing friends or acquaintances for office was a Lincoln pastime in this period, and indeed throughout his active life. In March, 1877, he wrote Secretary Evarts urging the appointment of George Schneider of Chicago as minister to Switzerland: "His appointment would reflect great credit on the government and I can only hope that it may be made."[16] To the President he suggested another friend as collector of Internal Revenue for the Chicago district.[17] Then he wrote Hayes asking that his cousin, Miss Mattie Todd, whom he had never met, be made postmistress of Cynthiana, Kentucky, where she lived.[18] He had started this practice in 1869 when he suggested to President Grant that Theodore Canisius, who had been consul at Vienna from 1861 until 1866, be returned to his post.[19]

April, 1876, found Robert Lincoln formally entered into poli-

---

12 Lincoln to Hayes, Oct. 10, 1877, *ibid.*
13 John Hay to Lincoln, Feb. 14, 1878, Thayer, *John Hay,* II, 20–21.
14 William Henry Smith to Rutherford B. Hayes, Aug. 9, 1878, Hayes Library.
15 Lincoln to John Hay, Dec. 12, 1879, Hay Papers.
16 Lincoln to William M. Evarts, Mar. 12, 1877, CHS.
17 Lincoln to Rutherford B. Hayes, July 9, 1877, Hayes Library.
18 Lincoln to Hayes, Nov. 19, 1878, *ibid.* On December 13, 1878, he thanked the President for making the appointment.
19 Lincoln to Ulysses S. Grant, Apr. 6, 1869, copy in ISHL.

tics, in that he himself was a candidate for public office. He was elected a supervisor of the town of South Chicago. This suburb of the large metropolis had been for some time under the control of a "gang of robbers," who practiced fraud and corruption by voting "themselves enormous salaries for doing nothing."[20] So successful were Lincoln's efforts that a decade later the press could say that he had "put the affairs of the town in good shape, and since then not a dollar of taxes had been levied for town purposes."[21] Unfortunately, the records of South Chicago, which was annexed to Chicago in 1889, have disappeared, and materials regarding this aspect of Lincoln's career have been lost.

At about the same time he was supervisor, a bill was introduced in the Illinois state legislature to make Lincoln, along with several others, a trustee of the monument to Stephen A. Douglas.[22] Governor Cullom appointed him a trustee of the Illinois Central Railroad in 1880.

As the presidential election of 1880 approached, Lincoln became active on behalf of the third-term attempt of Ulysses S. Grant. When a banquet was given in Chicago in December, 1879, to honor Grant on return from his world tour, Lincoln was present.[23] In Chicago on the evening of April 15, 1880, a mass meeting was held in the Central Music Hall, headlined as the "First Gun of the Third-Term in This State."[24] Colonel Frederick Grant, John A. Logan, Leonard Swett, Lincoln, and Stephen A. Douglas, Jr., were all in attendance. Governor Beveridge nominated Lincoln as the chairman of the meeting and he was applauded into the position. In a rousing bloody-shirt speech Lincoln alleged that "The Democratic party has by fraud and violence established for itself a majority in the National Senate and House of Representatives." He also raised the issue of Negro voting rights in the southern states. At last warming up to his main topic, Lincoln proclaimed, "We need a man who has before

20 Chicago *Tribune*, Jan. 11, 1887.
21 *Ibid.*
22 *New York Semi-Weekly Tribune* (New York City), Feb. 20, 1877, clipping in ISHL.
23 Chicago *Tribune*, Dec. 7, 1879.
24 *Ibid.*, Apr. 16, 1880.

this faced and cowed the hosts of rebellion."[25] One cannot help pondering Lincoln's change of heart on the subject of Grant nor being shocked at his poor taste in supporting probably the most inadequate of all the American Presidents. Still Lincoln proclaimed that Grant's courage and ability were known the world over. Then John A. Logan, whose support of Grant is not at all surprising, took over at the gathering and admitted that although the General had made some mistakes in the White House, he was more experienced now and was not likely to make them again.

The Republican county primary, which has been described as "riotous,"[26] was held May 8, 1880.[27] At issue was the control of the county convention that would, in turn, send ninety-two delegates to the state convention to be held later in Springfield. The Grant men did not do well, but Lincoln was elected a delegate from the Second Ward.[28] When the Cook County convention met on May 10, the anti-Grant forces were able to establish the unit rule, and thus shut out the General's forces. The Grant people withdrew and formed a rival delegation bound for Springfield. Lincoln himself was one of the "Palmer House" delegates, as the third-term supporters were called. When the credentials committee of the state convention met to attempt to settle the squabble, Lincoln presented the claim of the Grant delegates.[29] On the night of May 18, the Grant men gathered in the Representatives Hall of the State House for a meeting that was called "a notably enthusiastic one."[30] Lincoln was elected chairman and Stephen A. Douglas, Jr., was chosen secretary of the gathering. The rival claims of the two delegations from Cook County were settled by John A. Logan, who was in firm control, although he was accused of "bull-dozing" the convention. Seated were thirty-six Grant men and fifty-six anti-Grant men. The third-term supporters were in control of the state convention to the degree that

25 *Ibid.*
26 Don E. Fehrenbacker, *Chicago Giant*, 223.
27 Chicago *Tribune*, May 9, 1880.
28 *Ibid.*
29 *Daily State Journal* (Springfield), May 18, 1880.
30 *Ibid.*, May 19, 1880.

they bound the Illinois delegation to the national meeting to the unit rule, thus ensuring that Illinois would be solid for the General. Lincoln was suggested as a delegate to the national convention, but he declined this honor in favor of Stephen A. Douglas, Jr., who was sent instead.[31] Why Lincoln was not interested in going to the convention is not known. Perhaps he was too busy with his professional activities. At about this time he wrote John Hay relative to a possible trip to Washington, "It is too far to walk and I have no pass."[32]

In November, Lincoln was chosen by the voters of Illinois to be a presidential elector. His total state-wide vote was 318,037, which was the highest vote received by an elector.[33] It was said, "Not alone for the sake of his beloved father, but for his own worth, is Mr. Lincoln esteemed and honored by his associates, his clients and his friends."[34] Just before Lincoln went to Springfield to cast his ballot, he jokingly wrote to Hay that he had about made up his mind to vote for Garfield and Arthur.[35] (In the same letter he mentioned a railroad accident which he said had been "too close a call to be amusing."[36])

James A. Garfield and Chester A. Arthur had won office by the narrowest margins. Garfield presided over a Republican party still suffering from the aftermath of the Grant third-term attempt. He had been a dark-horse compromise candidate chosen from the anti-Grant forces. He had to heal the party's wounds. On November 16, 1880, not long after the election, Joseph Medill of the Chicago *Tribune* met with the President-elect. The editor was on friendly terms with Senator Logan, although they had been on opposite sides in the Grant movement. Medill told Garfield that Logan did not wish any position in the cabinet, but that it would be good to appoint some member of the Grant faction to that group. Garfield was most friendly with his caller, and it is

31 Chicago *Tribune*, Jan. 11, 1887.
32 Lincoln to John Hay, May 17, 1880, Hay Papers.
33 Andreas, *History of Chicago*, III, 852.
34 *Ibid.*, II, 469.
35 Lincoln to John Hay, Nov. 30, 1880, Hay Papers.
36 *Ibid.*

possible that the two men may have discussed Lincoln at this time.[37] There can be little doubt that Logan originated the idea of Lincoln's being in the cabinet, though others may have reached the President-elect with the notion first.

There was, however, a rumor that Grant himself did not wish Lincoln made secretary of war. To squelch the idea, Grant had his associate Adam Badeau write to Lincoln telling him that there was no truth in the story, that Grant would be happy to see Lincoln secretary of war, and that the letter might be made public if Lincoln so desired.[38] On January 10, 1881, Grant had written Senator Logan of his high opinion of Lincoln and said, "I believe it would strike the public most favorably to see him in the cabinet, and no one more than myself."[39] Later he expressed himself more fully:

> I write to you on the subject of a cabinet position for Illinois. I do not desire to give any recommendation. You mentioned in a letter to me the name of Robert Lincoln. There is nothing I could do for him, that would help him, that I would not do both for his own sake and for the profound respect and esteem in which I hold the memory of his father. But with no more means than he has, it would, in my estimation, be an injury to him to give him an office that would take him from his profession. To give him a position which he could not sustain himself well in might be still more injurious. Has he had the sort of practice that would enable him to prove acceptable as Attorney General? If so, it would help him in his practice when he retired. If otherwise it would hurt him. You can judge better of his fitness than I can.[40]

Grant ought not to have worried over Lincoln's fitness, for he would prove himself a better cabinet member than Grant usually managed to dredge up during his own presidency. Nor was Grant

---

[37] Robert G. Caldwell, *James A. Garfield*, 316.

[38] Adam Badeau in the Chicago *Tribune*, Mar. 6, 1887. In the Huntington Library there is a letter from Lincoln to "My dear General," dated February 27, 1881, which appears to be Lincoln's response to Badeau. The former speaks of his high regard for Grant and of his certainty that the newspaper story was not true.

[39] Ulysses S. Grant to John A. Logan, Jan. 10, 1881, John A. Logan Papers, Library of Congress.

[40] Grant to Logan, Feb. 15, 1881, *ibid.*

the only one who questioned Lincoln's appointment. Henry H. Keep on February 5 wrote that he objected to "a boy" being appointed to such an office. However, the tone of his letter indicated that he was really angry with Senator Logan and not Lincoln.[41]

On December 29, 1880, Garfield had another caller who wished to discuss cabinet appointments. He was Senator J. Donald Cameron, the Republican boss of Pennsylvania. Cameron also suggested the name of Robert T. Lincoln for a post, and evidently Garfield agreed with him.[42] Shelby M. Cullom of Illinois in his memoirs takes credit for the appointment of Lincoln.

> After General Garfield was elected to the Presidency, but before his inauguration, I determined that I would urge upon him the appointment of Mr. Robert T. Lincoln as a member of his cabinet. . . . With this purpose in view, I visited Garfield at his home in Mentor. . . . I at once told him the mission on which I had come. We had quite a long talk, at the end of which he announced that he would appoint Mr. Lincoln his Secretary of War.[43]

Cullom, undoubtedly, believed that he had been responsible for the appointment, but Garfield's biographer says:

> By February, R. T. Lincoln was definitely selected as a cabinet member from Illinois, especially after Logan in the interview of February 11, had approved his name. S. M. Cullom . . . takes credit for suggesting the name to Garfield on February 15, and inducing him to appoint him, but the journal [kept by Garfield] shows that he had been suggested by Cameron on December 29, was on the January 16 slate and had been approved by Logan, all before Cullom arrived.[44]

Of course, it is a sound politician who can make other politicians believe that he has been swayed by their opinions when, in fact, he has already made up his mind to do what his fellows propose before they come calling.

---

41 Henry H. Keep to James A. Garfield, Feb. 5, 1881, James A. Garfield Papers, Library of Congress.
42 Theodore C. Smith, *The Life and Letters of James Abram Garfield*, II, 1062.
43 Shelby M. Cullom, *Fifty Years of Public Service*, 124–25.
44 Smith, *Garfield*, II, 1080.

Others were busy on Lincoln's behalf. The Republican members of the Illinois delegation in Congress petitioned the Chief Executive to appoint Lincoln to a cabinet post.[45] Joseph Medill wrote Logan, "I quite agree with you that the selection of Robert Lincoln would please the people of Illinois and the whole nation and would be a happy compromise between rival aspirants. Unless this be done the chance of an Illinois man [entering] the cabinet is hardly worth considering."[46]

As for Lincoln while all this was going on, he was quietly going on about his business. In December he wrote John Hay that he would like to see Isham receive an appointment, although it had been so cold in Chicago that he was hoping for a job that would take him to Washington.[47] On January 29 he wrote the President-elect urging that Emery A. Storrs be appointed attorney general.[48] But on January 10, 1881, he wrote of his concerns for the future and for the appointment in a letter to Senator Logan:

MY DEAR GENERAL:

Your letter of Dec. 30th was duly received and should have had an earlier acknowledgment, at least to indicate to you my appreciation of the expression of friendship which has prompted your action and your letter to me. This, I answer you, I value very highly.

In the principal matter I am somewhat in doubt. I have strong faith that General Garfield's character, influenced by his broad culture and great political experience, will make his administration a marked one and that under it we may hope for an abatement of the subjects which have so long made our political contests discreditable to the country and for that reason I would certainly be glad to be associated with the administration. My own conviction however, is that situated as I am, I could not in justice to my family take any office which interfered with my present means of livelihood. This is perhaps not a patriotic way of looking at things and would not be justifiable in a situation which might arise but is not likely to do so again in our day. Mr. Isham and I have been together for eight years and our professional business is I think

45 Petition dated Jan. 14, 1881, Garfield Papers.
46 Joseph Medill to John A. Logan, Jan. 27, 1881, Logan Papers.
47 Lincoln to John Hay, Dec. 29, 1880, Hay Papers.
48 Lincoln to James A. Garfield, Jan. 29, 1881, Garfield Papers.

probably the largest in Chicago. I am 37 years old, in good health and am in receipt of a professional income which not only enables me to live in comfort but added to my other small resources encourages me to think that by handling my affairs properly I may be able to make a reasonable provision for my children. I like my present way of life and think I would not like a political career. If I should go into such a career, I think I would have to make up my mind to look out for my future. In such a place as you mention my income would be considerably reduced and my expenses largely increased and the outcome of the whole matter in its relation to those dependent on me would be a constant source of anxiety. Such positions are highly honorable of course and are proper objects of ambition but they seem to me to be in the nature of luxuries which can only be properly enjoyed by men of some fortune.

I am at the age in life at which I can best do the things I must do and I am not so old but that I could ten or twelve years later enjoy an honorable political place as well as now and I think it would not be more difficult to obtain them than now if I should be in a position to take it.

I think it very likely that you might be able to argue me out of my present notions by keeping my attention to the attractive side of the picture but sitting here cooly I think I am judging correctly for my own case. Feeling as I do now I should be compelled to decline any appointment and I think that inasmuch as my name has been mentioned to Gen. Garfield, he ought to know my feelings. I have a letter from Mr. Harlan this morning which made it necessary for me to telegraph him to see you and as he ought to know what I have written I enclose this to him asking him to give it to you.

I hope that nothing I have said will make you think that I do not feel under great obligations to you. These obligations I desire to express very warmly.

Believe me, My Dear General,
Very Sincerely yours
ROBERT T. LINCOLN[49]

To his friend Hay in February, Lincoln wrote much the same

---

49 Lincoln to John A. Logan, Jan. 10, 1881, Logan Papers.

type of letter. He said that if an office came his way it would embarrass him, for he would lose money on the proposition and would be eventually faced with no money and no business but with a wife and children to support. His children, "pretty well grown up," would want to know if their father could "keep them up in proper style and if not, why not."[50]

Whatever won Lincoln over to accepting the cabinet post is difficult to say, but on February 28, Garfield formally tendered the office of secretary of war to Robert T. Lincoln, and on March 2 the offer was formally accepted.[51] Lincoln was not present at the inauguration, but on March 8 he informed his chief that he would arrive in Washington shortly.[52]

The new cabinet was composed of: James G. Blaine, secretary of state; William Windom, secretary of the treasury; Robert T. Lincoln, secretary of war; Wayne MacVeagh, attorney general; Thomas L. James, postmaster general; William H. Hunt, secretary of the navy; and Samuel J. Kirkwood, secretary of the interior. The Senate confirmed all the appointments on March 5, 1881, and the officials took their respective oaths at their convenience. On the whole, the group was a reasonably good one, although in his attempt to pacify all segments of the Republican party, Garfield had made for himself some built-in problems. One soon came out into the open. Blaine was pushing the appointment of William E. Chandler as solicitor general, and Garfield made the nomination. Lincoln on calling upon Attorney General MacVeagh, who would be Chandler's superior, found him ready to resign if Chandler took office. The Secretary of War thereupon arranged for Chandler to decline the office and thus keep the cabinet intact.[53]

The appointment of Lincoln was generally well received, although, according to one newspaper, "The personal history of the new secretary of war is a brief one, except in so far as it falls

[50] Lincoln to John Hay, Feb. 7, 1881, Hay Papers.
[51] Lincoln to James A. Garfield, Mar. 2, 1881, Garfield Papers.
[52] Lincoln to Garfield, Mar. 8, 1881, *ibid.*
[53] Smith, *Garfield*, II, 1150.

within that of his father, the martyr President."[54] *Harper's Weekly* said of Lincoln that those who knew him considered him talented, and "His appointment has been received with favor all over the country."[55] According to the New York *Tribune*: "He is a member of a firm which represents the interest in the West of many Eastern insurance companies which have loaned large sums of money in Illinois and other Western states. The management of this business has developed in Mr. Lincoln a superior executive ability, and a capacity for the management of large interests involving many intricate details."[56]

When the Lincoln family arrived in Washington, they rented a house on Massachusetts Avenue, just east of the Thomas Circle.[57] The three children soon made themselves at home. Mary, the eldest, and Abraham II, called Jack by all, played at the White House with the younger Garfield children.[58] The proud father reported to his Aunt Emelie that he felt like a patriarch.[59] The writer Gail Hamilton, a member of Secretary Blaine's household, called on the Lincolns and observed:

> Robert Lincoln looks like his mother rather than his father. I called on his wife this morning, and she says she knows I shall like him, that he is thoroughly good, and honest, and noble. She has almost everything to make her handsome but health, and I told her so and that she ought to move Heaven and earth to get that, and she said it did her good to hear me talk,—it encouraged her so, and she meant to devote herself this summer to getting well, so as to come out strong next winter. She seems very sweet, and simple, and attractive.[60]

A few years later, after she had regained her health, Mrs. Lincoln was described as:

---

[54] Unidentified Boston newspaper clipping, dated 1881, Harvard University Archives.

[55] *Harper's Weekly*, Mar. 26, 1881.

[56] New York *Tribune*, Mar. 6, 1881.

[57] Chicago *Tribune*, May 31, 1884.

[58] Letter to the author from Abram Garfield, son of the President, June 14, 1958.

[59] Lincoln to Emelie Todd Helm, Jan. 5, 1881, copy in ISHL.

[60] H. Augusta Dodge, ed., *Gail Hamilton's Life in Letters*, II, 814. Diary entry for Mar. 3, 1881, which incorrectly reads 1880.

a slight, regular featured, delicate-faced lady, with very dark brown eyes. She is very simple and gracious in her manners. Her receptions this winter have been very popular, because Mrs. Lincoln appears to understand the work of making her guests comfortable.[61]

The Secretary had a workroom fitted up on the second floor of his home and spent many evenings there, "with a box of Henry Clay cigars at his elbow, for he is an almost incessant smoker, running over the papers from the department and the news of the day.[62] Unfortunately, the Garfield administration had barely started to settle into normal routine when tragedy struck.

On July 2, 1881, the President was shot by a disappointed office seeker as he stood in the Washington railroad station.[63] The trip on which the Chief Executive was embarking had been announced well in advance. *Harper's Weekly* in its June 18 edition reported that the President, together with Secretaries Blaine, Lincoln, and Hunt, would attend the commencement at Williams College.[64] The popular accounts of the shooting related that Secretaries Lincoln, Windom, Hunt, and Postmaster General James had seen their wives to the special train and were walking up and down the platform alongside the car when news reached them of the assassination.[65] This conflicts with a long account of the shooting written by Lincoln a few weeks after it occurred, in which he said "I was not going with him [the President] that day but was at the train to excuse myself for one day." From this it appears that Lincoln planned to join the Presidential party later. There was a cry "the President is shot." By his account Lincoln reached Garfield in fifteen seconds and found him lying on his back, eyes closed, and a terrible gray look about his face. Blaine and one or two strangers were standing by. Lincoln remembered that his driver was still waiting for him and so dispatched the man for a doctor. Eventually the wounded President

[61] Chicago *Tribune*, May 31, 1884.
[62] *Ibid.*
[63] Smith, *Garfield*, II, 1179–1201, contains a long detailed account of the shooting and continues the story to the death of the President.
[64] *Harper's Weekly*, June 18, 1881.
[65] *Ibid.*, July 8, 1881.

opened his eyes, his color improved, and he held out his hand to Lincoln. The Secretary of War thought the President the coolest man in the area. At first the extent of the danger to the Chief Executive was not known, but on the day of the shooting, the cabinet notified Vice-President Arthur that he should be prepared to take the oath of office as President in the event of Garfield's death.[66]

All this took place on Saturday morning, and Lincoln recorded that from then until Tuesday morning he was hardly away from the White House.[67] Lincoln was beseiged by requests for information regarding Garfield's condition. Former President Grant wired him from Long Branch, New Jersey, where Garfield was to have visited had the tragedy not taken place.[68] The Secretary telegraphed John A. Logan, "The President's condition is very alarming."[69] Garfield lingered from July 2 to September 19, 1881, and was eventually taken from Washington to Elberon, near Long Branch, New Jersey, where it was felt the climate would be more beneficial. At times there were hopes that the wounded man would recover, but on July 18, Lincoln wrote John Hay: "I wish I felt better about the President. He is an awfully wounded man."[70] During all those weeks the federal government appeared to function normally, but actually only the most routine business was transacted. Garfield fretted over this, and it was arranged for each cabinet member to have an interview with the President, where, by prearrangement, each "assured him that there was nothing calling for his action and that all things were going well."[71] Said Lincoln, the government was "running along— every man running his own Department and thinking he is doing so well that he may be President some day."[72] As far as his own

66 Smith, *Garfield*, II, 1179–80.
67 Lincoln to Norman Williams, July 28, 1881, Robert T. Lincoln Misc. Papers (hereafter cited as R. T. Lincoln Papers), Library of Congress.
68 *Harper's Weekly*, July 8, 1881.
69 Lincoln to John A. Logan, July 2, 1881, Logan Papers. Lincoln continued to keep Logan informed on July 3, 5, and 6, 1881.
70 Lincoln to John Hay, July 18, 1881, Hay Papers.
71 Smith, *Garfield*, II, 1195.
72 Lincoln to Norman Williams, July 28, 1881, R. T. Lincoln Papers, LC.

job, when Lincoln was interviewed by the press in August, he stated, "There is really nothing for me to tell you about the War Department. It goes on in a routine way." The Secretary hoped that there would be no new Indian troubles. He also optimistically predicted that the President would recover.[73]

James A. Garfield died September 19, 1881. Lincoln had been in New England and started for New Jersey on the day the President finally died.[74] When the end came, Arthur took the oath of office as Chief Executive at his New York City home, and a new administration began. The next day Robert T. Lincoln issued the following order:

> With profound sorrow the Secretary of War announces to the Army that James A. Garfield, President of the United States, died at Elberon, N.J., at twenty-five minutes before 11 in the evening of September 19, 1881.
>
> The great grief which is felt by the nation at the untimely death of the President will be especially felt by the Army, in whose services he bore so distinguished a part during the War of the Rebellion. In him the Army had lost a beloved Commander in Chief, friend, and former comrade.
>
> Proper honors will be paid to the memory of the late Chief Magistrate of the nation at headquarters of each military department and division and at each military station.
>
> The General of the Army will give the necessary instructions for carrying this order into effect.
>
> ROBERT T. LINCOLN
> *Secretary of War*[75]

At the same time, Lincoln sent another order to the army announcing that Arthur had now entered upon the duties of President.[76] On September 22, Arthur again took the oath in Washington, D.C. It was administered in the Capitol, by Chief Justice Waite, in the presence of the cabinet and several other persons.[77]

[73] New York *Tribune*, Aug. 15, 1881.

[74] Pendel, *Thirty-Six Years*, 102.

[75] Secretary of War, G.O. No. 71, Sept. 20, 1881, *Messages and Papers of the Presidents*, X, 4605–4606.

[76] Secretary of War, G.O. No. 72, Sept. 20, 1881, *ibid.*, X, 4606–4607.

[77] *Ibid.*, X, 4615.

Garfield was accorded an impressive state funeral, recalling to many, and no doubt to Robert Lincoln in particular, the sad memorials for his own father some years before. Lincoln took an active part in making the arrangements for the Garfield services, and, together with Secretary of the Navy Hunt, issued the final orders for the procession in Washington.[78] Later the second martyred Chief Executive was buried in Ohio, his native state.

When the Arthur administration began, Lincoln had little acquaintance with his new chief.[79] The Secretary of War, as well as the other cabinet officers, submitted his resignation, as is customary in such instances. At first, Arthur refused to accept the resignations,[80] but then, over a period of a few months, Arthur removed each cabinet official except Lincoln. Blaine was succeeded by Frederick T. Frelinghuysen, and Windom first by Charles J. Folger, then Walter Q. Gresham, and finally Hugh McCulloch, the latter having served as a member of the Lincoln and Johnson cabinets many years before. Secretary of the Navy Hunt was replaced by William E. Chandler; Secretary of the Interior Kirkwood by Henry M. Teller; Postmaster General James, first by Timothy O. Howe, then by Walter Q. Gresham, and finally by Frank Hatton; and Attorney General MacVeagh by Benjamin H. Brewster. It has been said that the Arthur cabinet was, on the whole, "a respectable one,"[81] and one that "worked together in harmonious and friendly fashion, diverse as were their tastes and characteristics."[82]

In some respects it seems strange that Lincoln did not follow his associates into retirement, but as time passed it became clear that he and the new President had high regard for one another. Decades later Lincoln spoke of Arthur as "my greatly beloved Chief, when I was in the War Department."[83] Still, there is some hint that Arthur may have hesitated in regard to keeping Lincoln.

78 *Ibid.*, X, 4611–12.
79 Chicago *Tribune*, Nov. 19, 1886.
80 Thomas Hunt, *The Life of William H. Hunt*, 242–43.
81 Hugh McCulloch, *Men and Measures of Half A Century*, 485.
82 Leon Burr Richardson, *William E. Chandler*, 335.
83 Lincoln to Charles Elmer Rice, Aug. 30, 1903, ISHL.

It was January, 1882, before Mrs. James G. Blaine wrote, "Arthur has at least asked Lincoln to remain."[84] A few days later she wrote to her son, undoubtedly with some bitterness, "Hunt and Delano [*sic*] and Lincoln are still in his cabinet, but I think he would be better pleased to have them where your Father is."[85]

The newspapers were given to much speculation on Lincoln's future. Early in 1882 it said that, although it had been understood that the Secretary of War would remain, "there are indications that the desire to retain him is not so strong that it overshadows all other considerations." This double talk was followed by the note that Lincoln could have an important foreign mission if he should leave the cabinet.[86] The Secretary himself may have had some thoughts about leaving, for in March, 1882, he complained to John Hay that his boy had had the chicken pox, his girls were not well, and he had had no fun in Washington: "I long for the independence of Chicago."[87] The following month it was again rumored that Lincoln would remain a short time longer and then give way to "some one more in accord with the present administration."[88] Then after this it was reported that, despite the various rumors, Arthur had asked Lincoln to remain and this he would do.[89] From time to time the rumors cropped up again, as in late August, 1882.[90] They were accompanied by reports that Lincoln would enter the senate race from Illinois to succeed Judge Davis. It was said that he had the backing of Davis, Logan, and the Administration.[91] However, nothing came of this and Lincoln remained in office until the close of the Arthur administration. That he was not overjoyed with his post, however, is

84 Mrs. James G. Blaine to her son Walker Blaine, Jan. 1882, in Harriet S. Blaine Beale, ed., *Letters of Mrs. James G. Blaine*, I, 282–83.

85 Mrs. Blaine to Walker Blaine, Jan. 17, 1882, *ibid.*, I, 288–90. Her reference to Delano is an error for it had been six years since Columbus Delano left the Grant cabinet as secretary of the interior.

86 *New York Times*, Jan. 4, 1882.

87 Lincoln to John Hay, Mar. 23, 1882, Hay Papers.

88 *New York Times*, Apr. 12, 1882.

89 *Ibid.*, Apr. 16, 1882.

90 *Ibid.*, Aug. 28, 1882.

91 *Ibid.*, Sept. 6, 1882.

quite evident and long afterward, when one of his friends was made secretary of war, Lincoln expressed a desire to manifest his gratification at the appointment but, "In doing this I should forbear in kindness to tell him from my experience some of the griefs and troubles which he will meet in his new and important office."[92]

[92] Lincoln referred to the appointment of Jacob M. Dickinson in 1909. See Lincoln to F. H. Rawson, Mar. 4, 1909, Dickinson Papers, Tennessee State Archives.

Chapter 8

The War Department

A NEWSPAPER ACCOUNT, dated June 1, 1883, described the personal appearance of the Secretary of War:

> A very good looking man, indeed, who just misses the right to be called handsome, having none of the gauntness of the martyr President, just passing from the roundness of limb that belongs to young and lusty manhood to be fullness of middle age; a white-skinned, blue-eyed, brown-bearded man, who seems to have more forehead when he tries to make a chimney-pot hat stay on his head than when it is off—larger headed than the President, or I believe, any other man in the cabinet, and possessing more vitality than any two of them. He looks you straight in the face, speaks promptly and decisively in a strong voice, which has a remarkable huskiness of tone—it almost crackles and if you heard it a good distance away and had never heard it before, you would know that it belonged to a strong, positive, efficient nature. He walks with a vigorous and rapid stride, and seems at all times to have a surplus of physical strength. He is 5 feet 10 inches high, and weighs fully 190 pounds, which will gradually increase to 200 as he grows older.[1]

His office routine was described in yet another newspaper account of the same date:

> In his office he sits most of the time, wheeling when he talks, generally to the left, so that his right arm rests on the handsomely-

[1] Unidentified newspaper clipping, dated June 1, 1883, Harvard University Archives.

125

carved border of the mahogany. His guests sit at the end of the desk rather than at the opposite side. As he wheels in his chair, he faces the corner of the room where sits Col. Barr, his military secretary. His private secretary, and a subordinate clerk are stenographers, to whom he dictates most of his letters. The official day begins with interviews with senators, members and the heads of bureaus or departments. Twice a week there is a cabinet meeting at noon to take him away from his desk. When at his desk he tries to devote the afternoon to the dispatch of business, and the last hour of the day, whether it ends at 4 o'clock or 6 o'clock, as is more often the case, is devoted to an examination of the papers which the chief clerk brings in his packet.[2]

Most of the work of the army, of which as secretary of war Lincoln had charge from 1881 to 1885, was caused by the occasional Indian uprisings on the frontier. The Secretary noted in his annual report for 1882, this year having been a fairly typical one, that the army had been called upon to deal with Apache uprisings in Arizona and in southwestern New Mexico. The military establishment was at this time limited to an army of only twenty-five thousand as fixed by law.[3]

The commanding general of the army was William T. Sherman, until late in 1883 when he was succeeded by General Philip Sheridan. Lincoln's relationship with Sherman appears to have been entirely satisfactory, but there is evidence that the same could not be said of his work with Sheridan. The latter general addressed Lincoln as "the Honorable Secretary of War," but his letters were always full of suggestions of one sort or another.[4] Even before Sheridan became commanding general, he addressed the Secretary regarding his future plans and contemplated "changes of command."[5] Shortly after Lincoln left office, the press reported that there had been trouble between the Secretary and his general over the latter's tendency to issue orders without

---

[2] Unidentified newspaper clipping, dated June 1, 1883, *ibid.*

[3] *Annual Report of the Secretary of War*, 1882, I, iv.

[4] Philip Sheridan to Lincoln, Nov. 28, Dec. 28, 1883, and Mar. 6, 1884, Sheridan Papers, Library of Congress.

[5] Sheridan to Lincoln, Sept. 25, 1883, *ibid.*

the approval of his civilian superior, Lincoln. It was said that Lincoln threatened to take the matter to the President if it continued. Evidently that settled the issue, although Lincoln's successor, Endicott, ultimately called his chief, President Cleveland, in on the problem.[6] If there was friction between Lincoln and Sheridan, it was not in evidence when Lincoln was given a dinner at Chamberlain's in Washington soon after his retirement from the War Department; Sheridan, as well as other military and civilian figures was in attendance.[7] When the General died, Lincoln was in London, but he cabled his condolences to the widow and was full in his praise of Sheridan.[8]

Many of the officers and men serving in the early 1880's were like Sherman and Sheridan, veterans of the Civil War. In fact, in many ways the army of 1881 to 1885 was very similar to the old wartime force. It was outmoded in many ways and badly in need of modernization. The weapons in use by the army were quite antique and Lincoln, together with President Arthur, pushed for necessary changes.[9] In 1883, Congress passed a law enabling the realization of some of the desired modernization, and Lincoln moved ahead with it.[10] Lincoln and Arthur also favored the idea of assisting the state militias to bring them up to date and started a plan whereby federal officers would work with each militia upon its request to instruct it in the ways of modern warfare.[11]

During his years in the War Department, Lincoln was frequently called upon to travel here and there, making inspection tours and sometimes political junkets. One such venture in June, 1881, involved a speech at a reunion of the Army of the Potomac. Lincoln was accompanied by General Sherman and on the return trip to Washington his party was enlivened by the presence of Mark Twain who was on the same train. The noted humorist

6 Washington *Evening Star*, Apr. 28, 1885.

7 *Ibid.*, Mar. 27, 1885.

8 Chicago *Tribune*, Aug. 7, 1888.

9 *Annual Report of the Secretary of War*, 1882, I, xix; *Annual Report of the President*, 1883, *Messages and Papers of the Presidents*, XI, 4766–67.

10 *Annual Report of the President*, 1884, *Messages and Papers of the Presidents*, XI, 4832.

11 *Annual Report of the Secretary of War*, 1882, I, v–vi.

joined the official party unannounced and became involved in a mock argument with the other two. Sherman asked Twain if he expected to pay extra fare for riding with him and the Secretary. Twain said he hadn't expected to pay any fare, whereupon the General said: "Oh you don't. Then you'll work your way." Sherman dressed the writer in his military coat and hat and at the next station pushed him out onto the platform to speak. The puzzled audience was at first amazed and then amused at the incident. This routine was continued through the trip, with Lincoln sometimes joining the other two in brief speeches to train-side crowds. The anecdote leaves the impression that the Secretary of the War too may have donned the military uniform.[12]

The great bulk of the work of the Secretary of War was of a very routine type, as is indicated by Lincoln's correspondence of this period. Sometimes it involved other departments as well as his own. In October, 1881, for example, Lincoln addressed the attorney general on the matter of the prosecution of a captain which he thought was "being improperly handled by the local law officers of the Government." After pointing out specific things, Lincoln concluded, "I think I should act differently if I was District Attorney here."[13] In June, 1881, the Secretary advised Congressman John Van Voorhis that he had no authority to lend a cannon for the use of the First Brigade of Veterans of Rochester, New York, in their Fourth of July celebration; in June, 1882, he wrote Senator Logan, the chairman of the military affairs committee, that although Congress had authorized the loan of one thousand army tents to Russian Jewish refugees at Vineland, New Jersey, unfortunately that many were not available; and then on another occasion he answered Senator Miller of California regarding a petition from the San Francisco Board of Trade to the effect that not enough army supplies were being purchased in that city.[14] Frequently the letters involved per-

12 Albert B. Paine, *Mark Twain, a Biography*, I, 720–21.

13 Lincoln to Wayne MacVeagh, Oct. 13, 1881, R. T. Lincoln Papers, University of Chicago Library.

14 Secretary of War, Letters Sent, 1881–85, Vols. 91–110, Record Group 107, National Archives.

sonnel. To the "War Governor" of New York, E. D. Morgan, Lincoln promised to put before the President the matter of the promotion of a Lieutenant Sawyer to the rank of captain, and again he agreed to consider the application of Captain Andrews as paymaster of the army.[15] To R. B. Latham of Lincoln, Illinois, the Secretary regretted that there was then no vacancy in the Quartermaster's Department and that, therefore, Lieutenant Beck could not be appointed to a position.[16] In April, 1882, Lincoln discussed several matters in a fairly typical letter to General James A. Ekin, the assistant quartermaster general:

I have your letter of the 6th instant.

I am glad you feel in the way I do about Col. Saunders. As to the other appointment you mention, I have nothing to say except that it would be perfectly satisfactory to me.

I have no desire to exercise in the case of Mr. Van Buskirk. I think him probably a good man: but I have no doubt that he is too deaf to be efficient in such a position and, therefore, if you had a vacancy, I would not think it proper to recommend him to your consideration.

> Very truly yours,
> ROBERT T. LINCOLN[17]

Once in a while his correspondents were old friends of his father: Lincoln wrote to Governor Alexander H. Stephens of Georgia regarding a lieutenant who was a military instructor at a Georgia college.[18] Personnel appointments naturally caused some unhappiness once in a while. The quartermaster general, Montgomery C. Meigs, had to be told that the President intended to put him on the retired list to make way for Colonel D. H. Rucker, the father-in-law of General Sheridan. Rucker was actually older than Meigs and only wanted the honor of having held the position before he himself was retired. He was soon succeeded by Colonel Rufus Ingalls.[19]

[15] Lincoln to E. D. Morgan, Oct. 24, 1881, and July 7, 1882, New York State Library.

[16] Lincoln to R. B. Latham, May 13, 1883, Lincoln College Library.

[17] Lincoln to James A. Ekin, Apr. 10, 1882, Duke University Library.

[18] Lincoln to Alexander H. Stephens, Jan. 26, 1883, *ibid.*

[19] Russell F. Weigley, *Quartermaster of the Union Army*, 356–58.

Other subjects of the Secretary's correspondence involved such matters as Indian affairs, sending out copies of the *War of the Rebellion* series, and answering frequent questions about the military service of a person at one time or another. Historical research had its limits, though, for Lincoln advised Simon Gratz of Philadelphia that the records of the Revolutionary War officers were in the State Department.[20]

Lincoln's job involved a variety of duties. When the Old Pension Office Building was erected in the north half of Judiciary Square, Lincoln had to approve the plans,[21] and when the Mississippi River went on a rampage, flooding a large territory from February to April, 1882, the Secretary prepared to help the victims. After Lincoln received a petition from citizens of a Missouri county requesting aid from the army, he wrote Senator Cockrell of that state that he had directed the assistant commissary general to furnish the needed rations.[22] Ultimately $349,958.88 worth of rations was distributed to flood victims, thousands of whom were homeless.[23] The Secretary's actions won praise from a Mississippi newspaper that first paid tribute to Abraham Lincoln and then commented:

> His son "is a chip off the old block." He has let no opportunity pass to show the Southern people kindness. He has worked side by side with the Southern Governors for the relief of the overflow sufferers, and we are sure Robert T. Lincoln has been praised oftener since he has been at the head of the War Department by Southerners than by Northerners. His thoughtful kindness, and his attention to the details, are proof that his heart was in the work. The Southern people are impulsive, warmhearted, and extremely grateful, and we are correctly expressing their sentiment for the Secretary of War.[24]

A considerable amount of Lincoln's time when he first took

20 Lincoln to Simon Gratz, June 24, 1881, Historical Society of Pennsylvania.
21 H. P. Caemmerer, *Washington, The National Capital*, 305.
22 Lincoln to Francis M. Cockrell, Mar. 24, 1882, Historical Society of Pennsylvania.
23 *Annual Report of the Secretary of War*, 1882, I, xi.
24 *New York Times*, May 8, 1882, quoting the Vicksburg (Miss.) *Herald*, May 2, 1882.

over his post was occupied with making changes in the office of
the secretary of war itself. For a number of years, in fact for the
most part since the service of Edwin M. Stanton, the secretaries
had been men of little knowledge of departmental affairs and
they generally tended to let the organization run itself.[25]

> Under the carelessness, the indifference and laziness of preceding
> Secretaries the Office of Chief Clerk became one of great import-
> ance. Crosby, an alert, active-minded man, who was Chief Clerk
> under Belknap, was a man who had very strong political influence
> back of him. For a number of years he was practically Secretary
> of War.[26]

Soon after Lincoln entered upon his duties, Crosby left office,
as did a number of other longtime employees.[27] A peculiar problem was that of army officers who were on "special" or "detached"
service and assigned to posts within the War Department. One
such officer was said to have never seen more than six weeks of
active duty with his regiment in over twenty years of service.[28]
Quietly, Lincoln went about cleaning up such matters amid vio-
lent protests from the officers involved.[29] For those civilian aides
in the department whom Lincoln found competent, he pressed
Congress for a pay raise and requested that more clerical help be
hired. He wrote, "From personal observation I am satisfied that
they deserve recognition for their faithful service, and I earnestly
recommend that the small increase may be appropriated."[30] In
time, Lincoln's handling of the War Department earned him the
respect of many, and General Drum, the adjutant general, was
quoted as saying, "He is the best secretary of war we have
had since Jefferson Davis."[31] (Such a statement was high praise
indeed and makes one wonder why Edwin M. Stanton was not
mentioned.)

[25] Chicago *Tribune*, May 31, 1884.
[26] *Ibid.*
[27] *Ibid.*
[28] *Ibid.*
[29] *Ibid.*, Aug. 29, 31, and Sept. 4, 1885.
[30] *Annual Report of the Secretary of War*, 1882, I, xxiv–xxv.
[31] Unidentified newspaper clipping dated June 1, 1883, Harvard University
Archives.

Lincoln was able to achieve certain accomplishments because he enjoyed the complete confidence of President Arthur, with whom he was always on the friendliest terms. Lincoln's influence on the President and on his fellow cabinet members was considerable, and on at least one occasion he used it to even a score with an old enemy. Ward H. Lamon was an applicant for the office of postmaster at Denver, and on May 3, 1883, he wrote Lincoln that he could not understand why Lincoln might have acted to prevent the appointment.[32] The Secretary of War fired back the answer, "I took an early opportunity to say to the Postmaster-General that your appointment would be personally offensive to me, and I explained to him, briefly the reasons." One of them was Lamon's life of the Civil War President, which Lincoln said contained the statement that Thomas and Nancy Lincoln had never been married. Lincoln cited chapter and verse on other alleged offenses and spoke of Lamon's statements as an "astonishing exhibition of malicious ingratitude on your part towards your dead benefactor."[33] Needless to say, Lamon never had a chance of receiving an appointment from President Arthur. Infuriated, Lamon threatened to publish a biography of Robert T. Lincoln that he had in preparation; this would even the score. To Lamon, Judge Davis wrote: "I appeal to you in the name of the great dead, and in the name of your living friends, not to publish anything concerning Robert T. Lincoln. It would grieve me beyond measure, and many besides, who have loved you and Mr. Lincoln."[34] If Lamon did write anything on the subject, he never published it.

Not all of the requests for help addressed to Lincoln received rebuffs. His Aunt Emelie Todd Helm became postmistress of Elizabethtown, Kentucky, by presidential appointment.[35] Through Lincoln, Judge Davis was able to secure positions for his associates, sometimes mutual friends of the jurist and the

32 Ward H. Lamon to Lincoln, May 3, 1883, Herndon-Weik Mss.

33 Lincoln to Lamon, May 10, 1883, Huntington Library; copy *ibid.*

34 King, *Lincoln's Manager*, 305.

35 R. Gerald McMurtry, *Ben Hardin Helm*, 69.

Secretary.[36] On at least one occasion Lincoln may have found himself in a situation in which he could not produce an appointment. Adam Badeau claimed that he had a promise from Garfield through Lincoln of a diplomatic appointment, but after Garfield died Arthur did not make the appointment.[37]

Not all of Lincoln's time as secretary of war was occupied by routine appointments and petty gripes; there was the case of Fitz-John Porter.[38] On January 10, 1863, Porter then a major general of volunteers, was court-martialed for refusing to obey the orders of his superior officer, General Pope, at the second battle of Manassas. He was convicted and sentenced "to be cashiered and to be forever disqualified from holding any office of trust or profit under the Government of the United States."[39] On January 21, 1863, President Lincoln confirmed the trial and approved the sentence. Over the years the case had received much attention. A century later most historians would agree that "Porter did nothing wrong at Manassas," and that he was not guilty of the charges against him.[40] In the 1870's and 1880's, however, the issue had political overtones. President Hayes in 1878 ordered an investigation of the case, and at that time Robert T. Lincoln appeared as a witness to uphold the sentence against Porter. The General's biographer and champion feels that Lincoln's testimony was quite damaging to Porter and concludes, "There could be no denying that Robert Lincoln's war record was despicable," and that the man himself was a "narrow-minded son of a broad-minded father . . . ."[41] At the time, Manning Force writing to President Hayes concluded from Lincoln's statement that President Lincoln thought Porter should have been shot.[42] Ultimately the case came before Lincoln and his superior, President Arthur. In December, 1881, Porter asked the Chief Execu-

36 King, *Lincoln's Manager*, 305.

37 Chicago *Tribune*, Mar. 6, 1887.

38 Otto Eisenschiml, *The Celebrated Case of Fitz John Porter* is a full account of the episode, although strongly biased in favor of Porter.

39 *Messages and Papers of the Presidents*, XI, 4712.

40 T. Harry Williams, *Lincoln and His Generals*, 163.

41 Eisenschiml, *Porter*, 238–40.

42 Manning F. Force to Rutherford B. Hayes, Oct. 23, 1878, Hayes Library.

tive to annul the court-martial, but, the General's champion argues, again Lincoln stood in the way.[43] There is no evidence offered to confirm or deny the statement that in Lincoln "Porter faced another stubborn opponent."[44] Arthur sent Porter's appeal to Lincoln, who transmitted it to Attorney General Brewster for his opinion on certain legal issues. Brewster in turn advised that Arthur did not have the power to restore the officer to the military. However, on May 4, 1882, the President used his constitutional powers to grant Porter a full pardon.[45] A bill then passed Congress for Porter's relief but on July 2, 1884, Arthur vetoed it. Once more the General's biographer implies, and again without any evidence one way or another, that Lincoln and the Attorney General were responsible for Arthur's actions.[46]

Another matter with which Lincoln was occupied, and a celebrated and controversial episode it was, concerned the Greely Arctic expedition and as an aftermath of it, another court-martial, this time of General William B. Hazen.[47] This project was "entirely an enterprise of the War Department."[48] In the late 1870's ten nations agreed to establish a circumpolar chain of posts in the Arctic for the purpose of meteorological and magnetic observations. Of the fourteen stations to be established, the one at Lady Franklin Bay in Grinnell Land, under the command of Lieutenant Adolphus W. Greely, was located the farthest north. It has been said that at the time of the organization of the Greely expedition, "Neither Garfield nor his new Secretary of War, Robert Todd Lincoln, was interested in the project." It has been further charged that Lincoln "did not make life easy for Greely," and that for weeks he neglected to sign the necessary papers to start the group on its way. Finally, Greely called on the Secretary and "Lincoln fuming at the temerity of the brash lieutenant

43 Eisenschiml, *Porter*, 268–69.
44 *Ibid.*
45 *Messages and Papers of the Presidents*, XI, 4712.
46 Eisenschiml, *Porter*, 296.
47 A. L. Todd, *Abandoned: The Story of the Greely Arctic Expedition* is the most recent account of the Greely expedition.
48 Richardson, *Chandler*, 326–27.

whom he considered a nobody, signed the necessary papers."[49]
Greely and twenty-five men reached the designated point in
August, 1881, with supplies to last them three years. However,
the party was to remain only two years and in the summer of
1882, more supplies would be sent, although if this failed the
group would still be in no danger, except, of course, if some of
the supplies were lost.

When in due time relief ships were sent north, they failed to
reach the explorers and by the fall of 1883, the situation was
critical. A cry went up to send out another ship, but all Arctic
experts said that this would be impossible because of the approach of winter. Lincoln and his counterpart in the Navy Department, Chandler, at this time conducted an inquiry into the
possibility of sending out more ships, but on the advice of authorities on the subject they dropped the matter.[50] In Lincoln's
annual report as secretary of war dated November 15, 1883, he
wrote that although no ships would be sent for the time being,
"Lieutenant Greely's case is considered by no means hopeless."[51]
On December 13, 1883, Lincoln called upon Secretary Chandler
to aid in the rescue of the stranded men, and a few days later
President Arthur set up a joint army-navy board to plan operations for the future.[52] The board met from December 20, 1883,
to January 22, 1884, and, after making its report, formally ad-
journed in February.[53] There was some argument about whether
the new relief measures should be undertaken by the army or the
navy, but the two secretaries decided in favor of the latter: "The
work of the relief expedition of 1884—and for that matter, of all
the relief expeditions—was as purely nautical as any work that
was ever entrusted to a seaman."[54] It was then up to Congress to
advance the money necessary for the project; the House promptly
voted the sum, but there was much debate and delay in the

[49] Todd, *Abandoned*, 16–17.
[50] Winfield S. Schley and J. R. Soley, *The Rescue of Greely*, 97–99.
[51] *Annual Report of the Secretary of War*, 1883, 22–23.
[52] Schley and Soley, *Rescue of Greely*, 103–104.
[53] *Ibid.*, 104.
[54] *Ibid.*, 108.

Senate.[55] As for Secretary Lincoln, it is often stated that he was convinced of the hopelessness of many more attempts since probably the men had already perished.[56] Further, "Secretary of War Lincoln was credited with saying that he did not see any use throwing away more money for dead men, that they must have perished by that time."[57]

After much delay Greely and the few living members of the party were rescued as starvation was imminent. After they were rescued, it became known that the Lieutenant had on June 6, 1884, ordered Private C. B. Henry shot, and when Greely returned to the United States, he requested a court of inquiry into the matter. He was told that Lincoln declined to order such an action, for "the Secretary of War entertains no doubt of the necessity and the entire proprietary of your action."[58] However, before making such a statement, the Secretary had thoroughly investigated the evidence, which consisted of diaries kept by several members of the expedition.[59] When the rescued men and their rescuers returned to the United States, they were given a warm welcome at Portsmouth, New Hampshire, where the ships arrived August 1, 1884. Secretary Chandler was in attendance, but Lincoln was not, although he did send his regrets to the officials gathered at the ceremonies.[60] A week later, when the ships arrived at New York, Secretary Lincoln and Generals Sheridan and Hancock were present at another ceremony.[61]

The aftermath of the Greely episode was a public controversy that led ultimately to the court-martial of an officer of the War Department. As has been mentioned, there was discussion of whether or not another relief ship should have been sent north in September of 1883. The Secretary of War was opposed but the chief signal officer of the army, General William B. Hazen, took

---

55 *Ibid.*, 109–12.
56 Richardson, *Chandler*, 328; William Mitchell, *General Greely*, 116.
57 Mitchell, *Greely*, 116.
58 Adolphus W. Greely, *Reminiscences of Adventure and Service*, 146.
59 *Ibid.*
60 Todd, *Abandoned*, 278–79.
61 Schley and Soley, *Rescue of Greely*, 276.

the opposite view. Hazen had been largely responsible for the organization of the Greely venture, and he issued the orders to the Lieutenant on June 17, 1881, that started off the operation.[62] In May, 1882, Hazen was the one who reminded Secretary Lincoln that it was time to send out a resupply mission.[63] The General continued to be very much involved in the Greely affair, and it was said that after Lincoln made his decision in the fall of 1883, Hazen never forgave Lincoln for what he considered his inaction.[64] The Chief Signal Officer gave voice to his opinions to such an extent that the Secretary of War in his annual report in 1884 stated that he felt Hazen's activities constituted "an intrusion of an official opinion . . . into an official jurisdiction beyond his own, and his dictum upon the exercise of a superior responsibility which he was not invited to share are extraordinary in their time and place, and are hardly excusable even under whatever . . . irritation may have been caused."[65] Lincoln's statement was in large part caused by General Hazen's own annual report in 1884, in which he discussed at some length the matter of the Arctic expedition.[66] Perhaps the most significant part of his lengthy discourse was: "I therefore trust that this whole matter . . . will be deemed worthy of a thorough investigation by Congress—a body that will perform its duty, and stand above the suspicion of being swayed by partisan considerations."[67]

In short, Hazen was calling for Congress to investigate his superior, the Secretary of War, and strongly implied that, if it did its duty, it would place the blame for the entire matter on Robert T. Lincoln. On the surface it may appear that Hazen was a deliberate troublemaker, but such was not the case. He has been described as "a conscientious professional officer," but also as a person who spoke and "wrote rather freely on controversial matters."[68] Indeed, there is no evidence of particular ill will be-

[62] *Ibid.*, 21–23.
[63] Todd, *Abandoned*, 47.
[64] "William Babcock Hazen," *Dictionary of American Biography.*
[65] *Annual Report of the Secretary of War*, 1884, I, 25.
[66] *Annual Report of the Chief Signal Officer*, 1884, ibid., IV, 14–21.
[67] *Report of the Chief Signal Officer*, ibid., IV, 18.
[68] "Hazen," *DAB.*

tween the two but rather an honest difference of opinion. There had been at least one other occasion when the two had clashed over a matter not related to the Greely episode. Hazen objected to the enlistment of a Negro man into the Signal Corps and asked Lincoln to sustain him. Instead, the Secretary used his position to help the man who was finally enlisted.[69]

In regard to the Greely expedition, Hazen maintained that after the wreck of the relief ship in the middle of September, there was still time to send out another expedition. Lincoln argued to the contrary, and he could quote in defense of his position several navy officers. As Commander Wildes was quoted, "To charter another foreign ship with foreign crew for this duty to go north at this late season would simply invite fresh disaster."[70] It would have been necessary to charter a foreign ship because no United States ship was available. Winfield S. Schley reported that the winter of 1883 was the most severe in thirty years and concluded, "Under the circumstances any vessel attempting this navigation would have come to grief, if she had not been totally lost."[71] He concurred with Lincoln in not sending out another expedition. As for himself, the Secretary of War reflected that "while deploring the terrible loss of life incurred by the . . . expedition, [he] has never seen reason to doubt the proprietary of these conclusions reached by the Secretary of the Navy and himself."[72]

Following publication of the report of the Secretary criticizing him, the General wrote a letter to the head of the War Department discussing the matter, but it was returned to him with a warning to keep the letter private. This he did not do; instead on March 2, 1885, Hazen told the whole story of the letter to a reporter and the matter was published the same day in the Washington *Evening Star*. In the newspaper account Hazen said

[69] "Secretary Lincoln and the Color Line," *Frank Leslie's Illustrated Newspaper*, Oct. 11, 1884.

[70] Statement of Wildes quoted in *Annual Report of the Secretary of War*, 1884, I, 23.

[71] Statement of Schley quoted *ibid.*, 25.

[72] *Ibid.*

he had written Secretary Lincoln blaming him for the loss of life to the Greely party and he further stated that it was a straightforward discussion of the matter with evidence to back up his statements.[73] This brought the matter to a head, for Lincoln had warned the officer that if he remained silent the matter would be forgotten, but if he continued his efforts in behalf of an investigation, it would constitute "a breach of military discipline which could not be overlooked . . . ."[74]

On March 3, 1885, President Arthur ordered Hazen to consider himself under arrest and suspended from duty.[75] The following day the names of those who would sit on the court-martial to try Hazen were announced. They included such noted personages as Winfield S. Hancock, John M. Schofield, and O. O. Howard.[76] The trial began just as the new President, Grover Cleveland, was about to assume office and it was rumored that Cleveland might dissolve the court-martial, but such was not the case.[77] On March 8, Lincoln filed the charges against Hazen and court proceedings began March 11.[78] The court-martial caused some editorial comment and brought from the Chicago *Tribune*, always loyal to Lincoln:

> At last the Chief Signal Officer of the Army, Brig. Gen. W. B. Hazen, has been ordered court-martialed. It is a tardy order, but better late than never. If ever an officer deserved to be court-martialed for infraction of army discipline and for disrespect to his superiors it is Gen. Hazen. . . . His persistence in giving vent to his personal pique and official ignorance has been properly rebuked. It is high time that it should be checked.[79]

The trial opened with the accused pleading not guilty to the charges against him.[80] The trial hinged not on whether or not

73 Washington *Evening Star*, Mar. 2, 1885.
74 *Ibid.*, Mar. 12, 1885.
75 *Ibid.*, Mar. 3, 1885.
76 *Ibid.*, Mar. 4, 1885.
77 *Ibid.*, Mar. 7, 1885.
78 Chicago *Tribune*, Mar. 8, 1885; Washington *Evening Star*, Mar. 11, 1885.
79 Chicago *Tribune*, Mar. 5, 1885.
80 Washington *Evening Star*, Mar. 11, 1885.

Hazen had openly criticized Lincoln and thus violated military rules of conduct, but upon the failure to send another relief ship to Greely.[81] On March 20 the defense rested and the prosecution summed up its position. The same day the proceedings ended.[82] The verdict, which was guilty, was not immediately announced officially. Lincoln's successor as secretary of war, William C. Endicott, received the record of the trial on March 30, but before acting upon it, he left for his home in Massachusetts on an extended trip.[83] Therefore, it was April 17 before President Cleveland confirmed the verdict and publicly reprimanded General Hazen. He noted the General's long service in the army and stated that the accused "has been adjudged guilty of indulging in unwarranted and captious criticism of his superior officer, the Secretary of War, thereby setting a pernicious example subversive of discipline. . . . Subordination is necessarily the principal duty of a soldier, whatever his grade may be."[84]

Hazen's punishment was limited to the public rebuke; he was allowed to resume his position, which he kept until his death in 1887.[85] It was rumored that the General was happy over the outcome of the trial for he felt that his position had been vindicated.[86] For his part, Lincoln kept completely silent, even in the face of rumor that he had stacked the court-martial against Hazen. However, the Washington *Evening Star* reported, "The published intimation that Secretary Lincoln packed the Hazen court is refuted by the fact that the President personally selected the members of the court and Mr. Lincoln had nothing to do with it."[87] The entire matter was soon forgotten and disappeared from the press and the public mind.

During the Garfield and Arthur administrations Lincoln had

81 An account of the trial, together with much supplementary material, is T. J. Mackey, *The Hazen Court-Martial*. Mackey defended Hazen and attempts to prove in print what he could not prove before the court-martial.
82 Washington *Evening Star*, Mar. 20, 1885.
83 *Ibid.*, Mar. 30, 1885.
84 Mackey, *Hazen Court-Martial*, 280.
85 "Hazen," *DAB*.
86 Washington *Evening Star*, Apr. 18, 1885.
87 *Ibid.*, Mar. 30, 1885.

little time for rest and relaxation. He did leave Washington the night of September 29, 1883, for Sandusky, Ohio, to spend a few days near there on the shore of Lake Erie.[88] In October, 1882, he combined a business trip with a vacation when he and Secretary Chandler left Washington and joined the President at his home in New York. From there the officials went to Massachusetts to attend the centennial of the birth of Daniel Webster.[89] A much longer trip, and one with political overtones, took place the following summer. It began with President Arthur and some of his cabinet officers—Folger, Lincoln, and Gresham—being present on July 31, 1883, to open the Southern Exposition held in Louisville, Kentucky.[90] From Kentucky the President and Lincoln went west and were joined by General Sheridan, Senator Vest of Missouri, and several others. Their destination, by way of Chicago, was Yellowstone Park. The party left for Wyoming on August 3, and it was not until September 4 that they returned to Chicago.[91] On the return trip the presidential party passed through Minneapolis. There a celebration was under way to commemorate the completion of Henry Villard's Northern Pacific, and the local citizens staged a parade for the President and his party. The city of St. Paul gave an elaborate banquet for the distinguished group assembled. Lincoln was in attendance, of course, and singled out General Herman Haupt, also present, to ask some details about the aftermath of the battle of Gettysburg.[92] Although President Arthur's health was not good, he returned from the trip much rested and relaxed. The tour had political implications because of the forthcoming election of 1884, and the assumption that Arthur would be a candidate for re-election. His triumphal return to Chicago had all the trappings of a political junket.

88 New York *Tribune*, Oct. 2, 1883.

89 George F. Howe, *Chester A. Arthur*, 177.

90 *Ibid.*, 247.

91 *Ibid.*, 247–48, contains a detailed account of the trip.

92 Herman Haupt, *Reminiscences of General Herman Haupt*, 224. For a description of the banquet, see Thomas J. McCormack, ed., *Memoirs of Gustave Koerner*, II, 679–80.

Chapter 9

Lincoln for President

CHESTER ARTHUR HAD MADE A GOOD PRESIDENT, much to the surprise of friend and foe alike. *Harper's Weekly* even wondered if Garfield would have done as well and concluded that he would probably not have excelled his successor.[1] The Republican party now owed Arthur renomination, and yet there was a sizable group within the party that would not support this idea. The old-line spoilsmen were alienated, while the reformers were still lukewarm. The race for the nomination in 1884 was a wide-open affair. Long before the campaign got under way John Hay wrote from Europe:

> Next year is still absolutely in the air. Arthur is gaining; Lincoln is much talked about, Sherman will have Ohio, and there is a new quiet boom for Blaine. But it is anybody's race as yet and, in view of the uncertainty of the event the candidates themselves hardly know whether they want the nomination.[2]

There had been some vague talk about running Robert Lincoln for President for several years, and in 1884 such a nomination seemed at least a possibility. John Hay, writing in January 1884, ran down a list of prospective candidates, among which was "Bob Lincoln, who has no organized following but a strong

[1] *Harper's Weekly*, Mar. 7, 1885.
[2] John Hay to Levi P. Morton, Aug. 17, 1883, Levi P. Morton Papers, New York Public Library.

though diffused sentiment for him—greatly to his annoyance as he is heartily for Arthur."[3] Never once did Lincoln even consider supporting another candidate, for he said of his favoring of the President, "if I did not do so, I should feel it my duty to resign my position as a member of his cabinet."[4]

Aside from Lincoln's own demonstrated abilities there was the all powerful name he bore. His family name was perhaps the most potent single force in late nineteenth-century American politics. Many would-be supporters brushed lightly over Lincoln's personal qualifications and then bore down heavily on his ancestry. Others reversed the order, but always the two were inseparable. In December, 1883, Judge S. Newton Pettis of Meadville, Pennsylvania, who had been Abraham Lincoln's minister to Bolivia, was in Cleveland, Ohio, sounding out Garfield's old supporters on behalf of Lincoln's nomination in 1884. From his point of view, Arthur, Grant, and Blaine were not possible as candidates. Although Pettis professed to be a Blaine man, he felt that the "Plumed Knight" could not carry New York and would have to be content with a cabinet post. As for Lincoln, Pettis told reporters, "the Secretary declares he is in no rush for a nomination and feels somewhat embarrassed by the action of his friends in pushing him while a member of Arthur's cabinet." The Judge also felt that Lincoln would have strong second choice support from other camps and that the Secretary alone could prevent southern Negroes from leaving the Republican fold. In the end, he predicted, the stalwarts would rally around Lincoln and so too would Arthur once he realized he could not obtain the nomination for himself.[5]

On June 2, 1884, the New York *Times* ran an editorial on the race and concluded that really Senator Edmunds was the best man for the nomination but that he could not possibly receive the nod. Therefore, being realistic:

---

[3] Hay to Morton, Jan. 19, 1884, quoted in Robert McElroy, *Levi Parsons Morton*, 155.

[4] Toledo *Blade*, quoted in Chicago *Tribune*, Aug. 31, 1887.

[5] *New York Times*, Dec. 29, 1883.

what stronger name could be presented to the convention, what name more certain to secure a hearty endorsement than that of ROBERT T. LINCOLN. MR. LINCOLN is an energetic and capable Secretary of War. His successful administration of that department gives the assurance of a creditable discharge of the duties of the Presidency. The supporters of all the other candidates, without exception, have claimed him for the second place on their tickets, showing clearly that he is entirely acceptable to every group and faction of the party and has the confidence of all Republicans. Moreover—and we consider the fact one of prize importance—Mr. Lincoln *has no political debts.* The office would come to him unsought, and he would be absolutely free to administer the great trust without bias of any kind, personal or political. Next to the name of EDMUNDS, the name of LINCOLN is the strongest that could be presented to the convention and to the country.[6]

Once committed, the *Times* went to work to generate support for its man. It printed a long article on how much the great masses of the common people loved Robert T. Lincoln. (One man supposedly interviewed mentioned that he believed Lincoln should be permitted to fill out his father's term.) Other citizens felt that Lincoln could unite the party and that he should be nominated because he was not engaged in an unsightly race for the post. A streetcar conductor told of a New York G.A.R. parade that had been all but rained out; others sought shelter, but Secretary Lincoln remained to the end though wet to the skin. "There ain't anything high-toned about him."[7] However, it must be noted that Lincoln's name was being presented because the *Times* hoped that it could thus prevent the nomination of Blaine.[8]

Lincoln had the support too of some differing groups within the party. William E. Chandler, the old-line Grant supporter, favored Lincoln's nomination.[9] So did such independent young

---

6 *New York Times,* June 2, 1884.

7 *Ibid.,* June 4, 1884.

8 E. Benjamin Andrews, *The History of the Last Quarter-Century in the United States,* II, 74.

9 Unidentified newspaper clipping, dated June 1, 1883, Harvard University Archives.

Republicans as Henry Cabot Lodge and Theodore Roosevelt, who at the same time harbored an intense hatred for Chandler and his group.[10] "Though nominally committed to Edmunds, Lodge had hopes of uniting all the anti-Blaine elements behind Robert T. Lincoln."[11] Former President Hayes was friendly. Speaking of Blaine, Hayes wrote, "Either Edmunds, Lincoln or Sherman would be a better President and a better candidate." Personally, "I still hope Edmunds may be the nominee, or Lincoln, or Sherman."[12]

Since Lincoln was not an active candidate there was little open opposition to him, although Joseph Pulitzer's New York *World* did speak out against him on the grounds that he was merely his father's son.[13] As the speculation continued, Lincoln himself was most careful never to encourage potential supporters. By 1884, Abraham Lincoln's birthday was already memorialized by banquets and speechmaking, and his son was forever being pressed to attend these functions. In a letter marked "personal and private" the War Secretary wrote General M. D. Leggett:

> Please accept my warmest thanks for your kind letter and your hospitable invitation to stay at your house if I should accept the invitation of the "Lincoln Club" for its dinner on my father's birthday anniversary. I am not, however, able to accept it. I have a personal engagement here as a host for the evening of the 11th, which of course could be postponed only under extraordinary circumstances.
>
> I may say to you privately that if I were free to go, I should hesitate, least in my wish to thank the young gentlemen of the club . . . for the honor they do my father, I should give occasion to misrepresentation to which no reply could easily be made—I trust that at some other time I may be free from any such possibility.
>
> I am very sincerely yours,
ROBERT T. LINCOLN[14]

10 John A. Garraty, *Henry Cabot Lodge*, 76.

11 *Ibid.*

12 Charles R. Williams, ed., *Diary and Letters of Rutherford Birchard Hayes*, IV, 146.

13 New York *World*, May 10, 1884.

14 Lincoln to General M. D. Leggett, Feb. 3, 1884, Indiana University Library.

Lincoln also sought to discourage another type of appeal:

> Please see the friend who writes the inclosed letter, proposing
> to organize a club in Chicago on my behalf for President. I am not
> a candidate for either President or Vice-President, and therefore do
> not wish any clubs formed for me. If you will kindly give this mat-
> ter your early attention and stop it you will much oblige me.
>
> Sincerely yours,
>
> ROBERT T. LINCOLN[15]

Despite all that Lincoln could do to discourage his supporters,
the speculation continued. If he did not receive the presidential
nomination, then surely he must at least be the vice-presidential
nominee. Lincoln's friend, General Nicholas Longworth Anderson, predicted, "From all I can gather, Blaine and Lincoln will
be the next Presidential ticket, combining the forces of the East
and West, the followers of Garfield and Lincoln, the enthusiasm
of two great names."[16]

If Lincoln had had political ambitions at this time, he would
have had an opponent in John A. Logan, who coveted the second
place on the ticket. As it was, in Illinois during the preconvention
politicking, Lincoln's name was often used by those who were
attempting to hurt Logan's chances. Carl Schurz, that sage observer of the political scene, wrote to Logan:

> To judge from what I see and hear, and from the expressions of
> sentiment which float through the press, there is in the Republican
> ranks an almost unanimous voice in favor of nominating Lincoln
> for the Vice-Presidency.[17]

In so far as the presidential contest was concerned, Schurz, writing from New York, believed, "Edmunds would probably be the

15 Lincoln to Leonard Swett, Mar. 28, 1884, quoted in the Chicago *Tribune*,
Apr. 16, 1884, and reprinted in the *New York Times*, Apr. 17, 1884. See also the
Chicago *Tribune*, May 31, 1884, for the motives behind the Illinois Lincoln boom.

16 Nicholas Longworth Anderson to his son Larz Anderson, Mar. 15, 1884, in
Isabel Anderson, ed., *The Letters and Journals of General Nicholas Longworth
Anderson*, 225.

17 Carl Schurz to John A. Logan, Feb. 29, 1884, in Frederic Bancroft, ed., *Speeches,
Correspondence and Political Papers of Carl Schurz*, IV, 194–95.

strongest here; but Gresham, Hawley, Lincoln and several others would, I have no doubt run well."[18]

It was said that at this time Blaine was not especially anxious to have the nomination and, instead, is supposed to have told George S. Boutwell of Massachusetts that his main concern was to defeat President Arthur and that Boutwell should work for the nomination of John Sherman for President and Robert T. Lincoln for Vice-President.[19] When the Republican convention finally met, Blaine was nominated for the top post and Logan was his running mate. Whatever reluctance Blaine may have had toward being the nominee was somehow overcome. It took four ballots to nominate the "Plumed Knight" and on each Lincoln had taken votes. On the first ballot he received four votes; on the second, one; on the third, eight; and on the last, two. Logan was virtually the unanimous choice of the party; hence, the Lincoln boom completely vanished.[20] Of course, Lincoln was still a young man and there would be other elections. However, when asked about them in December, 1884, he observed that 1888 was a long way in the future and "I think that time will only strengthen my dislike of the annoyances attending candidacy for, or the holding of, public office."[21]

The Secretary of War was at the White House when word of Blaine's nomination was received, and although later Arthur came to resent the convention's action, he at once telegraphed the candidate his "hearty support."[22] The suspense of the convention proceedings over, the President and Secretary Lincoln left Washington the next week for an inspection tour of West Point.[23] The nomination of Blaine split the Republican party and paved the way for the election of Grover Cleveland. Until March 4, 1885, Arthur continued to occupy the White House

18 Schurz to Preston B. Plumb, May 12, 1884, *ibid.*, IV, 200–202.

19 Alexander K. McClure, *Our Presidents and How We Make Them*, 288.

20 Frank A. Flower, *History of the Republican Party*, 372–75.

21 Lincoln to Colonel D. C. Pavey, Dec. 1, 1884, quoted in the *New York Times*, Mar. 9, 1887.

22 Howe, *Chester A. Arthur*, 265.

23 *Ibid.*

with almost universal respect from the general public. Lincoln and the other cabinet officers, too, continued their work until the inauguration of Cleveland. On February 25, 1885, the Arthur administration held a farewell reception with all of its members present, although, contrary to usual practice, Mrs. Lincoln "did not receive" and may not have even been present, although the Secretary was.[24] A few days later Robert T. Lincoln turned his office over to his successor. Justice Field swore in Secretary Endicott and Lincoln introduced the new man to those present.[25]

There was general agreement that Lincoln had done an admirable job as secretary of war and he could take pleasure in reading:

> Secretary Lincoln undoubtedly received his appointment through his family position, but the appointment has proved to be one of the best that could have been made. Mr. Lincoln stands today solely upon his own merits, and if he ever is to receive promotion in the public service he will prefer to owe this promotion to his record.[26]

Of course, even greater pleasure for Lincoln stemmed from the fact that he was a former secretary. A year after leaving the War office he wrote John Hay, "I am pretty happy just now." The reason was:

> I am let alone in the papers and I don't want my name in them again until I am assured of the regular complementary notes written by some member of my afflicted family with 'no flowers' attached. Like Nanki Pooh, I can't be there to see it, but I don't mind that. God willing I will never again be in the jaws of that damning hyena, the public at large.[27]

The hope that his name would remain out of the papers was just so much wishful thinking, for such was never to be the case. Not too many years after Lincoln left the War Department, there

24 Chicago *Tribune*, Mar. 1, 1885.
25 Washington *Evening Star*, Mar. 7, 1885.
26 Chicago *Tribune*, May 31, 1884.
27 Lincoln to John Hay, Mar. 14, 1886, Hay Papers. Unfortunately, at a key point in the letter, Lincoln's scrawl becomes illegible. It appears, however, that the public may be a "damning hyena."

was an uproar over the Confederate battle flags. It was said that at his order some flags were boxed up to be returned to the states. When asked about it, Lincoln demanded, "Well, what of it?" and then continued, "What if the old rags were boxed up?" He did not specifically remember any such order, "We had more important things to think about when I was there than the disposition that should be made of a few, rotten old rebel flags."[28] The controversy ultimately involved President Cleveland who first issued and then revoked an order for the return of the remaining flags. Not until 1905 were they at last sent back to the states whence they had come originally.

When Lincoln officially left the cabinet on March 7, 1885, he did not immediately leave Washington. When he first did, it was without his family and for only a few days. Late in March, General Anson Stager of Chicago died, and Lincoln, in company with Senator Logan, at once left for that city to attend the funeral. They arrived March 28 on a morning train.[29] After serving as a pallbearer at the funeral, Lincoln returned to Washington.[30] In June it was reported that "Ex Secy. Lincoln and family have gone to Fortress Monroe," presumably for a vacation.[31]

The Chicago *Tribune* of July 3, 1885, reported that Lincoln "has returned to Chicago and will resume the practice of his profession 'just as though nothing had happened.'" His return to Chicago was followed by what must have been a happy period in the life of Robert T. Lincoln: his children were growing up, and his wife had recovered her health. He was immensely proud of his son, whom he called Jack, and his daughters. When the wife of John Hay presented him with a daughter, Lincoln wrote his friend Nicolay, "my experience with girl babies makes me envy him. They are very nice."[32] Years before he had written, "My small wife is only tolerably well but the babies are small steam

---

28 New York *Tribune*, Jan. 13, 1888.

29 Chicago *Tribune*, Mar. 27 and 28, 1885.

30 *Ibid.*, Mar. 29, 1885.

31 *Ibid.*, June 23, 1885.

32 Lincoln to John G. Nicolay, Jan. 23, 1880, Nicolay Papers.

engines and such a circus as we have every night, you never see."[33]

In 1887 the Lincolns had built for themselves a new house, where they were to live for many years, located at 60 Lake Shore Drive near Lincoln Park. Also living in the neighborhood were Potter Palmer and Franklin MacVeagh. Just before the house was completed, Lincoln sought permission from the park board to have electric wires strung across the park grounds so that his residence and those of his neighbors might be lit by electricity. The board insisted that the residents also light the edge of the Park in return for the privilege.[34] Work on the home progressed slowly and in October, 1887, Lincoln reported to Nicolay, "I am camping in my new home and can't get the painters off the first floor though they promised to be done a month ago."[35] It was December before Lincoln could write, "We are now getting really settled after six years vagabondizing—nothing but the sheriff or undertaker shall ever move us."[36] When finally completed, the house was described as "pseudo-Romanesque," constructed of brown brick and reddish sandstone.[37] It contained twenty rooms in its three stories and had a reception hall paneled in oak and a parlor in mahogany.[38]

Mr. and Mrs. Robert T. Lincoln were much sought-after participants in Chicago social affairs. Typical of their activities were: a huge golden wedding party held in the summer of 1885 in honor of Judge and Mrs. John D. Caton, pioneer Illinois residents;[39] a "brilliant" reception given by Mr. and Mrs. George M. Pullman at their home the evening of February 2, 1886;[40] and acting as manager and patroness of the "Second Annual Chicago Charity Ball," held February 25, 1886, for the benefit of two

---

33 Lincoln to John Hay, June 6, 1875, Hay Papers.

34 Chicago *Tribune*, Feb. 16, 1887.

35 Lincoln to John G. Nicolay, Oct. 27, 1887, Nicolay Papers.

36 Lincoln to Nicolay, Dec. 18, 1887, *ibid*.

37 Chicago *Tribune*, Apr. 28, 1889.

38 *New York Times*, Jan. 18, 1959. At that time the house was threatened by wreckers but it was purchased by a Chicago couple who wished to preserve it. (Chicago *Tribune*, Jan. 31, 1959.) Later, however, it fell victim to "progress" and was demolished.

39 Chicago *Tribune*, July 29, 1885.

40 *Ibid*., Feb. 3, 1886.

Chicago hospitals.[41] Mr. and Mrs. Lincoln were part of a group described as the "most fashionable audience that ever gathered in Chicago," which witnessed a benefit performance of *The Rivals*, performed by the Histrionic Club at the Madison Street Comedy Theatre in February, 1887.[42] There were few important social functions held in Chicago between 1885 and 1889 at which the Lincolns were not present. They were a part of the élite of Chicago society and counted as their friends the families of George M. Pullman, Potter Palmer, Marshall Field, and others who made up the list of the most prominent families of the city.

Frequently there were "stag" social functions which Lincoln attended. In 1885, Grover Cleveland appointed a prominent Chicago resident, Lambert Tree, minister to Belgium. Lincoln, together with Potter Palmer, Lyman J. Gage, Lyman Trumbull, General John M. Schofield, and others, gave him a farewell banquet held at the Palmer House.[43] In the spring of 1886, Schofield himself was transferred to a new command post, and a banquet was tendered him at the Calumet Club. Lincoln was there and spoke for about five minutes, praising the departing officer and welcoming his successor, General Terry.[44] James Russell Lowell visited Chicago in February, 1887, and Lincoln was present when he spoke at the Central Music Hall.[45] The local Harvard Club honored the visitor at a banquet held the evening of February 25 at the Hotel Richelieu, at which it was reported, "Next to Mr. Lowell sat the Hon. Robert T. Lincoln."[46] President Eliot of Harvard visited Chicago in February, 1888, and at the banquet given him Lincoln sat at the head table.[47] Earlier the same day Mrs. Lincoln had held an afternoon reception for the visitor so that the ladies of the city might meet him.[48] On one occasion, as

41 *Ibid.*, Feb. 7 and 26, 1886.
42 *Ibid.*, Feb. 22, 1887.
43 *Ibid.*, Aug. 20, 1885.
44 *Ibid.*, Apr. 11, 1886.
45 *Ibid.*, Feb. 23, 1887. Lowell aroused a storm of protest by speaking on a literary topic instead of the political subject that had been announced.
46 *Ibid.*, Feb. 25, 1887.
47 *Ibid.*, Feb. 10, 1888.
48 *Ibid.*, Feb. 12, 1888.

Lincoln was entering a public dinner, he remarked gloomily, "This will be one of those heavy dinners with no wine to help us digest it."[49] Nevertheless, Lincoln attended such functions with amazing regularity.

Some occasions in which Lincoln took part after his return to Chicago were not as cheerful as those previously mentioned. Since, it seems, his associates were generally older than he, there were funerals of friends, associates, or relatives to attend. In time, he was left as almost the sole survivor of a past generation. In the summer of 1885, Lincoln went to Springfield to be present at the last rites of C. M. Smith, the husband of his mother's sister.[50] The year 1886 brought the deaths of three persons who had been very close to Lincoln: David Davis, Chester Alan Arthur, and John A. Logan. Justice Davis died June 26, 1886, at his home in Bloomington, Illinois, and to his survivors Lincoln sent this telegram:

CHICAGO JUNE 27—PLEASE CONVEY TO ALL OF JUDGE DAVIS' FAMILY MY SINCERE SYMPATHY IN A LOSS WHICH AFFECTS ME CLOSELY. I WILL BE AT THE FUNERAL.[51]

With Judge Walter Q. Gresham and Senator Logan, Lincoln left Chicago the morning of the twenty-eighth and arrived in Bloomington in time for the funeral, which was held June 29. Lincoln, as an active pallbearer, helped to carry his "second father" to his grave.[52]

In November of the same year, former President Arthur died after a long illness. Immediately, Lincoln telegraphed his condolences to the family, and on November 18 he and Judge Gresham, who had also been a member of the Arthur cabinet, boarded the afternoon train for New York.[53] Before leaving, the former War Secretary issued this statement regarding the former President:

My acquaintance with him really began with my official con-

---

49 Charles H. Dennis, *Victor Lawson, His Time and His Work*, 69.
50 Chicago *Tribune*, July 30, 1885.
51 *Ibid.*, June 28, 1886.
52 *Ibid.*, June 29, 1886.
53 *Ibid.*, Nov. 19, 1886.

nection. Not only did I learn to respect him most highly, but to have a great personal affection for him. It always seemed to me that he overcame in an admirable manner the difficulties surrounding him when he became President. While an earnest Republican, he was above all a patriotic citizen, and I know of no act in which he did not have at heart the public interest. I think it is universally conceded that, as far as he was actually responsible, he was able and dignified . . . He was a President of whom the country is proud and for whom it may well mourn.[54]

Senator John A. Logan of Illinois was reported ill around Christmas and Lincoln, hearing these reports, telegraphed the Senator's family in Washington.

CHICAGO, DECEMBER 26—WE ARE DEEPLY GRIEVED BY THE MORNING'S REPORTS, BUT HOPE WE MAY HAVE NEWS OF THE GENERAL'S IMPROVEMENT.

ROBERT T. LINCOLN[55]

But no improvement followed, and the newspapers of December 27 announced the death of "Black Jack," as the Senator was popularly known. At once, Lincoln gave a statement to the press in which he praised the deceased and spoke of him as a lifetime friend and associate.[56] John A. Logan is today remembered, if at all, as a third-rate party hack who owed much of his success to a constant "waving of the bloody shirt." However, in his day he was very popular, especially with the Union veterans groups. Upon his demise, Chicago Republican leaders gathered together and decided upon a memorial meeting to be held the evening of December 30, 1886. Robert T. Lincoln was called upon to be the principal speaker and presiding officer of the gathering. He accepted and at the appointed hour delivered a lengthy eulogy on the late Senator.[57]

Sometime later the Illinois legislature authorized the building of a statue of Logan, and Lincoln, along with Melville W. Fuller,

54 *Ibid.*
55 Chicago *Tribune*, Dec. 27, 1886.
56 *Ibid.*
57 *Ibid.*, Dec. 31, 1886.

John M. Palmer, and others, served on the Logan monument committee. Working with the widow, the group selected a site in Jackson Park, requested additional money contributions, and commissioned the sculptor Augustus Saint-Gaudens to do the statue. The artist took a very long time to complete the memorial, and it was not dedicated until 1903.[58] For the artist the Logan monument was "perhaps the most irritating" of all his commissions, and there were many letters which passed to and from the gentlemen of the committee.[59] Lincoln was somewhat unhappy, too, for quite a different set of reasons; characteristically, he had objected in 1887 to the campaign for contributions to build the monument: "Mr. Lincoln said he did not think it was dignified for the commission to beg for money."[60]

At the very moment that Logan was being eulogized and praised throughout Illinois, politicians were asking who would take Logan's place in the Senate? The Illinois state legislature contained a Republican majority in both houses so that it was a foregone conclusion that the successor would be a member of that party. The Chicago *Tribune*, always friendly to Lincoln, in the same edition that reported his speech to the meeting held December 30 printed in the "letters to the editor" column an interesting item signed only "P.B.K." It suggested Lincoln as the logical man for the vacant Senate seat in these words:

> He is a man who I believe to be fully equal to the responsibilities of the office and could represent the ideas of today in a way that would be an honor to our State. He has acquitted himself of one high office in our Government with distinction and honor. Let us have him again.[61]

However, Lincoln was by no means the only, or even the principal, candidate proposed to fill the vacancy. Almost a dozen men were under serious consideration and they included former Gov-

[58] *Ibid.*, Feb. 26 and June 19, 1887; Mrs. John A. Logan, *Reminiscences of a Soldier's Wife*, 432.

[59] Homer Saint-Gaudens, ed., *The Reminiscences of Augustus Saint-Gaudens*, II, 102–106.

[60] Chicago *Tribune*, Dec. 3, 1887.

[61] *Ibid.*, Dec. 31, 1886.

ernor Hamilton, Governor Oglesby, Joseph G. Cannon then in the House of Representatives, and Charles B. Farwell of Chicago.[62]

The senatorial contest created a good bit of excitement, not only in Illinois, but in other states as well. For example, the Omaha *Bee* observed that:

> The name of Robert Lincoln has not been prominently mentioned as a possible candidate for the United States Senate to succeed Gen. Logan and he may not desire the honor. But we are disposed to think if the selection of the Republicans of the Illinois Legislature should fall to him, the country would applaud the choice.[63]

According to the Denver *Republican*, "The Illinois Legislature cannot do better than elect Robert Lincoln to fill the vacancy in the United States Senate caused by the death of Gen. Logan."[64] The Chicago *Tribune* ran a series of biographical sketches of prominent candidates, and in the one on Lincoln it stated that he was "a man of vigor, ability, and executive capacity, . . . and is known for his good judgment and unaffected modesty. Besides, he is energetic and loves to work."[65] As usual, Lincoln did nothing to advance his candidacy, and the Republican members of the legislature decided in caucus held January 13, 1887, to present as their candidate, Charles B. Farwell. Five days later Farwell was formally elected United States senator.[66]

Lincoln was especially active on the local political level. He had returned home from Washington to find the city of Chicago firmly in control of the Democrats and dominated by an able mayor, Carter H. Harrison, usual designed as "the elder" to distinguish him from his son who also later served as mayor. Harrison, though a man of great ability, was well within the tradition of the big-city bosses.[67] First elected mayor in 1879, he was re-elected in 1881, 1883, and 1885, although in the latter race

62 *Ibid.*, Jan. 1, 1887.
63 Omaha *Bee*, quoted *ibid.*, Jan. 7, 1887.
64 Denver *Republican*, as quoted in the Chicago *Tribune*, Jan. 9, 1887.
65 Chicago *Tribune*, Jan. 11, 1887.
66 *Ibid.*, Jan. 14 and 19, 1887.
67 Claudius O. Johnson, *Carter Henry Harrison I*, 268–87.

he was nearly unseated by the Republican candidate.[68] After the 1885 contest the Republicans began working toward the adoption of new election laws, which they undoubtedly felt would help their cause. Lincoln took an active part in gaining their adoption. The Young Republican Club of Chicago held a mass meeting the evening of October 31, 1885, at the Central Music Hall for the purpose of getting support for the new election laws. The announcement of the meeting said that it "should be attended by all citizens who have at heart the interests of the Republican party and reform in the Election law."[69] When the appointed hour for the conclave to begin arrived, there was a much smaller crowd present than had been expected because of rain. Robert T. Lincoln was chosen chairman of the evening and delivered one of the principal speeches. "He felt that we were at one of the crises of our municipal life."[70] Lincoln presented the idea that national party principles and platforms had little to do with municipal affairs, although he concluded that it was a good idea to support the Republican party in this instance and help elect the Republican candidates to the city commission. The election was held November 4, 1885, and the new election laws were approved; at the same time, the Republicans scored some gains in the city government.

The following year, 1886, brought congressional elections, and in July, when the convention met in the Fourth Congressional District, Lincoln nominated Representative George E. Adams for another term. He was greeted with "enthusiastic cheers" and spoke warmly of Adams whom he said he had known for years.[71] When, in the spring of 1887, another municipal campaign opened and the Republicans had another chance at the mayor's office, Lincoln became active again. This time Carter Harrison suddenly withdrew from the race, leaving the Democrats without a candidate. On March 23, 1887, a "Grand Republican Mass Meeting" was held in the evening and Lincoln was selected by

68 *Ibid.*, 288.
69 Chicago *Tribune*, Oct. 31, 1885.
70 *Ibid.*, Nov. 1, 1885.
71 *Ibid.*, July 25, 1886.

the committee on arrangements to be a vice-president of the group.[72] With Harrison out of the way, John A. Roche, the Republican nominee, handily won the contest (only to be defeated two years later by another Democrat).[73] Some weeks later another election was held, this one for municipal judges. On the evening of June 4, 1887, the Central Music Hall was once again the site of a Republican rally and once again Lincoln spoke long and ably for his party and its candidates.[74]

For the most part, Robert Lincoln's political activities in the period 1885–89 have a partisan tone, but on at least one occasion he crossed party lines to help a friend. Following the death of Chief Justice Morrison R. Waite in 1888, it was rumored that President Cleveland was considering the Chicago attorney Melville W. Fuller for the vacancy. Lincoln had known Fuller for many years and, at the suggestion of mutual friends, Lincoln wrote the President urging the appointment.[75] It was made, but at once there began a fight over confirmation of the nominee. Charges that Fuller had been a Copperhead during the Civil War were made, but Lincoln, Lyman Trumbull, and others vigorously denied them.[76] Eventually Fuller's nomination was confirmed, and Lincoln was among those paying tribute to the new Chief Justice at a banquet held in his honor just prior to his departure from Chicago to take up his new duties.[77] On one other occasion, Lincoln helped to honor another Democrat, President Grover Cleveland, who visited Chicago in the summer of 1887. The visit was considered nonpolitical, hence Lincoln's service on the mayor's reception committee, which first met in the city council chamber July 26 to plan for the Chief Executive's arrival.[78]

In any discussion of Robert T. Lincoln's life during the late 1890's, it must be remembered that he was first and foremost a

72 *Ibid.*, Mar. 23, 1887.
73 *Ibid.*, Apr. 6, 1887.
74 *Ibid.*, June 5, 1887.
75 Willard L. King, *Melville Weston Fuller*, 108.
76 *Ibid.*, 116.
77 *Ibid.*, 121–22.
78 Chicago *Tribune*, July 24, 1887.

lawyer and to his profession he devoted his full energies. The law firm was one of the most influential and prosperous in Chicago and numbered among its clients many important individuals and firms. Chief among these firms were the various railroad interests represented by Isham, Lincoln and Beale. They had a part in the problems arising out of the Wabash receivership in 1886, and in 1888, Lincoln and others represented General John McNulta, the Wabash receiver, in a court action to determine the General's responsibilities under the new Interstate Commerce Commission toward another railroad whose workers were on strike.[79]

It has already been said that Lincoln drew up Walter Newberry's will. He was also a member of the original board of trustees of the Newberry Library, and it was in that capacity that he attended their meeting the evening of July 8, 1887, at the home of E. W. Blatchford to discuss their duties and to plan the location of the new library.[80] When John Crerar died, his will specified that "the following named friends" were to act as the board of directors of the proposed Crerar Library; Lincoln and Marshall Field were included in the list.[81]

[79] *Ibid.*, Apr. 2, 1886; Matilda Gresham, *Life of Walter Quinton Gresham*, I, 413.
[80] Chicago *Tribune*, July 9, 1887.
[81] Moses and Kirkland, *History of Chicago*, II, 142, 213–14.

Chapter 10

Another Presidential Election

AT THE SAME TIME THAT ROBERT LINCOLN was occupied with Chicago politics, his law practice, and his family, his name was being prominently mentioned in another but familiar area. Usually no sooner is one presidential campaign over than speculation about the next one begins. This was especially true in the late nineteenth century when politics was something of a national sport. Since the date of the elections was not standardized as it became later, there was almost constant political activity of one sort or another. As early as the spring of 1886, Lincoln's name was brought forth as a candidate for President in 1888. A Negro journal in Atlanta, Georgia, was well aware of the magic in the name Lincoln and suggested that the Republican party could not do better than to choose the man from Illinois as its standard-bearer.[1]

Several days later a Chicago reporter asked Mr. Lincoln how he felt about the matter. The reply was straightforward. After observing, "The editor knows more about that [the newspaper's statement that there was great clamor for Lincoln's nomination, especially among the Negro population] than I do," Lincoln said, "I'm entirely out of public life. I attend strictly to my private business and have no time, nor if I had time, any inclination to

[1] Atlanta *Defiance*, quoted in the Chicago *Tribune*, Apr. 13, 1886.

discuss public matters."[2] The interview took place in Louisville, Kentucky, where Lincoln was on business. The reporter next mentioned to him the matter of the "fishing vacation," which "Mr. Lincoln is accustomed to take about the first of June." Before Lincoln could answer, someone in his party interrupted by saying that President Cleveland's usual fishing trip was being canceled because of his impending marriage on June 2 to Miss Frances Folsom.

> "Cleveland couldn't catch a bass anyhow," said one of Mr. Lincoln's companions. "I don't know about that," replied the genial ex-Secretary. "Cleveland has been pretty successful at catching anything he wants. I think he could catch a bass if he wanted it."[3]

Lincoln's statement on the presidency by no means ended the matter, and by early 1888 he returned to his policy of refusing invitations to speak lest his appearances be interpreted as an interest in receiving nomination to office. Joseph B. Foraker of Ohio had asked Lincoln to speak at a birthday celebration in honor of his father in Columbus. The son replied that he wished to avoid any appearance that would encourage newspapers to use his "name in connection with public matters." However, he did very much appreciate the honors done to the President's memory.[4] Also in February there was a meeting of the Michigan Republican Club, but Lincoln declined to attend.[5]

During the Illinois senatorial contest the Buffalo *Courier* ran an editorial in which Lincoln was discussed not only as a possible senator but as a possible President. It noted that in 1884 certain persons had favored Lincoln, but at that time both Arthur and Logan had been in the way of Lincoln's candidacy. Now Arthur was dead, as was Logan, and:

> By the latter's death not only has a seat in the Senate been vacated but also room has been made for a new aspirant to the Republican

2 Chicago *Tribune*, Apr. 28, 1886.

3 *Ibid.*

4 Lincoln to Joseph B. Foraker, Jan. 27, 1888, Historical and Philosophical Society of Ohio.

5 Chicago *Tribune*, Feb. 23, 1887.

Presidential nomination. That as such Mr. Lincoln would have elements of strength no one would deny.[6]

There followed the usual reference to the "illustrious name which he bears" and an acknowledgment that although his official record had not been particularly remarkable, still his "political record is calculated to strengthen him."[7] The latter statement was mainly a reference to Lincoln's efforts in behalf of Grant's third-term attempt of 1880.

Later in January, 1887, the Knoxville (Tennessee) *Times* took up the cry and put forth Lincoln as its favorite candidate.[8] In late spring the Toledo *Blade* polled its readers on their choice of a nominee and found Lincoln in third place behind Blaine and John Sherman. It also discovered that he was almost the sole choice mentioned for Vice-President. Looking at the situation, it concluded:

> It is to be remembered that Mr. Lincoln . . . has made no effort whatever to work up a boom. He has no literary bureau, no lieutenants of any kind at work for him. His strength is entirely spontaneous. Those who know him personally are well aware that he has no wish to be either President or Vice-President. The two tragedies at the White House touched him very nearly, and he makes no secret of his distaste for public life. He enjoys the practice of the law, and lives quietly. He is building himself a home on the Lake-Shore drive, near the park which bears his father's name, and it is safe to say that he sincerely prefers that semi-urban and semi-suburban residence to the Executive Mansion in Washington. Like Richard Cromwell he has no taste for public life. But the American people are not accustomed to pay much attention to personal likes and dislikes in selecting a President. No man ever promoted his chances by "taking heed thereto," as the King James version puts it. It is evident that the Republican party has its eye on Mr. Lincoln, and in the event of a contest such as those of 1876 and 1880 his name will be placed at the head of the ticket without putting out the gas or the resort by his friends to any sharp prac-

[6] Buffalo *Courier*, quoted in the Chicago *Tribune*, Jan. 1, 1887.
[7] *Ibid.*
[8] Knoxville *Times*, quoted in the Chicago *Tribune*, Jan. 24, 1887.

tice. On the contrary, his personal friends and himself could not prevent that result if they tried. At least there never was a clearer indication of public sentiment that if there is to be a dark horse at all it will be the son of Abraham Lincoln and this is not altogether because he is the son of his father either. With the inauguration of General Garfield he came prominently before the public and during the four years he was at the head of the War Department he showed himself to be level-headed, honorable and modest. The people were well pleased to find the son of the Great Emancipator free from the vices and follies so often found in the sons of illustrious sires. He made no enemies. Alike popular with both wings of the Republican party, his candidacy would arouse no animosities. If he lacks magnetic power—one of the prime qualities of his father—he is particularly strong in the negative virtues. Should the convention find itself deadlocked it would make no mistake in taking him up and once more doing battle under the leadership of Lincoln.[9]

A mugwump paper, the Springfield (Massachusetts) *Republican* stated that Lincoln was "an honored son of an honored sire" and then went on to say:

In the absence of deep-rooted and exciting issues, such as called forth a master like the older Lincoln, the son belongs to the class of men who seem best fitted to the office of President in more tranquil times—not men who have been longest identified with the struggles and triumphs of the party in the past, nor the giants of past warfare, but the younger men of judicial mold, of liberal convictions as to the improvement of public administration and the reform of abuses and sympathetic with every section of a Union truly restored. . . . He made the best Secretary of War of all who have recently held the position. He knew no party lines in administration, and served only his country. His services were recognized broadly by the people of all parties. In his own party no faction claimed him as its exclusive possession. His personal independence, integrity, and sincere devotion to administrative reform would, if he were nominated, place an embarrassing assortment of attractions before the independent and mugwump vote which elected Mr. Cleveland.

9 Toledo *Blade*, quoted in the Chicago *Tribune*, July 16, 1887.

The *Republican* concluded that Robert T. Lincoln was the man to reunite the Republican party after its disastrous split in 1884.[10] Along similar lines *Harper's Weekly*, in discussing Lincoln as a candidate, said, "This favor is not due wholly to sentimental considerations, although they are of great weight in practical politics"; still, "Mr. Lincoln was an excellent Secretary of War."[11]

Other voices were raised in the discussion of Lincoln potentially as a nominee. The *Boston Herald*, another mugwump journal, considered the former Secretary of War "a sensible gentleman," and "yet we hardly see enough in his record to warrant the singling him out as a candidate for the Presidency."[12] The *Herald* thought that probably Lincoln would agree for it seemed as though he had no such aspirations. Yet the writer wondered about the source of Lincoln's popularity and found that the feeling of people that he should be considered for Chief Executive was genuine and could have been worse directed. It concluded:

> We are not disposed to accept Mr. Robert T. Lincoln as a great man, or as one fitted to be President beyond many others, because he is the son of his father, but the great dignity he exhibited in office, and the absence of obtrusive ambition he has shown out of it, afford an agreeable indication that he would make a sensible and patriotic President.[13]

Some few papers were violently hostile to Lincoln; witness the following from the Omaha (Nebraska) *Republican*:

> It is curious how some papers hang on to the name of young Lincoln in discussing Presidential possibilities. There is more sentiment than sense in the suggestion. There are a hundred men in Omaha his superior. He is simply a cipher in the name. When Abraham Lincoln died the ciphers in his family were left without a figure to the front.[14]

10 Springfield *Republican*, quoted in the Chicago *Tribune*, July 23, 1887.
11 *Harper's Weekly*, Sept. 3, 1887.
12 *Boston Herald*, quoted in the Chicago *Tribune*, July 23, 1887.
13 *Ibid.*
14 Omaha *Republican*, Feb. 13, 1887.

In a somewhat lighter vein the Chicago *Tribune* reported:

The Wichita *Republic* nominates Robert T. Lincoln for President and Roscoe Conkling for Vice-President. It requires the imagination of only the most commonplace order to conceive the lofty scorn that the upward curve of Mr. Conkling's patrician and mugwumpian nose would express on seeing this combination in print for the first time, or of the air of patient resignation with which Mr. Lincoln would bear the undeserved humiliation on seeing it himself.[15]

Some months later the same paper commented: "Conkling approves of Robert T. Lincoln as a Presidential candidate. This is the first serious setback Lincoln's boom has received."[16]

In the midst of the oncoming election, Lincoln was interviewed by a reporter in August, 1887, and when asked about the Vice-Presidency, he responded:

I simply could not accept the nomination to the Vice-Presidency. To take any office at all would be a great sacrifice of my business interests here in Chicago, and the Vice-Presidency is not an office of such importance that I could afford to think of such a thing. I most certainly should not accept the nomination for the Vice-Presidency were it tendered, which I have no reason to think it will be.

Continuing, the former Secretary of War observed:

I have seen too much of the wear and tear of official life to ever have a desire to reenter it. Though I was but a boy when my father became President, I can well remember the tremendous burden he was called upon to bear. True, the conduct of the war made the cares of office then infinitely more exacting; but I have seen enough of Washington official life to have lost all desire for it. The Presidential office is but a gilded prison. The care and worry outweigh, to my mind, the honor which surrounds the position.

He recalled that he had found life as a cabinet member wearisome and that when he left office he resolved to spend the rest of his

15 Chicago *Tribune,* June 28, 1887.
16 *Ibid.,* Sept. 11, 1887.

life in the practice of his profession. "I am now 44, and come of a long lived ancestry," which made it possible for him to hope for another twenty to twenty-five years to live.

I wish nothing better than to spend those years in my professional work. I am not willing, either, to have them embittered by an unsuccessful candidacy or to pass such of them as the wear of office would leave in the unpleasant position, to use no stronger word, of a retired President. There is a fascination about public office, especially one of high dignity, which I can understand, but the more fascinating the position, the more disagreeable is the inevitable defeat which retires one to private life. I have seen many men to whom it came after their aptitude for the ordinary affairs of life had passed away, as well as their opportunities, while their needs remained in full force, and I long ago resolved that I would never, if I could help it, be in such a position. I went to Washington in 1881, with reluctance, and was glad to come away.

Turning to some of the issues of the moment, Lincoln continued:

I am a thorough protectionist. In all the political speeches I have made, I have dwelt upon this theme chiefly. There is no doubt in my mind that this is the only policy for this country to pursue, and it is growing in popular favor as the people more clearly understand the issue.

As for the problem of the Negro voters in the South, the evaluation of the son of the Great Emancipator was:

There is a general denial that there is intimidation or fraud in the South on the part of the greater portion of the Democratic press. There is perhaps no bulldozing, no Ku-Klux outrages, no shot gun practice upon the negro voters; but this is because the latter understand that they are not to exercise the right of suffrage, and dare not attempt it.

If they did, Lincoln said, there would be violence. As for the future:

The Southern problem is a most difficult one, and the process of solution through education and enlightenment is very slow. There is a feeling too that to allow the negro his equality of rights as a citizen will involve his social equality, and there is nothing more repugnant than this to the Southern Whites. Of course there would nothing of this sort follow; but this confusion of ideas is not strange, as we had the same thing here in the North during the war among the anti-war Democracy.

Toward the conclusion of the interview, Lincoln was again asked if he would accept a presidential nomination. Observing that he had been trying to get across the idea that he did not want such a thing, he did say, nevertheless, "I will say this; a duty might be imposed upon a man which he could not honorably avoid."[17] Here is the essence of Robert Lincoln's approach to public life. Twice he would find duties he could not honorably avoid, but never would he go searching for another one.

The interview was widely read and widely reprinted. It provoked considerable comment. The *Blade* itself noted that Lincoln was a supporter of civil service and that he would rally the mugwumps in New York and, as a matter of fact, throughout the nation.[18] The *Boston Herald* commented, "Mr. Lincoln it is only just to assume is not naturally ambitious." However, it felt that he would accept a nomination if one were offered. "With a shrewdness worthy of the elder Lincoln also he manages for himself, amid all his disclaimers of ambition, to publish a platform well adapted to gain him favor with the Republicans."[19] In the weeks that followed, Lincoln's name continued to be pushed before the public. In Washington in September, an audience of one thousand gathered at the A. M. E. Metropolitan Church "loudly applauded" the suggestion that a good presidential ticket would be Lincoln for President and Frederick Douglass for Vice-President.[20] At the same time Governor Luce of Michigan, visiting that state's fair, said that many Michigan farmers he had talked to favored Lincoln for President.[21] Lincoln's old friend

17 Toledo *Blade*, as quoted in the Chicago *Tribune*, Aug. 31, 1887.
18 *Ibid.*, Sept. 7, 1887.
19 As quoted in the Chicago *Tribune*, Sept. 7, 1887.
20 *Ibid.*, Sept. 24, 1887.
21 *Ibid.*

from the War Department, Thomas F. Barr, was quietly working behind the scenes on the former Secretary's behalf. On September 13 he wrote confidentially to John D. Long asking his support. In all probability Lincoln did not know about his efforts.[22]

On September 24, Lincoln himself was again interviewed, this time in Pittsburgh:

> I have nothing to say today that would interest the public, but when I have I want time to say it thoroughly and deliberately. When a man talks for publication things sometimes get twisted around, though I do not say that it is done with the intention of misrepresenting a man.

Asked if John Sherman would make a strong candidate, Lincoln said yes. "He is an excellent man. . . . ," but this did not mean that Lincoln preferred him over Blaine or Allison. "I would vote for any good Republican who may be nominated." After the interview the reporter concluded, "Mr. Lincoln intimated that, while he did not seek the Presidential nomination, he would submit to the decision of the convention."[23]

The following March a Negro citizen from Mexico, Missouri, wrote Lincoln urging him to seek the presidency and in reply received the following:

> Chicago, March 8, 1888—Mr. Ervin W. Caldwell, Mexico, Mo.—
> Dear Sir: I could not fail to appreciate highly the feelings expressed in your letter. I am, however, sorry to see any mention of my name in connection with any political office, and I have said this so often that it is a matter of wonder to me that it does not stop. While I hope to retain and manifest an interest in public affairs, my interest will never again be official. Yours, Robert T. Lincoln.[24]

An interesting story has been circulated about the 1888 nomination, which may or may not be true. The tale was that before the Republican convention certain party leaders considered a ticket made up of Robert T. Lincoln for President, and Fred-

22 Thomas F. Barr to John D. Long, Sept. 13, 1887, Harvard College Library.
23 Chicago *Tribune*, Sept. 25, 1887.
24 *Ibid.*, Mar. 12, 1888.

erick D. Grant, son of the General, for Vice-President. It was to be called a "father's son" ticket and have presented "names to conjure with!" The reporter of the story claimed that the plan ended when Grant was defeated for election as New York secretary of state.[25] Commenting on the story, Grant's son Major General Ulysses S. Grant III has said:

> I can only say that I have no recollection of Mr. Robert Lincoln and my father, General Frederick Dent Grant, being candidates for the Presidency and Vice-Presidency, respectively in 1888. . . . I was present in Chicago at the time of the Republican convention, and although only a lad of seven, I was much interested and personally an enthusiastic backer of Judge Gresham. I am sure that, if there had been any serious consideration of a Lincoln-Grant ticket, I would have been for it and remembered it.
>
> Of course people were often saying to my Father that he should try for the Presidency; but he never believed that he should.[26]

The race for the Republican nomination was wide open. Indicative of the situation was the Chicago *Inter Ocean*'s question "Who will it be?," which was then answered:

GRESHAM

ALLISON

DEPEW

CULLOM

BLAINE

ALGER

JERRY RUSK

FORAKER

LINCOLN

HARRISON

HAWLEY

SHERMAN[27]

---

25 Henry L. Stoddard, *As I Knew Them*, 157.

26 Letter to the author from Ulysses S. Grant III, June 25, 1958.

27 Chicago *Inter Ocean*, June 22, 1887, quoted in Leland L. Sage, *William Boyd Allison*, 207.

Instead of waiting for the outcome of the preconvention wire-pulling, Lincoln took a trip to England. In June he was interviewed at his hotel in Grosvenor Square, London. Said he, "I am here to avoid the bother of politics and business and to get a rest." Lincoln hoped the contest would be a clean one, and he insisted, "I am not a dark horse." In so far as he was concerned, "My own preference is strong for Judge Gresham." Gresham could unite the party. Commenting on civil service, Lincoln said he felt that Cleveland had abandoned it. After all, the original law "was passed under a Republican administration, and I have reason to know that during the last two years of Mr. Arthur's presidency the principles of civil-service reform were carried out with the most rigid precision." In the operation of the War Department, "I never knew the political opinions of any man who was appointed to any position. The examination papers were our only criteria as to the candidate's fitness." Aside from the civil service issue, Lincoln commented:

> I anticipate Republican success for another reason. While the Democrats have not absolutely committed themselves to the doctrine of free trade, they have made such an advance in that direction as to awaken great uneasiness in the minds of businessmen who are interested in manufacturing. Capitalists hesitate to embark on ventures when they have reason to apprehend that in a few years free-trade legislation may render those enterprises valueless.

In conclusion the traveler said that he felt that the protection issue would win votes for his party in the South.[28]

When the suspense over the winner of the nomination was ended, former Senator Benjamin Harrison of Indiana had been chosen. Harrison's chief qualifications for the nation's highest office were that he was too obscure to have many enemies and that his grandfather had once been President.

On August 19, Lincoln and his "pretty daughter" Mary returned to New York. He was tanned and appeared to be the picture of health. Since he had been away for some ten weeks, it

---

28 Chicago *Tribune*, June 22, 1888.

was necessary for him to go home to Chicago and plunge into his accumulated work. As for the upcoming campaign and the Republican chances: "The ticket strikes me as having great strength, and I am confident that it will win at the polls in November."[29] What about Lincoln's plans? "Shall I do anything in the campaign? Well, yes, I suppose I shall have to, you know."[30] In so far as issues were concerned, Lincoln insisted:

> One cannot go through Europe with open eyes and be anything else than a protectionist, if he is an American to my way of thinking. . . . We cannot afford to throw open our doors to the products of the cheap labor of Europe.

Invoking the infant-industries argument, the former Secretary of War left the impression that he favored keeping up the tariff walls only "for a time." The reporters in concluding their story could not resist commenting that Lincoln, wearing a brown billycock hat and a suit of Scotch tweed from Poole's, which combined to give him "quite an English air," bore "a most striking resemblance to the Prince of Wales."[31]

Between the latter part of August and the November election, Lincoln was a busy man indeed. The Chicago *Tribune*, in its election day editorial titled "The Sons of Lincoln and Douglas," noted that both Robert T. Lincoln and Stephen A. Douglas, Jr., were for the Republican cause, and the paper concluded that the "nation cannot do better than follow the lead of these two." Praising Lincoln, it said that when he arrived home, he "plunged into the thick of the fight and has made twenty or thirty stirring speeches in Illinois, Indiana, Ohio, Michigan, Wisconsin and Iowa."[32]

When the ballots were counted, it was found that although President Cleveland had the edge in popular votes, the electoral college had thwarted the will of the majority and declared Ben-

29 *Ibid.*, Aug. 20, 1888.
30 *New York Times*, Aug. 20, 1888.
31 Chicago *Tribune*, Aug. 20, 1888.
32 *Ibid.*, Nov. 6, 1888.

jamin Harrison the chosen one. On March 4, 1889, another Republican administration was launched.

The new Chief Executive immediately set about the task of making appointments to the various offices that the President is required to fill. The appointments to foreign missions were then almost exclusively used to pay off political debts and to reward men who had rendered aid, frequently of a monetary nature, to the victorious political party. Shortly after his inauguration Harrison began secretly to sound out several western senators about appointing a minister to London. Word of this leaked out, and the rumor was started that the man to be appointed was Robert T. Lincoln of Illinois. Regarding the story, John C. New of Indiana, a friend of the President and a recently appointed consul general in London said:

> What blanked nonsense. There is not a word of truth in it. Such an appointment is impossible. Harrison has got more sense. Lincoln is a good fellow, but he represents nothing politically, and the appointment is too big a one to be thrown away. If the English mission is given to Illinois, Bob Hitt will be the man.[33]

As for Lincoln, he and his household were spending a quiet winter following the election. On November 23, Mr. and Mrs. Lincoln, together with the Marshall Fields and the George M. Pullmans, attended a wedding; on December 6, Mrs. Lincoln was one of more than 350 who attended a fashionable reception; on December 10 there was a ball described as "One of the most elaborate affairs of the season"; and on the fourteenth the Lincolns were at another ball, where Christmas was the theme and a Hungarian military band played dance music.[34] After the Christmas holidays there was no let up in the social rounds. Robert and Mary Lincoln were manager and patroness respectively for the third annual Chicago charity ball held January 3, 1889.[35]

As the weeks passed, there was some grumbling that Illinois

33 Unidentified Boston newspaper, Mar. 27, 1889, Harvard University Archives.
34 Chicago *Tribune*, Nov. 23, Dec. 7, 11, and 15, 1888.
35 *Ibid.*, Dec. 9, 1888, and Jan. 4, 1889.

was not receiving its fair share of federal appointments. The Chicago *Tribune* asked, "What Does Illinois Get?[36] The appointment of minister to England had not been made because there had recently been some slight complications in Anglo-American relations. Sackville-West had been duped into becoming a minor campaign issue with the famous "Murchison letter." Then there was the perennial problem of Irish-Americans who took the opportunity of a change in administrations to send a delegation to call on President Harrison. They felt that the last two ministers to London had been excessively pro-English and asked that Harrison "select somebody thoroughly in sympathy with American institutions and not likely to be moved from his Americanism by British flattery."[37] The Chief Executive replied that "he proposed to select just such a man, adding that, notwithstanding their Irish sympathies, any of them would probably, if brought within the influence of English social life, be less acceptable to his sturdy fellow patriots at home at the end of his term than at the beginning."[38]

At last the appointment mill began to grind. On the evening of March 26, Senators Cullom and Farwell received a note from the President asking them to call at the White House at ten the next morning.[39] They rightly suspected that the summons was in regard to the English mission and decided that if asked to make a suggestion they would name John N. Jewett. They had considered Representative Hitt but knew he would prefer to remain as chairman of the House foreign affairs committee.[40] The pair had already proposed Jewett to Secretary of State Blaine.[41] When the Senators arrived at the President's office, he greeted them warmly and immediately said: "I am thinking of sending Robert T. Lincoln over there. He has had experience in public life, he is well known and well thought of in all parts of the country. I

36 *Ibid.*, Mar. 17, 1889.
37 Beckles Willson, *America's Ambassadors to England,* 398.
38 *Ibid.*, quoting *The Times,* Mar. 22, 1889.
39 Chicago *Tribune,* Mar. 28, 1889.
40 *Ibid.*
41 Cullom, *Fifty Years of Public Service,* 126.

172

believe his selection would give satisfaction not only in your State but everywhere else."[42]

The Chicago *Tribune* reported that Cullom and Farwell were favorably disposed and that the two had "heartily endorsed it, and they congratulated the President on the sagacity he had shown." Regarding Lincoln, Harrison said, "He doesn't know anything about it yet." Indeed, the nominee learned of it when a reporter called at his office. When a reporter called later, Lincoln "wore a pleasant smile." Asked the reporter, "You have heard of your appointment as Minister P. and E. E. to the Court of Saint James?" Lincoln replied, "That's a high-sounding title for a plain man." When asked if he would accept the appointment, he said he had not yet had time to consider it. He did add, however, that he found London to be "A pleasant city."[43]

Lincoln's appointment caused some disappointments, even among his closest friends. There had been much talk of Chauncey Depew taking the post but he did not want it.[44] However, John Hay did want the position, and he felt that if John Sherman had won the Republican presidential nomination in 1888, he would have had it.[45] Instead of receiving the appointment himself, Hay was now given the task of convincing Whitelaw Reid that he should accept the French mission, instead of the English which he too had wanted.[46] Former Secretary of State William M. Evarts had been rumored as the possible appointee to England, but now he was also disappointed.[47] At the same time, others were expressing joy over the nomination. Theodore Roosevelt wrote to Henry Cabot Lodge, "The appointment of Lincoln is admirable."[48] Another disgruntled diplomat, John A. Kasson of Iowa, grudgingly conceded:

The great places have been filled; Robert T. Lincoln goes to

42 Chicago *Tribune*, Mar. 28, 1889.
43 *Ibid.*
44 Willson, *America's Ambassadors*, 398.
45 Dennett, *John Hay*, 172.
46 *Ibid.*
47 Chester L. Barrows, *William M. Evarts*, 456.
48 Theodore Roosevelt to Henry Cabot Lodge, Mar. 27, 1889, *Selections from the Correspondence of Theodore Roosevelt and Henry Cabot Lodge*, I, 75.

England . . . . Lincoln to England and Frederick Grant to Austria are largely made on account of public admiration and gratitude for the service of two eminent Presidents, their fathers. But Mr. Lincoln adds, as Grant does not, some personal qualification and experience.[49]

Editorial comment was almost entirely unrestrained in its praise of the new minister to London. The *New York Times* judged that Lincoln "is a good lawyer, a man of unblemished reputation, who showed judgment and candor in his conduct of the War Department, and who is not at all a politician of the ordinary type."[50] *Harper's Weekly* spoke of him as one who "has taken a prominent position at the bar, and in public and private life has acquired a reputation for solid qualities and freedom from pretence or sham. He is regarded as especially clearheaded, judicious, and upright in purpose, and courteous and unassuming in manners." It added that he had another essential qualification for an American diplomat: "He is credited with having a comfortable fortune."[51] According to the New York *Herald*, "A more fortunate and satisfactory selection on all accounts than Mr. Robert Lincoln . . . could not have been made." The New York *Sun* proclaimed: "The appointment . . . will be popular in this country, and we dare say it will give satisfaction to the mass of Englishmen. He is likely to prove a better minister than we have had in England since the late Charles Francis Adams."[52] The Chicago *Tribune* praised Lincoln, "In all walks of life, public and private, he has been conspicuous for his good judgment, tact, prudence, and discretion," and reprinted words of praise from other papers around the country.[53] In England the *Daily News* of London noted, "The American Minister to England will be welcome if only for the name he bears," while the prime minister was reported as saying the appointment was a

---

[49] Edward Younger, *John A. Kasson*, 353.

[50] *New York Times*, Mar. 28, 1889.

[51] *Harper's Weekly*, Apr. 6, 1889.

[52] Quoted in an unidentified newspaper clipping, dated Mar. 28, 1889, Harvard University Archives.

[53] Chicago *Tribune*, Mar. 29, 1889.

pleasant surprise.[54] The Illinois state legislature joined in the pleasantries by passing a resolution endorsing the nomination.[55]

The appointment of Lincoln was viewed as entirely the decision of President Harrison, acting upon his own initiative, and was said to emphasize "the fact that he controls his own administration" and was not bossed by his secretary of state, James G. Blaine.[56] Unfortunately, Harrison's independence created difficulty with the two Illinois senators. Although Cullom and Farwell were reported to be delighted with the appointment, they were, in fact, angry over the way in which it was made. Many years later Senator Cullom recalled, "Farwell was extremely angry, and wanted to fight the nomination." However, Cullom talked him out of it, although he, too, was hurt by not being really consulted on the matter.[57] As a result of this and other frictions, Farwell became quite hostile toward Harrison and later opposed his renomination.[58] Cullom himself believed that Lincoln's appointment was in part made to "humiliate" Blaine.[59]

Senator Hoar of Massachusetts recorded that the President did mention Lincoln's name, along with several others, in a discussion prior to making the appointment.

> I said that I had known Mr. Lincoln pretty well when he was in President Garfield's and Mr. Arthur's Cabinet, and thought very highly of him. He was a very modest man indeed, never pressing any claim to public consideration or office, either on his own account or as his father's son, and never seeking responsibility. But I had noticed that when he had anything to say or anything to do, he always said or did the wisest and best thing to be said or done under the circumstances. I do not know how much influence what I said had, but it seemed to gratify President Harrison exceedingly, and he stated that he was strongly inclined to appoint Mr. Lincoln.[60]

54 *Ibid.*, Mar. 29, 1889.
55 *Ibid.*
56 Unidentified newspaper clipping, dated Mar. 27, 1889, Harvard University Archives.
57 Cullom, *Fifty Years of Public Service*, 126.
58 George F. Hoar, *Autobiography of Seventy Years*, I, 216.
59 Cullom, *Fifty Years of Public Service*, 126.
60 Hoar, *Autobiography*, I, 216.

The senator from Massachusetts felt that Harrison should have consulted Cullom and Farwell in advance, which actually he did, but it was done as a *fait accompli*.

On March 30, 1889, Lincoln's appointment was confirmed by the Senate, and word of the possible invoking of senatorial courtesy leaked out.[61] The Minister-designate went to Washington, arriving the morning of April 4. First he met Senator Cullom and the two went to call on the President. They stayed for "several minutes," and Lincoln as he came out of Harrison's office was smiling and greeted a number of old White House employees "with considerable warmth." Then Lincoln went to call on Secretary Blaine, and the two greeted each other cordially.[62] On the ninth he started home for Chicago.[63] On the fifteenth he took his oath of office, and that same day from Chicago he informed Secretary Blaine:

> I shall at once upon my arrival in London request an audience of Her Majesty the Queen for the purpose of presenting my predecessor's letters of recall and my own letters of credence. I need not assure you that my best efforts will be used to maintain the good relations which now exist between the two countries, and to discharge the duties which may devolve upon me in a manner satisfactory to the President and honorable and useful to the country.[64]

The five Lincolns were making plans to leave Chicago, but the head of the household found time for a Union League Club banquet, attended by some two hundred, the evening of April 30 in honor of the centennial of the inauguration of George Washington. Among the toasts and responses was Lincoln's answer to the toast proposed to John Marshall. In it, he spoke of the Chief Justice as a man especially created by Divine Providence to head

---

[61] Chicago *Tribune*, Mar. 31, 1889.

[62] *Ibid.*, Apr. 5, 1889.

[63] *Ibid.*, Apr. 9, 1889.

[64] Lincoln to James G. Blaine, Dispatches from U.S. Ministers to Great Britain, microfilm roll 155, National Archives.

the judiciary, and of the nation that would not have been what it was then without Marshall's work.[65]

There was another Union League Club banquet held the evening of May 7, and this one was for Lincoln himself. The president of the club announced that the guest of honor had extracted from him a pledge that there would be no speeches. However, when Lincoln himself rose to make a few remarks, he said he had merely asked if there were going to be speeches. The banquet attended by some two hundred lasted until just before midnight.[66] The next night the Chicago Club gave its departing member a reception, which was described as "a vision of fairyland." Lincoln shook hands all around and had a pleasant word for the more than five hundred who attended. All the while an orchestra serenaded the group with selections by Strauss, Suppé, Schubert, Rossini, and De Koven.[67]

The Lincoln family left Chicago on May 9 and arrived in Washington the evening of May 10, after a hot, uncomfortable trip.[68] Minister Lincoln once again called on the President and Secretary of State; on May 12 his party left for New York.[69] They stopped there at the Fifth Avenue Hotel, where many friends called upon them and they spent a few days visiting and dining with them.[70] Accompanied by Mr. and Mrs. Robert S. McCormick, the Lincolns sailed May 15, 1889, on the *City of Paris*.[71]

65 Chicago *Tribune,* May 1, 1889.
66 *Ibid.,* May 8, 1889.
67 *Ibid.,* May 9, 1889.
68 *Ibid.,* May 11, 1889.
69 *Ibid.,* May 12, 1889.
70 *New York Times,* May 14, 1889.
71 *Ibid.*

Chapter 11

Literary Matters

Over the years Robert T. Lincoln and John Hay continued to be firm friends. Their relationship lasted for nearly a half century, until the death of Hay in 1905. While Lincoln was busy carving a legal and political career for himself, Hay was occupied with a literary and political one. To Hay, whom he saw in person only infrequently, Lincoln wrote long letters, which must have overtaxed his friend's abilities to decipher Lincoln's horrible handwriting, unless, of course, Hay finally mastered the scrawl. In May, 1871, Lincoln commented on his friend's literary success, "I don't know whether you care a tinker for my opinion but I can't help telling you that I am delighted with the way in which you are carving out a place for yourself and I sincerely congratulate you upon it."[1] A few months later Lincoln observed, "I have enjoyed the renewal of acquaintance with the papers that came out in the Atlantic as well as making friends with those I had not seen before."[2]

When Hay was to be married in 1874, Lincoln dashed off a note saying that he was amazed that Hay was at last to be "tied," and that unless he was there to see the ceremony in person, he would probably never be able to believe that it had actually happened.[3]

[1] Lincoln to John Hay, May 25, 1871, Hay Papers.
[2] Lincoln to Hay, Sept. 26, 1871, *ibid.*
[3] Lincoln to Hay, Jan. 17, 1874, *ibid.*

Throughout the 1870's and into the next decade, Lincoln and Hay continued their correspondence. When Hay anonymously brought out his antilabor novel *The Bread-Winners*, Lincoln wrote that he had read it and asked that Hay if he was acquainted with the author to tell him please how much he enjoyed the work.[4] Often the letters dealt with the daily happenings of family life, of wives, of children, of work, and on occasion of Lincoln's troubles with one problem or another.

There was also the biography of Lincoln's father. Less than two years after the death of the President, Hay wrote his friend and collaborator John G. Nicolay:

> A—— is making a collection of Lincoln's letters, speeches, etc., but on his own hook. B—— encourages it, but will not give him the key to the boxes. He will keep them for the present, and still hopes for our assistance in classifying them.[5]

In the spring of 1872, Lincoln himself raised the subject again when he wrote Hay:

> I hope that when the proper time comes to have you use the material taken from Washington and make a respectable book— It is absolutely horrible to think of such men as Herndon and Lamon being considered in the light they claim.[6]

In November of that same year, Nicolay, then marshal of the United States Supreme Court, wrote to Hay:

> I am convinced that we ought to be at work on our *Lincoln*, you might as well be putting in your time collecting material as not. I don't think the time for publication has come, but the time for preparation is slipping away.[7]

It was not long after that work was begun in earnest, in either late 1872 or early 1873.[8] Robert Lincoln turned over to the pair the bulk of his father's papers, and they were, in effect, given a

---

4 Lincoln to Hay, Jan. 9, 1884, *ibid.*
5 Hay to John G. Nicolay, Mar. 18, 1867, Hay, *Letters and Diary*, I, 278–80.
6 Lincoln to Hay, Apr. 7, 1872, Hay Papers.
7 Nicolay to Hay, quoted in Mearns, *Lincoln Papers*, I, 67.
8 Dennett, *John Hay*, 134.

monopoly on the Lincoln story. There would be no competing works in so far as Robert Lincoln was concerned. In return for this, the subject's son required but one thing: he would have the right to review the work before publication. This right of review has evoked considerable discussion. While certainly no formal contract existed between the writers and the younger Lincoln, it is clear that an understanding did.

William H. Herndon heard about the Nicolay and Hay efforts, and once again he and Robert Lincoln were feuding. Herndon wrote that the authors were "afraid of Bob; he gives them materials and they in turn play hush."[9] Herndon's biographer refers to the ultimate work as "Authorized by Robert Todd Lincoln, filio-pietistic in tone, and arch-Republican in politics."[10] Without doubt this latter statement is true, and yet the work was as it was not because of Robert T. Lincoln, but because of John G. Nicolay and John Hay. Years later, Nicolay's daughter wrote:

> My father, John Hay, Robert Lincoln, and Judge David Davis—whose opinion had great weight with the President's son—were of one mind concerning Mr. Lincoln's greatness, but they did not always see eye to eye on the best use to be made of the documents. Even so, there is no evidence to uphold a statement made, from time to time, to the effect that Robert Lincoln persistently "edited" the Hay-Nicolay biography.[11]

That same lady concluded that Nicolay and Hay were " 'Lincoln men all the time,' but from conviction, not compulsion."[12] Of the charge of censorship, David C. Mearns has written:

> In other words, it could hardly be said, on the basis of a single instance, that Robert Lincoln had purged his father's papers. . . . Nevertheless, future critics would abuse him . . . . This would be unfair; he was more proficient as an editor than as an addicted censor.[13]

9 Donald, *Lincoln's Herndon*, 352.
10 *Ibid.*, 311.
11 Nicolay, *Lincoln's Secretary*, 274.
12 *Ibid.*, 303.
13 Mearns, *Lincoln Papers*, I, 76.

From time to time over the years, Lincoln was drawn into the research for the biography. In February, 1878, Hay wrote:

> I have been spending a fortnight in Washington with Nicolay and am very much gratified at the work he has done in arranging your papers and in preparing for our history. Besides putting the MS. in admirable order, he has made a first rate beginning at the chapters allotted to him. I also have had pretty good luck during the last season and we now consider the big job well begun. It will take a long time yet, but we are in no hurry and I presume you are not. We have made such arrangements that in case either of Nicolay's death or mine your property is safe and the work done is available for the survivor.[14]

While on the subject of death, Hay mentioned that on his way home he had heard of the passing of Gideon Welles and that he was interested in Welles's diary. Considering that Lincoln and Welles's son, Edgar, were close friends, could Lincoln obtain the diary? ". . . we should, of course, pledge ourselves to regard it confidentially until our history is published, and even then to be guided by his wishes in regard to what should be used."[15] Lincoln responded by saying that he would write the younger Welles and, referring to the magnum opus, "I think you both want it, as I do, to be the *one* book on the subject." Then turning to everyday matters, Lincoln wrote, "I am plodding along with an excellent law business but like any lawyer I manage to live up to all I make."[16]

A decade later, for the writing of the biography involved some sixteen years, Nicolay wrote to Lincoln asking him to check with the Chicago Historical Society and see if they had files of the old *Sangamo Journal.* He needed the issue of January 27, 1837, which contained a speech delivered by Abraham Lincoln.[17]

Early in 1884, Hay wrote to Lincoln:

> N——— tells me that he had laid before you or is about to do so,

---

14 Hay to Lincoln, Feb. 14, 1878, Hay, *Letters and Diary*, II, 28–29.
15 *Ibid.*
16 Lincoln to Hay, Apr. 15, 1878, Hay Papers.
17 Nicolay to Lincoln, May 4, 1887, CHS.

the first volumes of our history containing the chapters in which I have described the first forty years of your father's life.

I need not tell you that every line has been written in a spirit of reverence and regard. Still you may find here and there words or sentences which do not suit you. I will write now to request that you will read with a pencil in your hand and strike out everything to which you object. I will adopt your view in all cases whether I agree with it or not, but I cannot help hoping that you will find nothing objectionable.[18]

In April, 1885, Lincoln wrote that he had not had time to read the work until he retired from the War Department. Now that he had, he was "delighted with the way you have done your work." As to specifics, Lincoln observed:

It is beyond doubt that my departed grandfather Lincoln was not an enterprising man and it is likely that your graphic assaults upon him *passim* are not undeserved but I could not help feeling better if you "let up" on him a little in a final version. He didn't have much chance to prepare to pose in the reflection of his son's fame and I feel sorry for him.[19]

On another occasion Robert Lincoln spoke of his grandfather's era in understanding terms: "It was a rough life, the Lord knows."[20] There were other suggestions offered by Lincoln. For instance, "the genealogy business which in my opinion is of little warrant."[21]

In reply Hay wrote:

Yours of the 17th received. I will do what you suggest in final revision. It is better, even as a matter of taste and without regard to your wishes which would, of course, be conclusive.

18 Hay to Lincoln, Jan. 27, 1884, Hay, *Letters and Diary*, II, 87–88.

19 Lincoln to Hay, Apr. 17, 1885, Hay Papers. Lincoln had a monument erected over the grave of his grandfather, located near Farmington, Illinois. (Hay and Nicolay, *Lincoln*, I, 74) To put it in the colorful language of Dennis Hanks, "After Sairy [Sarah Lincoln] died Bob—that's Abe's boy—he came down from Chicago and put up a tombstone for her and Tom and they lay thar together." (Chicago *Tribune*, Jan. 28, 1889.)

20 Lincoln to Hay, Jan. 10, 1886, Hay Papers.

21 Lincoln to Hay, Apr. 17, 1885, *ibid.*

There followed a brief discussion of technicalities, and then Hay concluded:

> The only question about going to press is whether we shall wait until we are virtually through or not. We could print three volumes now if thought advisable. All the publishing houses in the country want it.[22]

Evidentally there continued to be minor points of friction about one thing or another for in January, 1886, Hay was again writing:

> I was very sorry to see by a letter you wrote to N—— the other day that you were still not satisfied with my assurance that I would make those first chapters all right. Even before you read them I had struck out of my own copy here nearly everything you objected to and had written N—— to make the changes in his which he had not time to do. Since then I have gone over the whole thing twice again, reading every line so far as possible from your point of view, and I don't think there is a word left in it that would displease you. But of course before final publication I shall give you another hack at it, with plenary blue pencil powers.[23]

The writer ended by mentioning that he and Nicolay had finished the fifth volume of their work and that if they lived two years longer they would at last be through.

Several months later, as work continued, *Century Magazine* prepared to issue a part of the work in serial form, commencing with the November issue of 1886 and running to February, 1890. As that version was about to appear, Lincoln wrote Hay:

> I do not care to see the proofs of what I saw in MSS. I know that you have noted what I suggested & that I would have nothing to say on your opening chapters—I mean nothing of criticism—It is a great pleasure to me . . . to see the *magnum opus* launched . . . . My expectations of it are much greater than your blushing modesty would permit. I know it will be the book.[24]

22 Hay to Lincoln, April 20, 1885, Hay, *Letters and Diary*, II, 92.
23 Hay to Lincoln, Jan. 6, 1886, *ibid.*, II, 100–102.
24 Lincoln to Hay, Sept. 7, 1886, Hay Papers.

A few weeks later Lincoln wrote, "I suppose the Century will be out tomorrow with the first part of your work—I shall look at it with interest."[25]

By early March, 1888, the entire work was nearly finished, and Hay wrote Lincoln:

> Thank you for the corrections—all of which I have of course adopted. The MS. of all the articles goes to the publisher today. I was sorry to bother you but I thought it was best in every way to consult you—and it was.[26]

There remained now only the tying together of certain loose ends. Hay again wrote Lincoln:

> I own a few of your father's MS. which he gave me from time to time. As long as you and I live I take it for granted that you will not suspect me of boning them. But to guard against casualties here-after, I have asked N—— to write you a line saying that I have never had in my possession or custody any of the papers which you have entrusted to him.
>
> I have handed over to N—— to be placed among your papers some of those which your father gave me. The rest, which are few in number, are very precious to me, I shall try to make an heirloom in my family as long as one of my blood exists with money enough to buy a breakfast.
>
> We are nearly at the end of our lifelong task and I hope you will think your father's fame has not suffered any wrong at our hands.[27]

Lincoln was already launched on his career as minister to London when Hay sent him the final magazine installment of the work. The publisher was then putting it into type and it would appear two volumes at a time "rather rapidly." One other matter remained to be mentioned, and Hay wrote, "It will be dedicated to you."[28]

The dedication pleased Lincoln, who wrote to Nicolay:

25 Lincoln to Hay, Sept. 30, 1886, *ibid.*
26 Hay to Lincoln, Mar. 5, 1888, Hay, *Letters and Diary*, II, 141–42.
27 Hay to Lincoln, Apr. 12, 1888, *ibid.*, II, 145–46.
28 Hay to Lincoln, Dec. 22, 1889, *ibid.*, II, 183–84.

As you and Colonel Hay have now brought your great work to a most successful conclusion by the publication of your life of my father, I hope and request that you and he will supplement it by collecting, editing, and publishing the speeches, letters, state papers, and miscellaneous writings of my father. You and Colonel Hay have my consent and authority to obtain for yourselves such protection by copyright, or otherwise, in respect to this whole or any part of such a collection, as I might for any reason be entitled to have.[29]

The gift of potential royalties from the sale of not only the biography but also the works of Abraham Lincoln represented no small sum. Robert Lincoln was also generous in his praise to Hay, who, no doubt, passed it along to his partner:

Without being the proper critic, I can express my delight with the last part & with the whole of the work & I shall never cease to be glad that my father had two such devoted & exceptionally competent, friends as you & Nicolay to make this memorial.[30]

At approximately the same time that the Nicolay and Hay work appeared, the life of Abraham Lincoln written by William H. Herndon was published. As had been noted before, Herndon and Robert Lincoln engaged in a running feud for many years. Throughout the years after 1865, Herndon had gone about his business of collecting materials dealing with the life of the sixteenth President of the United States. When the first edition of his work appeared in 1889, it presented a picture of Abraham Lincoln quite different from that given by Hay and Nicolay, and in some ways it was a more truthful portrait. Despite the ill will between Herndon and the son of his subject, the older man did hold back material which he knew would particularly rile Lincoln. In 1888 he wrote to one who was also interested in Abraham Lincoln:

When you come back to Boston, I will write to you and will then send you some important notes which I drew up solely for my own

[29] Lincoln to Nicolay, quoted in Mearns, *Lincoln Papers*, I, 85–86.
[30] Lincoln to Hay, Jan. 7, 1890, Hay Papers.

satisfaction. I hope that they will assist you; when they come to hand, copy and send back to me. Give any person copies of the notes with the understanding that they, nor the facts in them, are not to be published for years. You may do the same with any or all of my letters. Robert Lincoln is living and the publication of them or the facts of them would offend "Bob," who religiously hates me for telling the naked truths about his noble father. "Bob" came from Chicago once raging to be somehow satisfied. He had some extra fool advisers in Chicago, nice, dainty, finical kid-gloved asses who loved smooth literature with no admixture of truth in it, no robust truth.[31]

Herndon's biography was published by the firm of Belford, Clarke and Company. "From the day his book was published, Herndon received dozens of letters complaining that no copies of *Herndon's Lincoln* could be obtained in any of the book stores."[32] To complicate matters, in September, 1889, the publishing firm went into bankruptcy, after having printed only fifteen hundred sets of the work.[33] Many would have been content to rage against the publisher, but not Herndon; he blamed it all on Robert T. Lincoln. In January, 1889, Herndon already had the idea that Lincoln was attempting to suppress the work when he wrote to his literary collaborator Jesse W. Weik: "What do you think of Bob's acts? I'll tell you what I think, I think he's a d——d fool. He has the insane rage of his mother without the sense of his father. Robert Lincoln is 'a wretch' of a man."[34]

After Lincoln went to England in 1889, Herndon's friend Truman H. Bartlett then in Paris attempted to buy a set of the Herndon biography and was "told by the booksellers that the President's son . . . had purchased and destroyed every copy of the small English edition."[35] Furious, Herndon wrote to Bartlett:

31 Herndon to Truman H. Bartlett, Nov. 10, 1888, Hertz, *Hidden Lincoln*, 221–22.

32 Donald, *Lincoln's Herndon*, 335.

33 *Ibid.*

34 Herndon to Jesse W. Weik, Jan. 15, 1889, Hertz, *Hidden Lincoln*, 237–38.

35 Donald, *Lincoln's Herndon*, 335.

Your letter dated the 17th ult., was duly received, for which I thank you. I fear what you say about Robert Lincoln is true; he has his mother's insane temper without his father's discretion. I have a tender feeling for the man, first, because of the "boy," and secondly, on account of his father; and yet I must say that Bob is a "wee bit of a man." I am sorry that he did as you were informed he did. It is just like Bob, however. A book cannot be put down by such methods. Such acts will, if known, add to the sale of the Life of Lincoln, the sale of any book.[36]

As to this charge of suppression, Herndon's biographer says:

There is no doubt that Robert Todd Lincoln found the Herndon-Weik biography objectionable, but I have found no evidence to show that he tried to suppress it, either in England or in America. . . . the fault lay squarely with his [Herndon's] publishers. Belford, Clarke & Company had no standing in the publishing world—no agents, no list of authors, no outlets. The firm was not equipped to distribute Herndon's book.[37]

After going into bankruptcy, the publishing firm was reorganized, but Charles Scribner's Sons purchased the plates for the biography from the other company and planned a new edition. When Herndon died March 18, 1891, he believed that Scribner's would shortly bring out his story of Abraham Lincoln. At that point Robert Lincoln did definitely enter the picture. The publishing firm informed Jesse W. Weik, who took over the Herndon work, that "with sincere reluctance" they were going to drop the biography from their publication schedule.[38] A Chicago journalist, Horace White, wrote Weik that the reason was that Robert T. Lincoln had objected to the head of the firm, Charles Scribner, and that the firm "did not wish to be instrumental in putting out a book that was objectionable to the son of the subject of the book."[39] To make the book acceptable to Lincoln,

---

[36] Herndon to Truman H. Bartlett, Dec. 20, 1889, Hertz, *Hidden Lincoln*, 244–45.

[37] Donald, *Lincoln's Herndon*, 335.

[38] Charles Scribner's Sons to Jesse W. Weik, Oct. 1, 1891, quoted *ibid.*, 341.

[39] Horace White to Jesse W. Weik, Oct. 6, 1891, quoted in Donald, *Lincoln's Herndon*, 341–42.

Scribner felt that such extensive changes would have to be made they would "spoil it or seriously impair its selling qualities."[40] However, in 1892, Weik secured a contract from D. Appleton and Company and a new edition was published.[41]

It is unfortunate that Lincoln bothered himself at all with the matter of the Herndon work, for certainly there was room for various interpretations of the life of Abraham Lincoln. However, he undoubtedly felt justified in objecting to the work. Robert Lincoln was essentially a Victorian gentleman with the moral code and ideals that term implies, and he felt Herndon guilty of impropriety. Herndon raised issues that ought not to have been raised. There was, for example, the question of Abraham Lincoln's legitimacy, to say nothing of the Ann Rutledge story. Also, there was the matter of President Lincoln's religious views. Herndon felt that since his law partner had never joined a church, he was automatically a nonbeliever, regardless of his personal convictions. This is not the only instance of a biographer being involved in difficulty with a family over the subject of a study; this is merely one of the more celebrated affairs. Yet, there is no question that Robert T. Lincoln was a good hater when he wanted to be, and he wanted to be in this instance. However, the Herndon affair followed Robert Lincoln throughout his life. Years later Brand Whitlock wrote to thank a correspondent for sending him a copy of Herndon's *Lincoln*. He had one copy already but:

> The copy I have is one of the later, expurged and fixed up editions, done to suit Robert Lincoln, who is a distant relative of Abraham Lincoln, and that only physically. He bought up, you know, all the Herndon's he could; the price on them must now be pretty nearly up to where he would be willing to part with some.[42]

As the only surviving member of the immediate family of

40 *Ibid.*, 341–42.
41 *Ibid.*
42 Brand Whitlock to Octavia Roberts, Mar. 28, 1909, Allan Nevins, ed., *The Letters and Journal of Brand Whitlock*, I, 89–90.

Abraham Lincoln, Robert Lincoln was almost constantly bombarded by inquiries and questions of all sorts concerning the President. In general, he followed a policy of not speaking or writing for publication on the subject of his father. A typical letter was one written in 1910:

> I can only say that I have always been careful to refrain from making any expressions concerning my father for publication; and in responding to the inquiries which have been very many, similar to your original question, I have invariably asked that my reply should be considered as personal and confidential. I appreciate all that you say on the subject; but I would prefer not to take, in this instance, an exception to my rule.[43]

Robert T. Lincoln was extremely conscious of his position and went to great lengths to avoid appearing to traffic on his heritage.

This does not mean that Lincoln refused all help to those who were interested in his father's life, for quite the opposite was true. Frequently he would answer questions, almost always of a factual, not of a subjective, nature. When asked in 1885 about the Gettysburg Address, he wrote what facts about its writing he could remember, noting, "It gives me pleasure to answer your inquiry."[44] When James Shouler was doing research about Abraham Lincoln's visit to Boston in 1848, Lincoln wrote that his assistant had gone through the Lincoln papers and found nothing that would help the writer.[45] Regarding Robert T. Lincoln's help to serious scholars, David C. Mearns has written:

> What gives a special force of kindness to his many acts of willing and earnest co-operation is the knowledge that nearly every question submitted to him involved matters personally unfamiliar and required, therefore, recourse to records and research.[46]

After all, here was a man who had to ask his aunt in 1918 for the date of his own mother's birth![47]

43 Lincoln to John W. Starr, Jr., Nov. 8, 1910, Lincoln Memorial University.
44 Lincoln to Belle F. Keyes, Dec. 16, 1885, ISHL.
45 Lincoln to James Shouler, Oct. 22, 1908, Harvard College Library.
46 Mearns, *Lincoln Papers*, I, 94.
47 Lincoln to Emelie Todd Helm, Mar. 22, 1918, copy in ISHL.

Occasionally the questions posed concerned photographs or portraits rather than manuscripts. Once he wrote Ida Tarbell:

> The picture (which I return to you) is an extraordinarily bad result of a photograph of my mother, with my brothers, William & Thomas. I know nothing of the original except that it must have been taken before February, 1862, as my brother William died in that month.[48]

Lincoln at one time hoped that the Hay and Nicolay work would be definitive and that no new works would be necessary, but such was not to be the case. In 1895 he observed, "It will not perhaps surprise you that I am sorry that the Publishers & the Public are not satisfied with what has been already done."[49] With the passage of time, the "Lincoln mania" gripped not only the United States but foreign nations as well. But Robert T. Lincoln did not frown upon all of the writers. In 1900 he wrote Ida Tarbell:

> Very many thanks for your two volumes which have brought out my family. It seemed to me at first that this field had been too many times gleaned to hope for much from the work you were undertaking and I must confess my astonishment & pleasure upon the result of your untiring researches—I consider it an indispensable adjunct to the work of Nicolay & Hay.[50]

Then in 1912 he wrote Helen Nicolay that he liked her book, *Personal Traits of Abraham Lincoln*.[51] A decade later Lincoln, nearing the end of his own life, acknowledged to Ida Tarbell:

> I have just received from your publishers, Harper & Brothers, an autographed copy of your book, *In the Footsteps of the Lincolns*. We are in the midst of getting ready to leave for our summer home in Manchester, Vermont, but I have found time to glance over the book. It seems very interesting, and I am sure I will greatly enjoy

48 Lincoln to Ida Tarbell, Apr. 27, 1895, Indiana University Library.

49 Lincoln to H. W. Alden, Nov. 21, 1895, R. T. Lincoln Papers, University of Chicago Library.

50 Lincoln to Ida Tarbell, Feb. 11, 1900, Tarbell Lincoln Collection.

51 Lincoln to Helen Nicolay, Nov. 7, 1912, Nicolay Papers.

reading it more carefully after we have settled down at Manchester.[52]

However, Lincoln continued to have trouble with biographers of his father. He apparently resented the famous life of Abraham Lincoln by Lord Charnwood. Around the time of the first World War, it was suggested that Charnwood ought to be made a corresponding member of the Massachusetts Historical Society, but he was denied admittance because "someone reported Robert Lincoln had sneered at the biography because Charnwood had repeated one of old 'Billy' Herndon's stories of Lincoln."[53] In the closing years of his life, Lincoln was troubled by the persistent former senator from Indiana, turned historian, Albert J. Beveridge. Following the success of his life of John Marshall, Beveridge turned to Abraham Lincoln as his next subject:

> But at the very beginning he was to encounter obstacles in his search for the whole truth. Eager to examine the Lincoln manuscripts in the possession of Robert T. Lincoln . . . he sent his request to the latter. . . . There was no reply. Assuming the letter had miscarried, he wrote again and sent it by special delivery, and this brought a petulant refusal.[54]

Whereupon Beveridge wrote that he was "willing to use dynamite, or chloroform, soothing syrup, or quinine, cocaine, or T.N.T."[55] to get hold of the papers. There is no evidence that Lincoln had anything in particular against the former Senator, although certainly they were never on the same side of the political fence. During the next year and a half Beveridge tried by various ways to approach Lincoln, once through Nicholas Murray Butler and once through Lincoln's old friend Henry White.[56] These attempts resulted in failure, and Beveridge gave up.

[52] Lincoln to Ida Tarbell, May 21, 1924, Tarbell Lincoln Collection.

[53] William R. Thayer to Henry Cabot Lodge, Oct. 11, 1918, quoted in Charles D. Hazen, ed., *The Letters of William Roscoe Thayer*, 337–39.

[54] Bowers, *Beveridge and the Progressive Era*, 563.

[55] Albert J. Beveridge to Worthington C. Ford, Jan. 20, 1923, quoted *ibid.*, 563.

[56] *Ibid.*, 563–64.

Chapter 12

The Years in London

W**HEN** R**OBERT** L**INCOLN'S** **APPOINTMENT** as minister to Great Britain was announced, John Hay wrote to him:

> I congratulate you most cordially on the great decoration. It is the most conspicuous compliment in the gift of a President, and I am delighted to see it go to you. I have had some inkling of it for several days, but did not dare speak of it till the nomination went to the Senate.
>
> I hope you will retain Henry White as Secretary of the Legation. He and his wife know their England better than any Americans have ever hitherto done, and I am sure they will be of very great use to you. It would not be possible to find anyone offhand who would do the routine and social work so well. Mrs. Hay joins me in warm congratulations to Mrs. Lincoln. When will you be here? If I can be of any service to you in any way do *not* hesitate to command me![1]

Hay's neighbor, Henry Adams, wrote to an English friend: "Our new minister to London, who is known familiarly here as Bob Lincoln, will, I hope, be liked. He is a good fellow, rather heavy, but pleasant and sufficiently intelligent." But Adams could not help mentioning, "Unless Hay himself were to have the place, Lincoln was as good a man as was likely to be sent."[2]

[1] John Hay to Lincoln, Mar. 27, 1889, Hay, *Letters and Diary*, II, 163.
[2] Henry Adams to Charles Milnes Gaskell, Apr. 21, 1889, Worthington C. Ford, ed., *Letters of Henry Adams, 1858–1891*, 398.

Lincoln and his party docked at Liverpool on May 22, 1889, where he was met by a flag-decorated tender bearing the mayor of the city. The mayor took the new arrival in his carriage to the railroad station where Lincoln took the train to London. There he was met by members of the American legation. On May 23 he was received by Lord Salisbury at the Foreign Office, and two days later he went to Windsor Castle to present his credentials to Queen Victoria. Accompanied by Henry White, Lincoln went from London by train and was met at the railroad station by a court carriage. In his account of his reception to Secretary of State Blaine, the Minister reported that he told Her Majesty of "the desire of my country for the prosperity of Great Britain," and that he would personally spare no effort to cultivate friendly relations between the United States and her nation and subjects. The formalities concluded, the two chatted informally for a few minutes before the American returned to London.[3]

William E. Gladstone had indicated a desire to become acquainted with the new diplomat as soon as he arrived, and a meeting was arranged. Throughout dinner Gladstone kept up a running conversation, giving no one a chance to say anything, and continued his monologue until he had to leave. On the way home a companion asked the great man what he had thought of Mr. Lincoln. The reply was, "Mr. Lincoln is a charming personality, but does not seem to have much conversation."[4]

Robert T. Lincoln's first public appearance in his new post was on June 13, 1889, when he spoke at a banquet given for a group of American engineers. It was said that the examples of Ministers Lowell and Phelps had given the English the notion that the American diplomat was sent over mainly to make after-dinner speeches. The new man measured up to the set standards: "He bore himself admirably and spoke with an excellent manner and marked felicity of ideas and words."[5]

Lincoln thoroughly enjoyed his first months in London. One

3 Lincoln to Blaine, May 27, 1889, *Dispatches*, m.r. 155. See also the *New York Times*, May 23 and 25, 1889.
4 Chauncey M. Depew, *My Memories of Eighty Years*, 260.
5 *New York Times*, June 16, 1889.

of his first dinners was with Andrew Carnegie, who had invited him to social events even before he left the United States.[6] He wrote a friend at home that he had attended a Fourth of July celebration and functions for visiting foreign dignitaries, but that he had found time to take two of his children, Mary and Jack, to watch boating on the Thames.[7] The summer of 1889 was probably the height of happiness for Robert T. Lincoln.

That summer of 1889, Abraham Lincoln II was sixteen, a charming, well-liked, and intelligent boy just approaching maturity. He had a great love of the sea, and during the years of the family's residence in Washington, Jack liked nothing better than to travel on President Arthur's yacht.[8]

There is a story about Jack and some friends playing baseball. As in all such stories, the baseball broke a window in a nearby house. When the angry owner of the house came out with the ball, Jack alone remained on the lot. The man angrily asked the boy's name, but, when the boy replied, "Abraham Lincoln," the man left as though he had seen a ghost.[9]

Perhaps it was because of his name that Jack was so interested in the period of his grandfather's presidency. As William G. Beale described it:

> He was fond of the history of the late war. I have seen him lie on the floor in his father's library with war maps spread out before him, a book open, and studying a battle by the hour. He was ready to discuss this situation or that in which General Grant and others had found themselves.[10]

Robert Lincoln had high hopes for his heir. He was to follow his father, first to Phillips Exeter, then Harvard, and then without doubt into the firm of Isham, Lincoln and Beale.[11]

While Jack was on a holiday in France in the autumn of 1889,

6 Lincoln to Andrew Carnegie, Mar. 22 and May 24, 1889, Andrew Carnegie Papers, New York Public Library.
7 Lincoln to "My dear Doctor," July 7, 1889, CHS.
8 Chicago *Tribune*, May 31, 1884.
9 *Illinois State Register*, Feb. 28, 1937.
10 *Lincoln Lore*, Oct. 16, 1939.
11 *New York Times*, Feb. 28, 1890.

his parents received word that he had blood poisoning in his arm. The sickness persisted; periods of hope were followed by times of despair. The concern expressed by John Hay in the following letter was indicative of that felt by the family and their friends:

> We were very very anxious all day yesterday—the morning papers having announced the dangerous illness of your boy in Versailles—yet we hoped for better news today; and this morning he still lives and there is further hope. We trust and pray the improvement may continue and that his youth and strength may soon restore him to perfect health again. Any other result would be too dreadful to contemplate.[12]

Near Christmas, Jack's condition had so improved that Hay was writing: "I congratulate you most cordially in the recovery of your boy. We were very anxious till we heard the good news."[13] After the first of the year, Jack was brought to London, but his father expressed continued anxiety over "our boy."[14]

One morning Lincoln was sitting in his home with Henry White when his daughter Mary rushed in and told her father, "Go upstairs quickly." In ten minutes Lincoln came back down the stairs with the news that his only son was dead. It was March 5, 1890.[15]

The impact of Jack's death on Robert T. Lincoln is impossible to calculate. Henry White wrote that following the funeral services:

> Mr. Lincoln asked me to go in the carriage with him and the clergyman which, of course, I did, returning with him alone. When we got to Kensington Gardens, I persuaded him to send away the carriage and walk there, which he did for an hour and enjoyed it.

Lincoln confided to White that his interest in his law firm and business affairs "was for Jack's sake only, and to keep the place

---

12 John Hay to Lincoln, Nov. 30, 1889, Hay, *Letters and Diary*, II, 182–83.

13 Hay to Lincoln, Dec. 22, 1889, *ibid.*, II, 183–84.

14 Lincoln to Hay, Jan. 7, 1890, Hay Papers.

15 An excellent account of the illness and death of Abraham Lincoln II is found in Nevins, *Henry White*, 72–73.

open for him."[16] Now there would never be another Lincoln in the firm of Isham, Lincoln and Beale.

Writing to John Hay a month later, Lincoln called his son's death "the hardest of many hard things," and continued:

> Jack was to us all that any father and mother could wish and beyond that, he seemed to realize that he had special duties before him as a man, and the thoroughness with which he was getting ready was a source of the greatest pride to me. I did not realize until he was gone how deeply my thoughts of the future were in him.
>
> .   .   .   .
>
> My wife has surprised us all, in not breaking down. . . . I would not have believed that any human could have stood the strain of the months as she did with apparent cheerfulness, even when she had no hope.[17]

Many people sent their condolences to the bereaved family. Their friends came forward to try to help fill the void left by Jack's death. Andrew Carnegie invited the Lincolns to come to Scotland; however, it was late September before Lincoln went—by himself.[18] His wife and daughters had left for a six-months stay in the United States on August 6.

On November 5, 1890, Robert Todd Lincoln arrived in New York on the steamer *City of New York*. He brought with him the body of his son. A private Pennsylvania Railroad car took him to Springfield. There on the morning of November 8, Abraham Lincoln II joined his grandparents and his three uncles in the presidential vault. Only Edgar Welles accompanied Robert Lincoln that morning, and although Lincoln greeted Senator Cullom, former Governor Oglesby, and Governor Fifer who were present at the entombment, he left that same day for Chicago.

After spending Christmas at Mount Pleasant with Senator Harlan, Lincoln stopped in Washington before proceeding, early in January, to the estate of Frank Thomson near Merion, Pennsylvania.

16 *Ibid.*, 72.
17 Lincoln to Hay, Apr. 8, 1890, Hay Papers.
18 Lincoln to Andrew Carnegie, July 17 and Aug. 27, 1890, Carnegie Papers.

Immediately after Jack's death, there were rumors that Lincoln would resign his ministry. According to William G. Beale, he had reluctantly accepted the post and only because his family would derive "social benefits" from their stay in England.[19] The rumors were renewed after Lincoln's return and persisted as he remained. Upon arriving in Pennsylvania, Lincoln made a statement:

> I arrived in this country the day after the election, and heard some unpleasant news [Republican losses in the congressional elections]. I expect to start on my return to England on Wednesday, and I hope to arrive in London the next week. I see by the papers I am expected on the other side next week, and they expect me to turn things upside down. As to the truth or falsity of that, of course, you will have to excuse me from commenting.[20]

Lincoln stopped briefly in Washington before he returned to his post and plunged into his work.

During his London years Lincoln was most fortunate in having a congenial staff to work with him. Henry White, the first secretary of the legation, who also acted as chargé d'affaires in the absence of the minister, enjoyed a long friendship with Lincoln. In 1891 young Larz Anderson, son of Lincoln's old friend General Nicholas Longworth Anderson of Cincinnati, arrived to become second secretary. One can imagine that the presence of this young man somewhat cheered the Minister and in some ways took the place of Jack. Lincoln thought highly of Larz Anderson and wrote to the young man's father: "after six months of intimate associations, both official and social with your son, I am prepared to say that he is one of the finest types of the American gentleman I have ever seen. He is a man to be proud of."[21]

On July 21, 1891, Mr. and Mrs. Henry White gave a ball to announce the engagement of Miss Mary Lincoln to Mr. Charles Isham. The young man had been Lincoln's secretary and was a distant cousin of his law partner. The immediate families were

19 *New York Times*, Mar. 7, 1890.
20 *Ibid.*, Jan. 5, 1891.
21 Isabel Anderson, ed., *Larz Anderson, Letters and Journals of a Diplomat*, 60.

the only Americans attending the ball, but it was well attended by members of English society.[22] The couple was married the afternoon of September 2 at Brompton Parish Church. Only Mr. and Mrs. Edward S. Isham and Mr. and Mrs. Marshall Field attended in addition to the families of the bride and groom.[23] Bombarded by "the London reporters, who tried to find out every detail of the alliance and wedding," Larz Anderson grumbled, "Reportorial cheek is as great here as in America."[24]

Robert T. Lincoln spent Christmas of 1891 in England with the Henry Whites, Larz Anderson, and other friends. Young Anderson noted that Lincoln was beginning to feel better "and his sunny disposition began to show itself again. It was very enjoyable to see him happy and talking at a tremendous rate. He insisted on sitting up till all hours."[25]

Much of the work of the minister and others at the legation was purely routine. A legation in a foreign land is a place around which swarm visiting citizens, and so it was then in London. Lincoln was constantly being called upon to look after distinguished guests, a time-consuming task. Some thought of this as being the minister's most important duty. For example, the noted attorney Joseph H. Choate told his wife, "I have also written to Mr. Lincoln that you would be in London, and would not hesitate to call upon him if you needed any advice."[26] In 1890, Mrs. John A. Logan visited England. Of the trip she later wrote, "Hon. Robert T. Lincoln was our American minister to England, and it goes without saying that we had every consideration and enjoyed many invitations to social functions."[27] Sometimes the object of Lincoln's care was an important congressman. Nelson Dingley,

22 *New York Times*, July 26, 1891.

23 *Ibid.*, Sept. 3, 1891.

24 Anderson, *Larz Anderson*, 76. To the Ishams was born one child, Lincoln Isham, in New York, June 8, 1892. McMurtry, *The Harlan-Lincoln Tradition*, 15.

25 Anderson, *Larz Anderson*, 88.

26 Edwin S. Martin, *The Life of Joseph Hodges Choate*, I, 428.

27 Logan, *Reminiscences*, 438. Lincoln was able to secure three hard-to-get tickets for a garden party so Mrs. Logan might attend, but in view of the fact that everyone else wanted tickets, he asked her not to mention the source of her good fortune. Lincoln to Mrs. Logan, July 1, 1889, Yale University Library.

Jr., of Maine "through the courtesy of Minister Lincoln was enabled to hear the closing debates on the Home Rule bill in the house of commons."[28] Even members of President Harrison's own family—Larz Anderson called them the "American Royalties"—were at one time the responsibility of the legation. Anderson dutifully conducted Mrs. Harrison, daughter-in-law of the Chief Executive, and Mrs. McKee, his daughter, through Westminster Abbey.[29] Now and then Lincoln's personal friends came to visit. John Hay arrived in May, 1891, but had the misfortune to come down with the grippe, and it was some days before he was up and around to see Lincoln.[30]

Many of the problems of the minister had to do with the ordinary American visitor, frequently one in trouble. Anderson noted in his diary:

> Another typical Legation incident occurred a day or two ago. A young girl called . . . . She had run away from home . . . with an English actress who promised her a stage career in London. The actress fell sick soon after arriving, died, and had just been buried, and the girl was alone and penniless. . . . She seemed to be telling the truth and looked so like a New England girl that I was sorry for her. I told the Minister and he saw her, too, and promised to advance her a passage home. She seemed grateful and promised to go right away, though of course, it remains doubtful till we hear of her safe return.[31]

There is no conclusion to the story, for the second secretary never mentioned it again.

Anderson wrote of another episode: "Curious people sometimes haunt the Legation. Yesterday, an elderly woman insisted that she must see 'President Lincoln,' and could not be convinced that he had long since been dead."[32]

Curious events occurred at the legation too. On the evening of July 18, 1891, while a guest of the Minister, Mrs. Bradley Martin

28 Edward N. Dingley, *The Life and Times of Nelson Dingley, Jr.*, 361.
29 Anderson, *Larz Anderson*, 74–75.
30 Hay, *Letters and Diary*, II, 217.
31 Anderson, *Larz Anderson*, 77.
32 *Ibid.*, 75.

lost a grape-shaped cluster of diamonds, including one nine-carat clear diamond. The butler, John Thompson, later turned himself in to Scotland Yard, but Lincoln thought him insane. The man later committed suicide and with him died the secret of the jewel theft.[33]

Frequently during his four years in England, Robert T. Lincoln was called upon to speak to different groups on a variety of subjects. In September, 1889, he addressed a group of workingmen.[34] In July, 1891, Lincoln addressed a dinner given by the Society of Authors to celebrate the new United States copyright law. Included among those who heard the Minister express satisfaction with the long-overdue legal step were Huxley, Bryce, and Wilde.[35]

The communications that passed between Lincoln and the State Department verify that much of his work was purely routine. Frequently questions about special passport problems arose that required Lincoln's attention. Even a matter as minor as a request for more passport blanks was the subject of a communication from London to Washington.[36] All United States consular appointments in the entire British Empire were first cleared through the London legation; the British government cleared the appointments of its American consuls through the same office. Other matters routinely handled were claims by American citizens to property in the British Empire and estates of Americans who died abroad.

During Robert T. Lincoln's tenure as minister to England a new extradition treaty was signed between the United States and Great Britain. It was largely a modernization of a similar long-standing treaty. Lincoln participated little in the agreement for

33 *New York Times*, Dec. 18, 1891; Frederick T. Martin, *Things I Remember*, 197–98.

34 Lincoln to Blaine, Sept. 19, 1889, Dispatches, m.r. 156. Complaining that he had been misquoted in the newspaper accounts, Lincoln himself wrote a letter to Secretary of State Blaine. Fortunately for readability, communications were usually penned by Henry White or another member of the staff.

35 *New York Times*, July 17, 1891.

36 Lincoln to Blaine, May 13, 1891, Dispatches, m.r. 159.

it was concluded in Washington on July 12, 1889. Ratifications were exchanged March 11, 1890, and the treaty was proclaimed in effect March 25. It was then published in both nations on April 5, 1890.[37]

Although not really involved with arranging the treaty, Lincoln did become involved in extradition cases. He was frequently requested to ask for the detention of an American who had fled to England, or, on behalf of the British government, he would request the detention in the United States of a fugitive. Once Lincoln had requested British authorities to detain a forger only to have New York authorities decide that they did not wish the criminal returned. When the matter was over, Lincoln advised the State Department that it had caused him some embarrassment which, he hoped, could be avoided in the future by a more careful handling of the problem.[38]

While Lincoln was in London, preparations were started for the World's Columbian Exposition to be held in Chicago. In February, 1891, Lincoln extended to Lord Salisbury, British foreign minister, an invitation for the British to participate in the exposition.[39] Immediately Salisbury raised the question whether United States contract labor laws would bar foreign workers employed to install British exhibits. Lincoln could only say that he did not think there would be any barrier, but that he would consult Washington.[40] There was a considerable delay in getting a final answer, but at last Blaine telegraphed Lincoln confirming the Minister's belief in the matter, and the latter, in turn, informed Salisbury.[41] The Minister's general attitude toward the fair caused some comment. Some in Chicago complained that, as a Chicagoan, Lincoln should be more actively promoting the event in England. The reply to such criticism was that any reluctance shown was the result of the Minister's desire to avoid

---

37 Lincoln to Blaine, Apr. 5, 1890, Dispatches, m.r. 157.
38 Lincoln to Blaine, Aug. 10, 1889, Dispatches, m.r. 155.
39 Lincoln to Blaine, Feb. 14, 1891, Dispatches, m.r. 159.
40 Lincoln to Blaine, Mar. 14, 1891, Dispatches, m.r. 159.
41 Blaine to Lincoln (telegram), May 8, 1891, Dispatches, m.r. 159.

the squabbles resulting from the planning and opening of the exposition.[42]

Of all the chores that Lincoln performed as minister perhaps the most absurd was his involvement in some lengthy correspondence about a picture by an obscure American artist, Mrs. William W. Carson. The incident not only illustrates the caliber of work a diplomat was generally called upon to do, but also shows how involved diplomatic proceedings can be. In June, 1891, Lincoln wrote Blaine about Mrs. Carson's picture, which she wished to present to Queen Victoria. Blaine had originally mentioned the subject the preceding January, but as Lincoln explained, the Queen had been traveling in France and he had not had an opportunity to discuss the matter with her private secretary, Sir Henry Ponsonby.[43] Now the Minister reported that Sir Henry had at last told him that Her Majesty would be delighted to have the gift. Mr. Lincoln next posed the question whether the work of art should be given directly to the Queen at Windsor Castle or be sent to him and then he would take the gift to Windsor. To this Ponsonby replied that it should be sent directly: "As Mrs. Carson is only a private person I think it would be making too much of her present if it were given through the Minister."[44] At this point Blaine put in an objection, although why he did is not at all clear. Lincoln informed Sir Henry and sent along the Secretary of State's letter.[45] Two days later the secretary informed Lincoln that his first statement regarding presentation was, of course, only a private opinion and perhaps he should consult the Queen again.[46] After more delay came the reply, "The Queen will be happy to receive you with the picture some day after the 15th of July."[47] At last the matter was settled, undoubtedly much to the relief of Lincoln, who probably never cared what happened to the picture in the first place.

[42] *New York Times*, June 12, 1892.
[43] Lincoln to Blaine, June 20, 1891, Dispatches, m.r. 160.
[44] Sir Henry Ponsonby to Lincoln, *ibid.*
[45] Lincoln to Ponsonby, June 3, 1891, *ibid.*
[46] Ponsonby to Lincoln, June 6, 1891, *ibid.*
[47] Ponsonby to Lincoln, June 16, 1891, *ibid.*

On August 12, 1891, Lincoln's predecessor and former teacher, James Russell Lowell, died. A memorial service was to be held in Westminster Abbey, but, unfortunately, the time was incorrectly given in the papers. The legation itself received the correction only two hours before the service was to begin. Lincoln "scurried home to get ready," and Larz Anderson rushed about the city telling Americans about the ceremony.[48] The impressive service was well attended; Mr. and Mrs. Lincoln were joined by the President's daughter and daughter-in-law. Lowell was memorialized as a poet and man of letters rather than a political figure. Lincoln explained that otherwise the services could not have been held in the Abbey at all.

Shortly after Robert T. Lincoln arrived in England, Mrs. Florence E. Maybrick, an American citizen, was convicted in British courts of having poisoned her husband, and the death sentence was imposed. Her home in the United States had been Portland, Maine, and several hundred citizens of her native land who believed her innocent petitioned Queen Victoria for clemency. The group included Mrs. Benjamin Harrison, Mrs. James G. Blaine, and a journalist relative of the Blaines who wrote under the pen name "Gail Hamilton."[49] Blaine sent the petition to Lincoln with instructions to present it to Lord Salisbury.[50] However, as Blaine informed the President, he was careful "to present no request from the Government but simply it was to be noted that the document only transmitted the wishes of a very large number of our Citizens."[51] The day before Blaine sent the petition, Lincoln sent to Blaine, who was vacationing at home in Maine:

> Had an interview with Lord Salisbury. Authorized to express, for your private information only, until public announcement of final decision, his belief that death sentence will not be executed.
>
> LINCOLN[52]

48 Anderson, *Larz Anderson*, 73.

49 Albert T. Volwiler, ed., *The Correspondence Between Benjamin Harrison and James G. Blaine, 1882–1893*, 77n.

50 Blaine to Lincoln, Aug. 23, 1889, *ibid.*, 78.

51 Blaine to Benjamin Harrison, Aug. 23, 1889, *ibid.*, 77.

52 Lincoln to Blaine, Aug. 22, 1889, Dispatches, m.r. 155.

The death sentence was reduced to life imprisonment but that did not end the clamor for the woman's release. At one point, Lincoln felt it necessary to tell Blaine that, contrary to published reports, he had not joined in any such appeal.[53] In May, 1891, Lincoln, probably at the request of Blaine, saw the British home secretary and discussed the case with him. Lincoln reported that the home secretary was convinced of Mrs. Maybrick's guilt and was of the opinion that if a mistake had been made in the case, it was in not carrying out the death sentence in the first place. The Minister concluded that he saw little hope of any release of the prisoner as long as that particular home secretary remained in office.[54] As it developed, Mrs. Maybrick was finally released fifteen years after her original conviction.[55]

A foreign legation functions as a listening post for the nation it represents, and Lincoln was sometimes called upon to secure information for the State Department. The enactment of the McKinley tariff law raised American duties to new heights, and Secretary Blaine asked Lincoln to order the consul general and consuls to investigate the effect that the law had had on English exports to the United States. Blaine said, "Let it be done privately, promptly, and with accuracy."[56] Immediately Lincoln contacted Consul General New and the survey was started.

Later in the same year Blaine asked the Minister to sound out the members of the British cabinet on the bimetallism controversy then raging in the United States, as well as in other countries. Lincoln replied with a long report of what his private talks had revealed.[57] Early in 1892, Lincoln discussed the proposed international monetary conference with Lord Salisbury and then proceeded to prepare for it.[58] That fall, while in the United States on leave, the Minister told reporters:

My personal relations with the British Government have been

[53] Lincoln to Blaine, Sept. 19, 1889, Dispatches m.r. 156.
[54] Lincoln to Blaine, May 16, 1891, Dispatches m.r. 159.
[55] Volwiler, *Correspondence*, 77n.
[56] Blaine to Lincoln, telegram, Feb. 1, 1891, Dispatches, m.r. 159.
[57] Lincoln to Blaine, Aug. 11, 1891, Dispatches, m.r. 160.
[58] Lincoln to Blaine, Jan. 27, 1892, Dispatches, m.r. 161.

very pleasant. There is nothing connected with my official duties that I feel I can properly speak about except the forthcoming International Monetary Conference, in arranging for which it has fallen to me to have some share.[59]

Robert T. Lincoln was involved in two important matters of diplomacy. One was the Bering Sea Controversy, which grew out of the possession by the United States of the Pribilof Islands, the summer home and breeding ground of a vast herd of fur seals. Certain groups, particularly Canadians, began to capture the seals when they left the territorial waters of the United States. The United States government countenanced the reduction of the surplus male population of the polygamous seals. However, capturing the animals at sea also destroyed the females, which then "caused the death of one dependent pup and one unborn."[60] If unchecked, this practice could in time lead to the extinction of the entire herd.

Eventually the United States Treasury Department instructed revenue cutters to seize Canadian ships on the grounds that the United States maintained jurisdiction in the Bering Sea regardless of the traditional three-mile limit. When offenders were taken to Sitka, Alaska, for trial, a federal judge held that the Sea was mare clausum. In the furor that followed, Secretary Blaine engaged in a verbal and written duel with the British government. He did not hold that the Bering was a closed sea, but he argued that taking the seals at sea was contrary to good practice and that in this one regard the United States's jurisdiction extended beyond the three-mile limit.

Lincoln in London was well aware of the controversy; occasionally he sent to the State Department clippings from British newspapers in regard to the dispute. In August, 1890, he became involved in a more direct way. Blaine asked Lincoln to search British libraries and the like for early maps of the Bering Sea area, for the Secretary wished to argue that the Russians, during their period of ownership of the area, had exercised similar

59 Randall, *Lincoln's Sons*, 309–10.
60 Julius W. Pratt, *A History of United States Foreign Policy*, 357.

powers to those that the United States was attempting to exercise. On August 20, Lincoln replied that he would begin the requested inquiry.[61] Three days later the Minister reported difficulties[62]: the Royal Geographical Society Library was closed and would not immediately be reopened. He was afraid to work in the House of Commons Library for fear that the British would become aware of his official interest in the matter. For the moment, about all that could be done was to have his private secretary (and future son-in-law), Charles Isham, engaged in "working the [British] Museum discreetly."[63]

In mid-September, Lincoln made a report to the Secretary of State. Isham had at last been able to get into the Royal Geographical Society Library, but the results of that and other attempts at finding helpful material were disappointing. Several pages of notes were transmitted to Washington, but Lincoln said he was amazed that in most early British maps Russian possessions in the area of the Bering Sea were not even shown.[64] The report must have been disappointing to Blaine, for although his stand had support from conservationists, it lacked support from international law and historical precedent.

"After a prolonged diplomatic wrangle the British and American governments on February 29, 1892 agreed to submit the whole controversy to arbitration."[65] There then followed some additional dispute over the United States's position that, pending a final settlement on the matter, it would continue to enforce its rules concerning the seals; however, if its position was found to be incorrect, the United States would in no way be responsible for damages. An editorial in the London *Times*, which Lincoln sent to Blaine in March, saw the American stand as an example of "twisting the lion's tail" for home political consumption.[66] The court of arbitration did not meet in Paris until February, 1893,

[61] Lincoln to Blaine, Aug. 20, 1890, Dispatches, m.r. 158.
[62] Lincoln to Blaine, Aug. 23, 1890, Dispatches, m.r. 158.
[63] *Ibid.*
[64] Lincoln to Blaine, Sept. 13, 1890, Dispatches, m.r. 158.
[65] Pratt, *United States Foreign Policy*, 357.
[66] Lincoln to Blaine, Mar. 26, 1892, enclosing a clipping from *The Times*, Mar. 25, 1892, Dispatches, m.r. 161.

and Lincoln took no further part in the proceedings. Indeed, when certain tangles developed over the matter in the fall of 1892, Lincoln was in the United States and it fell to Henry White to straighten out the trouble.[67] The final outcome of the controversy was to uphold virtually in entirety the British position in regard to taking the seals.

The other significant diplomatic matter to which Lincoln was a part was the celebrated Venezuelan boundary dispute between that nation and British Guiana. The issue had been unimportant for a long time until gold was discovered in the area and the region was settled. In 1840 a boundary had been surveyed by a British explorer, Sir Robert Schomburgk, but Venezuela refused to accept it. However, at one time or another each party had seemed friendly toward the idea of arbitration, which the United States also favored. Looking toward settlement of the dispute, Blaine on May 1, 1890, asked Lincoln to "use his good offices with Lord Salisbury to bring about a resumption of diplomatic intercourse between Great Britain and Venezuela as a preliminary step towards the settlement of the boundary dispute by arbitration." Specifically, the Secretary of State told Lincoln to propose a three-power conference to be held in Washington or London.[68] A few days later, Lincoln reported:

> Lord Salisbury listened with attention to my statement, in making which I was careful to keep within the lines of your instruction, and after remarking that the interruption of diplomatic relations was Venezuela's own act, he said that her Majesty's Government had not for some time been very keen about attempting a settlement of the dispute in view of their feeling of uncertainty as to the stability of the present Venezuelan Government and the frequency of revolutions in that quarter. . . . if the matter had been entirely new and dissociated from its previous history, I should have felt from his tone that the idea of arbitration in some form . . . was quite agreeable to him.[69]

In June the Venezuelan agent in England, Palide, called and

[67] Nevins, *Henry White*, 70.
[68] Willson, *America's Ambassadors*, 400.
[69] *Ibid.*

urged Lincoln to present him to Lord Salisbury. Lincoln thought this useless but asked Blaine his position in the matter.[70] Blaine promptly replied that Lincoln should try to get Palide in to see Salisbury.[71] A meeting was arranged but nothing came of it. From time to time, the issue was raised, but by the time Lincoln left office, the matter was still a stalemate. It was not until 1895 that the controversy reached a climax and involved the Cleveland administration and the British in a serious wrangle.

[70] Lincoln to Blaine (telegram), June 17, 1890, Dispatches, m.r. 158.
[71] Blaine to Lincoln (telegram), June 20, 1890, Dispatches, m.r. 158.

Chapter 13

Return to Chicago

THE YEAR 1892 WAS a presidential election year, and once again Lincoln was discussed as a potential nominee. In London the wife of the French ambassador described a dinner she attended in February of 1892:

> Mr. Lincoln, the American Minister, was there, and we all teased him about the Presidential election (the papers say he is to be the next President). Mdme. de Bille and I told him we were racking our brains to think what we could ask him for our friends at home when he would be at the White House. He assured us there was no possible chance of it, and no one would be as sorry as he himself if ever the thing came to pass. It certainly would be difficult to be a second President Lincoln.[1]

As it developed, President Harrison was easily renominated, and in the Republican convention Lincoln received but one vote.[2] When the campaign opened, Lincoln felt obligated to return home and participate.

Just before he left, Larz Anderson's father, an old friend of the Minister, died. On September 16 young Anderson wrote to his mother: "The Minister dined at home and I dined with him, and afterwards he sat and talked, oh, so sympathetically, encourag-

[1] Mary King Waddington, *Letters of a Diplomat's Wife, 1883–1900*, 339–40.
[2] Charles A. Church, *A History of the Republican Party in Illinois, 1854–1912*, 171.

ingly, consolingly, for no one has been touched more by grief and sorrow than Mr. Lincoln, and I felt strengthened by the words and advice of this brave man."[3] Characteristically, Lincoln offered Anderson any financial help he might have needed.[4] Mrs. Lincoln had returned to the United States in May to visit their daughter, Mrs. Isham, and her father, Senator Harlan. Her return had occasioned rumors then that her husband planned to resign.[5] Lincoln arrived in New York the morning of October 16 and announced that he would go briefly to Washington to report to the State Department and to the President before going on to Chicago.[6] A few days later he was home and attending a banquet connected with the opening of the great World's Columbian Exposition. Vice-President Levi P. Morton was the ranking governmental official present but there was also a host of cabinet officials, governors, and other dignitaries.[7] On October 22, Lincoln was present when the buildings were formally dedicated.[8]

Turning from the ceremonies of an exposition, Lincoln waded into the political situation of the moment. Speaking at a Republican rally held in Chicago the evening of October 24, Lincoln told the audience he appreciated the warm welcome it had accorded him and reported that during his years out of the country he had kept up with political developments. He turned to the theme of the great prosperity brought to the nation by the Republicans and held Chicago up as a shining example of government by that party. Amid laughter he proclaimed that if Columbus had been alive then, he certainly would have been a Republican and not a Democrat. Referring to the more immediate past, Lincoln told the gathering that the nation had been saved during Cleveland's presidency only because the Senate was controlled by the Republican party. The son of the first Republican President increased the highly partisan tone of his

---

3 Anderson, *Letters*, 307.
4 *Ibid.*, 308.
5 *New York Times*, May 25, 1892.
6 Chicago *Tribune*, Oct. 17, 1892.
7 *Ibid.*, Oct. 21, 1892.
8 *Ibid.*, Oct. 22, 1892.

speech when he proclaimed, "Thirty years ago the Democratic party brought this country to the verge of bankruptcy, and staking its all upon the extension of human slavery . . . ," it had been forced from power. What had saved the nation? The Morrill tariff enacted by the Republican party, of course.[9] Mr. Lincoln's historical facts may seem a bit questionable to readers now, but, nonetheless, they sounded good to his audience.

The name of Lincoln commanded no little political influence, and the minister to England was soon out on the campaign trail. On November 1, 1892, he wrote Mrs. Potter Palmer, "I am leaving town today for a little speech-making but am to be here again next Friday morning."[10] The Republicans were depending on Lincoln, Secretary of the Treasury Charles Foster, and Senator Sherman of Ohio to carry Illinois for the Grand Old Party.[11] Lincoln himself had high hopes for a Republican victory; in February he had written Murat Halstead, "Pretty much all the fresh news we get here about affairs at home is from the Democratic or Mugwump (if there is any difference) standpoint but I cannot help hoping that the Hill business is another of those political gifts to us which was so important in 1860."[12]

While in London two years before, Lincoln had been involved in an incident that showed, among other things, his extreme party loyalty. In Pennsylvania certain Republicans who opposed Senator Quay organized the Lincoln Independent Republican Committee. Robert Lincoln at once objected.[13] His words were sharp:

> The movement you mention recalls up here the old story of the Highland clan that deserted its friends and went over to the enemy on the field for no better reason than that it was not given the place of honor in the line of battle.[14]

Lincoln's letter brought an immediate reaction from the news-

9 *Ibid.*, Oct. 25, 1892.
10 Lincoln to Mrs. Potter Palmer, Nov. 1, 1892, CHS.
11 George H. Knoles, *The Presidential Campaign and Election of 1892*, 222–23.
12 Lincoln to Murat Halstead, Feb. 28, 1892, Historical and Philosophical Society of Ohio.
13 *New York Times*, Oct. 23, 1890.
14 *Harper's Weekly*, Nov. 8, 1890.

papers. He was roundly denounced by many and, as usual, was attacked as being only the son of his father.[15] When Lincoln was asked about the letter, he answered: "I wrote such a letter, and that is about all there is to it. The whole thing is a dead horse now."[16] The *New York Times* editorialized: "We venture to think, however, that this new despised corpse will be found across the path of Mr. LINCOLN'S political ambition to the close of his own life."[17]

Unfortunately for the Republicans, in November, 1892, Harrison was soundly defeated by Grover Cleveland, who was once again returned to the presidency.

There was little left for Lincoln to do but await the appointment of a successor. He returned to England just after the new year, arriving in London on the evening of January 4, 1893.[18] A month later Lincoln gave a dinner for a group of dignitaries, including the visiting Supreme Court justice, John M. Harlan.[19] On March 11, 1893, Mr. and Mrs. Lincoln dined with Queen Victoria at Windsor Castle. Her Majesty found Mr. Lincoln "very pleasant and sensible."[20] The same month an elaborate luncheon was given on board the American Line steamship *New York*, anchored in the harbor at Southampton. With some two hundred persons in attendance, various toasts were offered, including one to the newly inaugurated chief executive, Grover Cleveland. Before offering a toast to the American flag, Lincoln spoke of the celebration being held and commented: "If I were an Englishman, I would be proud of the commercial supremacy of my country, but as an American I congratulate America on the immense success it has reached within hardly more than a century. The sight of one's flag in a foreign port is thrilling. It is grand to see the flag borne abroad by the Queen of the seas."[21]

15 *Ibid.*
16 *New York Times*, Nov. 6, 1890.
17 *Ibid.*, Nov. 7, 1890.
18 *New York Times*, Jan. 5, 1893.
19 *Ibid.*, Feb. 11, 1893.
20 *The Letters of Queen Victoria*, 3rd ser., II, 238.
21 *New York Times*, Mar. 8, 1893.

The new secretary of state, Walter Q. Gresham, informed Lincoln on March 30, 1893, that he had given the President Lincoln's letter of resignation dated March 25, and that it had been accepted. Cleveland sent his "high appreciation" of Lincoln's service and wished him well. He requested that if possible Lincoln remain at his post until James A. Bayard could enter upon his duties.[22] On April 8, 1893, the Turkish embassy was the scene of a "Dinner d'Adieu" given jointly for Lincoln and William Henry Waddington, the retiring French diplomat.[23] Mary Harlan Lincoln left for home that same day.[24] On May 3, Lincoln and Henry White dined with Lord Rosebery, the foreign minister. The following day he went to Windsor to present his letter of recall, his last official act.[25] Lincoln arrived in New York on May 13,[26] where he was the guest of Edgar T. Welles. When he learned that his successor was also in the city, he called on Bayard. The next morning, Sunday, Bayard returned the call, and the two talked of the position in London. The meeting was described as most warm and cordial.[27] Lincoln attempted to arrange for Henry White and Larz Anderson to retain their respective positions. The latter was kept on,[28] but Henry White was succeeded as first secretary by James R. Roosevelt, elder half-brother of Franklin D. Roosevelt.[29]

The succession of Lincoln by Bayard did bring with it one long-overdue change: Robert T. Lincoln was the last United States minister to Great Britain. There had long been sentiment for raising this chief diplomatic post from a legation to an embassy, but nothing was done until 1893. The distinction was entirely ceremonial, but, as Henry White complained, Lincoln was often forced to stand in line at functions until the ambassadors of small, insignificant nations were received, and then he,

22 *Ibid.*, Mar. 31, 1893.
23 Waddington, *Letters*, 380–81.
24 *Ibid.*
25 *New York Times*, May 4, 1893.
26 *Ibid.*, May 15, 1893.
27 *Ibid.*, May 15, 1893.
28 Anderson, *Larz Anderson*, 98.
29 *Ibid.*; Nevins, *Henry White*, 74.

the representative of an important world power, would have his turn.[30] Senator George F. Hoar of Massachusetts, visiting Lincoln in London and T. Jefferson Coolidge in Paris, found them both complaining about their situations. He was instrumental in getting through Congress an amendment to the consular and diplomatic appropriation bill providing that when a foreign nation sent an ambassador to Washington the President at his discretion could do likewise when he appointed the chief of a foreign mission.[31]

On the whole, the period of Robert T. Lincoln's service as minister to England was calm, with little of great importance taking place. Lincoln was well liked by the English and his service was praised at home. Theodore Roosevelt, it is said, once remarked that all United States ministers to England had been pro-British except "Bob" Lincoln.[32] Speaking of this period, the British statesman Asquith wrote:

> For twenty years and more before the War [World War I] we had been very fortunate in the succession of eminent Americans whom the United States had sent as their representatives at the Court of St. James, whether the Republicans or the Democrats were for the time being in power at Washington. It was difficult to follow men like Motley and Lowell; but it would be impossible to find a more distinguished list of contemporary names than those of Phelps, Robert Lincoln, Bayard, John Hay, Joseph H. Choate, Whitelaw Reid, and Walter Hines Page.[33]

H. C. Allen, in his work on Anglo-American relations, speaks of the period 1872 to 1898 as the "Quiet Years," and notes that Edmund J. Phelps (1885–89) and Robert Todd Lincoln (1889–93) "carried out their duties with efficiency but without ostentation, the latter, indeed, with all the simplicity of his father which to some extent counteracted the flamboyance of his Secretary of State, Blaine."[34] Although Lincoln's diplomatic career was over,

30 *Ibid.*, 64–65.
31 Hoar, *Autobiography*, 227–28.
32 M. A. De Wolfe Howe, *James Ford Rhodes, American Historian*, 121.
33 Asquith, Herbert Henry, *Memories and Reflections*, I, 331.
34 H. C. Allen, *Great Britain and the United States*, 519–20.

he was later considered for another appointment. When John Hay resigned the post in London, Lincoln was among those mentioned as a possible successor.[35] However, Lincoln was deeply involved with business activities and the post did not interest him.

EXCEPT FOR A TRIP TO CHICAGO—for the dedication on June 22 of a monument to those who perished in the Chicago Massacre of August 15, 1812—Lincoln spent the summer following his return from England in the East.[36] In July the New York *Tribune* reported that Lincoln had taken a cottage at Rye Beach, New Hampshire, for the summer, adding that the area had been a favorite of his since his days at Exeter.[37] Writing to a friend, the former diplomat said, "Here we are settled down for the summer in a 'cottage' which you can easily find and I hope you will find when you come to visit your daughter."[38]

During the summer of 1893, Lincoln visited his alma mater, and it conferred upon him an honorary Doctor of Laws degree.[39] Speaking at the annual dinner of the alumni, he was described by an English observer:

> Mr. Robert Lincoln, the son of the great President, when once he had shaken himself free from his jokes, was vigorous enough. . . . The prolonged applause with which Mr. Lincoln was welcomed bore testimony not only to his own worth, but also the deep feeling of reverence with which his father's memory is cherished.[40]

Lincoln took the occasion to review the recent action of Governor John P. Altgeld of Illinois in pardoning the "anarchists" who had been involved in the Haymarket Riot of 1886. His view of Altgeld's action was, if nothing else, forthright:

> This act of a demogogic governor with a little temporary power, this slander upon justice I must denounce. . . . If I did not I would

---

35 John Hay to Whitelaw Reid, Nov. 13, 1898; Thayer, *John Hay*, II, 194–95.

36 Moses and Kirkland, *History of Chicago*, I, 62.

37 New York *Tribune*, July 1, 1893.

38 Lincoln to "My dear Marsten," July 4, 1893, New Hampshire Historical Society.

39 Harvard College, *Class of 1864, Secretary's Report*, No. 8, 98.

40 George Birkbeck Hill, *Harvard College by an Oxonian*, 105–106.

consider myself an apostate to my own State of Illinois. It is for you Harvard men to stand firm in the midst of such dangers in the republic.[41]

Unfortunately for Lincoln, the verdict of history has been that Altgeld performed a fair and courageous act in favor of those unjustly sentenced in the first place.

With his vacation over, Robert T. Lincoln returned to his home in Chicago and resumed work. A change that had begun to show right after the death of his son was taking place in the man. Before leaving England, Lincoln wrote to an old friend that he had received a letter from his daughter Mary, telling him of her son's first teeth, and the grandfather noted, "I feel about 900 years old."[42] Early in 1894, Lincoln told John G. Nicolay, "I am trying to get to work again but the shop has ceased to interest me I am sorry to say."[43] Sometimes he sought change by traveling. In the latter part of January, Lincoln attended a Young Republican Club meeting in New York City,[44] and a while later took a trip to California.[45] Still, at the end of the year, Lincoln complained: "I wonder if you are getting to feel so miserably old as I do. My daughter and her baby live a thousand miles away and the whole future seems, miserably, so many days to be passed."[46] A year later the situation was not much changed, for to John Hay, Lincoln wrote, "I am plugging away at a little law and a little business . . . ."[47]

When Lincoln returned to Chicago, he did not resume his association with Isham, Lincoln and Beale. Instead, he "found himself sufficiently occupied in the business affairs of various companies in which he had an interest."[48] Lincoln had been one of those interested in the organization of the Western Edison

41 Harry Barnard, *"Eagle Forgotten,"* 248.

42 Lincoln to "My dear Marsten," Jan. 27, 1893, New Hampshire Historical Society.

43 Lincoln to John G. Nicolay, Jan. 3, 1894, Nicolay Papers.

44 New York *Tribune,* Jan. 20, 1894.

45 Lincoln to Nicolay, May 15, 1894, Nicolay Papers.

46 Lincoln to Nicolay, Dec. 6, 1894, *ibid.*

47 Lincoln to Hay, Jan. 20, 1896, Hay Papers.

48 Harvard College, *Class of 1864, Secretary's Report,* No. 8, 98.

Light Company, as well as the Chicago Telephone Company.[49] In time, Lincoln became a director of the Chicago Edison Company, which in 1892 employed Samuel Insull as a manager. Although Lincoln is sometimes credited—or blamed, as the case may be—with giving Insull his start in Chicago, it is difficult to see how he played a major part in this for he was in England when Insull came to Chicago in July of 1892.[50] However, Lincoln's main interest for the next several years was the Pullman Palace Car Company. He had known its founder, George M. Pullman, for many years and now became "Special Counsel" for the company. Lincoln's title was to distinguish his position from that of the "General Counsel," John S. Runnells.[51] In 1893 the company was, as it had been since its founding, under the firm control of George M. Pullman. No sooner was Lincoln settled into his work than he was caught up in the most celebrated episode in the firm's history, the great strike of 1894.

The key to George M. Pullman's philosophy was his paternalistic attitude toward his employees.[52] He had built a model town—named, of course, for himself—in which many of his workers lived. Although the town was well regarded by sociologists, its residents lived in fear:

> If they spoke of the Company, they did so in a half whisper, and with a furtive glance behind them very much as "a Russian might mention the Czar." Everyone felt that he was spied upon, and that an incautious word might lead to his discharge and get his name upon the "blacklist."[53]

In May, 1894, the company dismissed a large number of workmen and cut the wages of those remaining. However, Pullman at the same time refused to lower rents in the town of Pullman or to reduce prices of commodities sold in company stores. He was approached by an employees' committee, which requested that

49 Bessie L. Pierce, *A History of Chicago*, III, 225, 228–29.
50 Forrest McDonald, *Insull*, 55–56.
51 *Who Was Who in America, 1897–1942*, 730, 1066.
52 See Almont Lindsey, *The Pullman Strike*, especially pp. 19–35 for a discussion of Pullman and his beliefs.
53 Harry Thurston Peck, *Twenty Years of the Republic*, 376.

wages be restored to their former level. Mr. Pullman responded by discharging at least part of those who had called upon him. The American Railway Union led by Eugene V. Debs now entered the picture. Many, even those who were far from being friends of labor, urged Pullman to settle the matter by arbitration. Mark Hanna observed, "a man who won't meet his men half-way is a God-damn fool."[54]

The company's answer to those urging arbitration was: "We have nothing to arbitrate."[55] Beginning on June 26, 1894, the 150,000 members of the American Railway Union refused to handle Pullman cars. The great strike was on. The company was in a very favorable position, for it must be remembered that the company did not operate railroad facilities, but instead leased its sleeping cars to railroads. Thus, the other companies would fight its battle. A former president of the Chicago Great Western Railroad, J. M. Eagan, became chairman of the General Managers Strike Committee. He was quoted as saying, "Mr. Pullman is not considered in this controversy."[56] Indeed the Pullman Company, as well as its founder, remained silent, although earlier a statement that the cut in wages had been the result of the existing economic depression had been issued.[57] The statement was made when "stock of the company was selling above par; its dividends for the preceding year on a capital of $36,000,000 had been $2,520,000, while it had a surplus of undivided profits amounting to $25,000,000."[58]

On July 4, 1894, the Chicago *Tribune* quoted Mr. Pullman—who, with his family, was vacationing at the fashionable seaside resort of Elberon, New Jersey—as saying that the strike would be broken in a week. It was not, and when disorders broke out, Governor Altgeld of Illinois used troops to maintain order. A few days later, over the vigorous protests of the Governor, federal troops were ordered out by President Cleveland. Still, Mr. Pull-

---

54 Thomas Beer, *Hanna*, 132–33.
55 Peck, *Twenty Years*, 378.
56 Chicago *Tribune*, June 29, 1894.
57 Peck, *Twenty Years*, 377.
58 *Ibid.*

man remained silent, for now, not only were the railroads fighting his battle, but so was the United States government. Criticism of Pullman became more pronounced. Secretary of State Walter Q. Gresham told a reporter that Pullman ought to resign the presidency of the company because of his attitude.[59] Even the Chicago *Tribune*, which had been perhaps the most violently antilabor newspaper in Chicago, now ran an editorial titled "Mr. Pullman's Absurd Stubbornness," in which it called for Pullman to act.[60]

Within a few days Pullman at last appeared in public, whereas he had previously refused to leave his vacation retreat. On the morning of July 13, he and Robert T. Lincoln arrived in New York on an early train. Reporters were on hand to question them but neither had much to say. Lincoln ended the interview by saying to Pullman, "Shall we take a cab to the Brevort House?"[61] Pullman agreed and they crossed the street as if to take a cab, but then dodged a few horse cars and other moving vehicles, recrossed the street, and walked to the Murray Hill Hotel. After breakfast they went to the Pullman offices for a conference with General Horace Porter and John S. Runnells.

The strike was ultimately broken and gradually calm returned to the city, but considerable bitterness toward the company still existed. Part of the aftermath was the conspiracy trial of Eugene V. Debs, which began in Federal Court in January, 1895.[62] Clarence Darrow defended the labor leader and during the proceedings George M. Pullman was subpoenaed to testify. A deputy marshal attempted to serve the businessman but he went into hiding and did not return to Chicago until after the proceedings ended because of the illness of a juror.[63] When Pullman did return, he called on Federal Judge Grosscup to explain his absence.

---

[59] Chicago *Tribune*, July 11, 1894.

[60] *Ibid.*

[61] *Ibid.*, July 14, 1894.

[62] This trial is not to be confused with the contempt trial, which was a separate matter. Conviction was obtained in the contempt case and Debs's sentence was upheld by the United States Supreme Court in *In re Debs*, 158 United States 564 (1894).

[63] Lindsey, *The Pullman Strike*, 303.

With him went Robert T. Lincoln and the matter "was quietly and amicably adjusted."[64]

Throughout the entire strike period, the role that Robert T. Lincoln played is not known. One may presume that he was in agreement with Pullman's stand since he was close to Pullman during this time. However, none of Lincoln's correspondence or public utterances ever made reference to the strike. Indeed, only once is Lincoln known to have written anything on the relationship between employer and employee, and that was in a letter written in 1907 to a friend. At a time when workmen's compensation legislation was first being sought, he wrote:

> I may agree that the State must not permit to starve a worthy man of the working class, but I am not moralized up to the point of thinking it right that if my chauffeur at $90 per month who calls himself skilled, is injured by his lack of skill ("not carelessness") in his first week, I may have to pay him $45 per month for the rest of his life. It is true that the accident had caused a loss, but should *I* (guiltless) stand it all? If the answer is that insurance is cheap, why could not the employee pay this insurance for himself, as I do for myself?[65]

Robert Lincoln continued his work as special counsel for the Pullman Company and to see the Pullman family socially. In April, 1896, Mr. and Mrs. Lincoln were among the guests at the lavish wedding of George M. Pullman's daughter Florence to Frank O. Lowden, later governor of Illinois.[66]

On October 19, 1897, George M. Pullman died suddenly.[67] Because of the hatred that Pullman's name aroused, his remains were buried in a deep concrete and steel vault to prevent any attempt to steal the body. This manner of burial impressed Lincoln and he determined to have his father reburied in the same manner. There had been several attempts to violate the tomb of Abraham Lincoln, and one attempt in 1876 nearly succeeded.[68]

[64] *Ibid.*
[65] Lincoln to Charles Louis Strobel, Nov. 14, 1907, CHS.
[66] William T. Hutchinson, *Lowden of Illinois*, I, 49.
[67] Chicago *Tribune*, Oct. 20, 1897.
[68] Lewis, *Myths After Lincoln*, 266–81.

In 1899 the Lincoln tomb in Springfield was rebuilt, and in February, 1901, Robert T. Lincoln paid seven hundred dollars to have the President reburied ten feet below the ground in a poured concrete and steel vault.[69]

By the terms of Pullman's will, Robert T. Lincoln and Norman B. Ream were made executors of the estate.[70] The principal persons mentioned in the will were the widow and two daughters. Mr. Pullman had two sons, but since both "had not fulfilled his hopes" for them, they were cut off with but a lifetime income of $3,000 a year.[71] In addition to persons named in the will, $130,000 was divided among several worthy projects, including the Chicago Historical Society and the Pullman Universalist Memorial Church at Albion, New York.[72] One and one-quarter million dollars went to endow a "free manual training school." The first problem which the executors faced was the desire of Mrs. Pullman and her daughters to provide more generously for the two sons. This was accomplished in 1899. Almost four years after the death of Pullman, the estate was at last settled. In 1900 the total amount of the estate was estimated at about seventeen and one-half million dollars; Lincoln and Ream received $425,000 for their work as executors.[73]

The manual training school took longer to establish. Under the terms of Pullman's will, Lincoln, Lowden, Ream, and "four other men were to be its directors or trustees."[74] There was no manual training school then in existence, and as a result of having no pattern to follow, the trustees disagreed about what they should do. After seeking the advice of outsiders—among whom was William R. Harper, president of the University of Chicago—the group turned much of the work of establishing the school over to their secretary, Duane Doty, and let him proceed with plans for the project.[75] Doty, in discussing the proposed institution with

---

69 *Ibid.*, 287.
70 Hutchinson, *Lowden*, I, 64.
71 *Ibid.*
72 Lincoln to Charles C. Terry, Feb. 26, 1898, ISHL.
73 All details unless otherwise noted are from Hutchinson, *Lowden*, I, 64–65.
74 Hutchinson, *Lowden*, I, 65.
75 *Ibid.*, I, 65–66.

Lincoln, insisted that "manual training" should "not mean hand-work only but a broad curriculum of technical or industrial education comparable with the best afforded overseas."[76] The trustees concluded that the amount of money provided for the school was inadequate and that they must wait for their resources to grow. In 1909 a site for the school was purchased; in 1914 construction was started. When the school opened in 1915, George M. Pullman's wish was finally fulfilled.[77]

The same newspaper that announced the death of Pullman carried an article about his possible successor as president of the company he had founded.[78] Several names were mentioned, including Thomas H. Wickes, a company vice-president, John S. Runnells, and Robert T. Lincoln. Special attention was paid to Lincoln (who for once was not referred to as the son of his father). It was noted that Lincoln's law firm had "had close business relations with the company for a number of years, and the ex-Secretary of War is familiar with its business in most of its details."[79]

The members of the board of directors of the company in 1897 were: Marshall Field, O. S. A. Sprague, Norman Williams, J. W. Doane, H. R. Reed, and H. C. Hulbert. When George M. Pullman died, several members were out of town, and the board did not hold a meeting to determine the future of the company until almost the middle of November.[80] When it did convene, its first action was to set up a three-man executive committee composed of Robert T. Lincoln, Marshall Field, and H. C. Hulbert. Since Lincoln was the only member of the group who could devote his full efforts to the management of the corporation, he was designated its president pro tempore and given power to sign documents and transact business normally handled by the permanent president.[81] There was speculation about whether the board

[76] Duane Doty to Lincoln, Feb. 17, 22, and 23, 1900, *ibid.*, I, 66.
[77] *Ibid.*, I, 67.
[78] Chicago *Tribune*, Oct. 20, 1897.
[79] *Ibid.*
[80] *Ibid.*, Nov. 12, 1897.
[81] *Ibid.*

would name a railroad man as the president. Rumors that Lincoln would not consider the position on an indefinite basis were authoritatively denied by the Chicago *Tribune*.[82]

In 1901, Robert T. Lincoln became the permanent president of the company. Although he often grumbled about his ill health,[83] Lincoln found himself quite busy and often declined outside activities on the grounds that he was "so much engaged."[84] In 1893, Pullman had acquired the Wagner Sleeping Car Company, and later the name of the corporation was changed from the Pullman Palace Car Company to simply "The Pullman Company."[85] Its operations continued to be of a two-fold nature: manufacturing sleeping cars and leasing the cars to operating railroads. Lincoln remained the head of Pullman until 1911, when he was succeeded by John S. Runnells. The firm's board of directors was ever changing, and among those who served after 1897 were William K. Vanderbilt, Frederick K. Vanderbilt, J. Pierpont Morgan, and Frank O. Lowden.[86]

The Pullman Company underwent its greatest period of growth during the period of Lincoln's tenure as president. Its gross revenue from leased cars over the years was: $8,598,000 in 1898; $12,720,000 in 1900; $21,772,000 in 1904; and $35,365,000 in 1910. Earnings after taxes from the same amounted to $384,000 in 1898; $4,321,000 in 1900; $6,645,000 in 1904; and $10,418,000 in 1910. The other part of the business, manufacturing, produced gross revenue of $10,368,000 in 1898; $16,704,000 in 1900; $22,838,000 in 1904. No figures for 1910 are available. Earnings after taxes from manufacturing amounted to $2,076,000 in 1898; $2,302,000 in 1900; $3,016,000 in 1904; and $8,899,000 in 1910.[87]

Robert T. Lincoln plunged into his work as president of Pull-

82 *Ibid.*

83 Lincoln to Emelie Todd Helm, Mar. 27, 1898, copy in ISHL; *see also* Lincoln to John G. Nicolay, Apr. 28, 1898, Nicolay Papers.

84 Lincoln to Charles E. Rice, May 4, 1901, Lincoln National Life Insurance Company.

85 "Pullman, Inc.," *Fortune*, Vol. XVII, No. 1 (Jan., 1938), 45.

86 Hutchinson, *Lowden*, I, 65.

87 All figures are from "Pullman, Inc.," *Fortune*, Vol. XVII, No. 1 (Jan., 1938), 41.

man and found himself confronted with matters both large and small. Some issues, such as the disposition of the old company town of Pullman, were held over from an earlier day. In May, 1900, Lincoln advised Mayor Carter Harrison of Chicago that the company was under court order to discontinue lighting the town street lamps and although he had addressed the Mayor on the matter in March, he had received no reply to date.[88] Lincoln was also concerned with the problems of employees, or potential employees, some presented to him by old political associates. To Senator John W. Daniel he wrote:

> Upon my return from California, your letter of February 20th, in relation to the application of John W. Southall for restoration to the position of conductor in the service of this Company, was duly received.
>
> I am advised that the action of the operating department in the case was only taken when the officials became convinced that the duties of the position were not being satisfactorily performed, and that the interests of the service required a termination of the employment.
>
> Because of your interest in the case, I have given it personal examination, and as a result, I am reluctantly compelled to say that I could not consistently direct a reinstatement, as I could only do so against the protest of officials of the operating department; and this I do not feel that I can properly do.[89]

When Senator Joseph B. Foraker wrote pressuring for the appointment of a friend as company agent in Baltimore, Lincoln replied:

> The considerations which govern a matter of this kind are these: When a vacancy occurs in one of our districts, which is a rare event because of the limited number of local employees, the selection to fill it is carefully made, and, as a rule, is made in accordance with civil service regulations which have been in effect with us for many years; and unless there may be adequate reasons to the contrary, seniority in service is a controlling element. This policy is regarded

[88] Lincoln to Carter H. Harrison, May 9, 1900, Newberry Library.
[89] Lincoln to John W. Daniel, Mar. 1, 1899, Duke University Library.

Robert T. Lincoln, 1905.

PULLMAN BUILDING,
CHICAGO.

Manchester, Vermont,
August third, 1905.

Arthur F. Hall, Esq.,
Secretary, The Lincoln National Life
Insurance Company,
Fort Wayne, Indiana.

Dear Sir:
Replying to your note of July
28th, I find no objection whatever to the use
of a portrait of my father upon the letter-
head of such a life insurance company named
after him as you describe; and I take pleasure
in enclosing you, for that purpose, what I regard as a very good photograph of him.

Very truly yours,

Robert T. Lincoln

Courtesy the Lincoln National Life Insurance Company

Robert Lincoln's favorite photograph of his father, made
in 1864, in the Mathew Brady Gallery in Washington, D. C.,
and a facsimile of a letter about it.

as an entirely equitable one to employees, and furthermore, our experience has shown that it operates as an incentive to growth in comprehensive district work.[90]

Then, just in case Foraker had not gotten the point, Lincoln wrote that the vacancy in question had already been filled.

Now and then problems arose over other matters. A Troy, New York, newspaper editor complained in 1900 to Lincoln about the loss of his annual pass, which had originally been granted by the Wagner Company. Lincoln replied that it was not possible for the Pullman Company to give free passes to all members of the journalistic community but that he would be happy to consider passes for special occasions.[91] When asked why the company did not make contributions to the Y.M.C.A., Lincoln answered that it did not because of the great number of requests the corporation received for funds, although he personally did appreciate the good work done by the organization.[92] The president of Pullman frequently wrote letters of recommendation. One written in 1900 urged Mayor Carter Harrison of Chicago to appoint William R. Manierre as a civil service commissioner: "Mr. Manierre is so well known that it is unnecessary to say anything regarding his fitness for the position, or in respect to his zeal and interest in municipal public affairs."[93]

In connection with his work with Pullman, Lincoln traveled frequently. He attended social functions such as the Golden Jubilee celebration of the Illinois Central Railroad held the evening of February 9, 1901.[94] Typical of these trips was one to Charleston, South Carolina, in March, 1908. Word was received by the station master that the railway official would arrive from Florida on his private car, the *Mayflower*.[95]

[90] Lincoln to Joseph B. Foraker, Mar. 7, 1902, Historical and Philosophical Society of Ohio.
[91] Lincoln to Arthur McArthur, Mar. 3, 1900, R. T. Lincoln Papers, Library of Congress.
[92] Lincoln to Bruce Haldeman, Dec. 13, 1910, ISHL.
[93] Lincoln to Carter H. Harrison, Nov. 8, 1900, Newberry Library.
[94] Corliss, *Main Line of Mid America*, 318.
[95] Clipping from unidentified Charleston, S.C., newspaper, Harvard University Archives.

Mr. Lincoln is making a tour of the country and it will be gratifying to Charlestonians to learn that he has decided to stop over
in this city. At present it is not known exactly how long his visit
will last but it is expected that he will be urged upon to linger
here awhile.[96]

Charles G. Dawes noted in April, 1899, that he had returned from
the Springfield funeral of former Governor Oglesby of Illinois
in the private car of Robert T. Lincoln, and that he had had
dinner on board with Lincoln, Frank O. Lowden, and others.[97]
At times business was combined with pleasure. In January, 1897,
Lincoln, Marshall Field, N. K. Fairbank, Horace Porter, and
others left Chicago on a special train and headed west. Passing
through Arizona Territory, they stopped in Phoenix. When interviewed by a reporter, Lincoln observed that theirs was not the
usual railroad inspection party, "today we got out and walked
several miles for exercise, the day being so fine, the train following at our own gait." As for their future plans, the president of
Pullman said:

> We have no plans. We left Chicago last Saturday, just ahead of
> the great blizzard, and came to Arizona both for a taste of milder
> winter climate and relaxation. We have found no plans ahead;
> will probably stay [at] Phoenix over Sunday; may go from here to
> Coronado and may shift over to the Southern Pacific and work
> back east.[98]

96 *Ibid.*
97 Bascom Timmons, ed., *Charles G. Dawes*, 189–90.
98 *Arizona Gazette* (Phoenix), Jan. 29, 1897.

Chapter 14

Politics and Personal Life

As ONE OF THE EMINENT BUSINESSMEN of the nation, Robert T. Lincoln was, in the middle and late 1890's, still occasionally drawn into politics. As early as the summer of 1893, a newspaperman friend of Lincoln's had urged him to begin laying plans for the presidential election of 1896, but Lincoln replied, "I have been unduly honored by this [Harrison's] administration. . . . I wish for the few remaining years of my active life to perform my duties as a private citizen and not those of any public office."[1] As time passed, Lincoln's personal feeling was that "In the absence of any accident we ought to have either Harrison or McKinley. There never was a better President than Mr. Harrison and if he wants it, the Country owes him a second term."[2] In June, 1894, his former cabinet colleague Thomas L. James spoke out in favor of Lincoln's nomination for the presidency.[3] A year later when he was still urging Lincoln's candidacy, he offered evidence of his candidate's party loyalty. James said that he had visited Lincoln in London, and as he was leaving, the Minister shook hands with his guests and said, "Goodbye; God bless you all, and d——n a mugwump."[4]

[1] Lincoln to William L. Shearer, July 5, 1893, in Charles V. Darrin, "A Lincoln Family Friendship," *JISHS*, Vol. XXXXIV, No. 3 (1951), 210–17.
[2] Lincoln to Shearer, July 24, 1894, *ibid.*
[3] *New York Times*, June 25, 1894.
[4] *Ibid.*, May 17, 1895.

Although Lincoln's support of his party never wavered, he admitted in the summer of 1895 a grudging admiration for President Grover Cleveland. When asked by a reporter about a possible third term for Cleveland, Lincoln recalled that he had favored a third term for Grant. "I have not given the matter any particular thought, but I think Mr. Cleveland has made a remarkably good President in many respects, and I am glad the country has such a good President, even if he is a Democrat and although I do not agree with him politically."[5] Lincoln regarded Cleveland favorably because of their mutual devotion to the gold standard in the midst of the great silver crusade. In April, 1895, Lincoln was one of several prominent Republicans who wrote Cleveland congratulating him on his "sound money" stand.[6] When at last the Republican convention of 1896 did meet, Lincoln was optimistic. Just before leaving on a fishing expedition on Lake Erie, he wrote, "It looks now as though the delegates at St. Louis would have little to discuss except the platform and there ought not to be much trouble about that if it is not to be shifty."[7]

In the midst of the presidential campaign of 1896, Lincoln consented to speak at ceremonies commemorating the thirty-eighth anniversary of the Lincoln-Douglas debates. Also present at Knox College, Galesburg, Illinois, were Chauncey M. Depew and John M. Palmer, the Gold Democratic candidate for President. Lincoln's part in the proceedings was short, but it was probably the only time in his life that he spoke publicly about his father. He began, "On an occasion of this peculiar significance it would suit me far better to be a listener . . . witnessing this demonstration of respect for my father." The son then wondered what his father's reaction would have been had he known that his memory was honored so widely. Continuing, Lincoln observed that the issues of 1858 had long been decided. His father had felt that those issues were the struggle between right and wrong, and no one could deny that right had triumphed.

5 New York *Tribune*, Aug. 18, 1895.
6 *New York Times*, May 14, 1895.
7 Lincoln to William L. Shearer, May 6, 1896, in Darrin, "A Lincoln Family Friendship," *JISHS*, Vol. XXXXIV, No. 3 (1951), 210–17.

This should give us confidence in our battle against the evils of our own times. Now, as then, there can be but one supreme issue, that between right and wrong. In our country there are no ruling classes. The right to direct public affairs according to his might and influence and conscience belongs to the humblest as well as to the greatest. The elections represent the judgments of individual voters. Perhaps at times one vote can destroy or make the country's prosperity for thirty years. The power of the people, by their judgments expressed through the ballot box, to shape their own destinies, sometimes makes one tremble. But it is times of dangerous critical moments, which bring into action the high moral quality of the citizenship of America. The people are always true. They are always right, and I have an abiding faith they will remain so.[8]

His remarks take on significance when recalled against the background of the hard-fought election of 1896, when to him William McKinley was the "right" and William Jennings Bryan, representing the Populist-Democratic cause, was the "wrong." Lincoln wrote to John Hay, "If Bryan succeeds it seems to me it would have been better for us all if Bull Run had been the last battle of the war."[9] In the end, Mr. Lincoln's candidate won, and he could retain his faith that the people were always "right."

Lincoln continued to be much in demand as a speaker, but because of the press of business—and personal inclinations—he usually declined. When he received an invitation to address the "Lincoln Banquet" in New York in early 1898, he replied. "I very much regret that I do not feel able to accept the invitation, but I wish to express most earnestly my grateful appreciation of this many-times renewed honor to my father's memory."[10] Two months later, when asked to speak at Montclair, New Jersey, he wrote, ". . . my business engagements are so pressing, that it will be impossible for me to undertake any public duty of that kind

---

[8] *Speech of the Honorable Robert T. Lincoln Made at the Celebration of the 38th Anniversary of the Lincoln-Douglas Debates, Galesburg, Illinois, October 7, 1896*, 1–3.

[9] Lincoln to John Hay, Nov. 1, 1896, Hay Papers.

[10] Lincoln to William D. Murphy, Jan. 14, 1898, Yale University Library.

for a good while to come."[11] In 1904, when asked to a similar affair, he answered:

> Although, for reasons to which I have so often given expression, it seems better that I should refrain from availing myself of invitations of this character; they are none the less gratefully received by me, and I beg you will convey to the members of the Club the assurance of my heartfelt appreciation of the sentiments which prompt them to honor the memory of my father by these annual observances of the anniversary of his birth.[12]

THE DECADE OF THE 1890's in the United States saw the rise of imperialism which culminated in the Spanish-American War. Robert T. Lincoln was not sympathetic to the jingos and their notions of new worlds to conquer. Nowhere is his attitude more evident than in his remarks after the battleship *Maine* was blown up in Havana harbor. Interviewed while visiting in Mount Pleasant, Iowa, Lincoln noted that possibly the ship had been blown up by accident or by the act of some fanatic, but in neither case would Spain be liable.

> Giving international law the widest latitude and stretching precedents to their limit there would be no liability against the government of Spain. It is an elementary principle of international law that a government is in no way responsible for the acts of private citizens. If it were not so, complications would be arising continually which would keep nations in a turmoil and arbitration continually.
>
> It is another primary principle that no nation is responsible for accidents. As to the right of a nation to fortify its harbors as it sees fit there cannot be the slightest doubt. This right is a conceded one and is exercised by all nations. The matter and manner of harbor defenses and fortifications are well known and perfectly understood. Whenever a vessel, therefore, enters the harbor of a foreign power it is with notice of such defenses and with an assumption of the chances they involve. It would not do to say that one nation is bound to give another notice of where and how its harbor de-

11 Lincoln to S. C. G. Watkins, Mar. 18, 1898, *ibid.*
12 Lincoln to Robert N. Kenyon, Jan. 23, 1904, Indiana University Library.

fenses are arranged, as the result of such a rule would be obvious. In entering the harbor of Havana the Maine did so with full knowledge that it was a fortified harbor and took all the chances of accident or the acts which might be done by those for whom Spain is not responsible.

The newspaper article concluded with the statement "Mr. Lincoln seems to speak more as an employed attorney for Spain than as a patriotic citizen of this country."[13] Actually Lincoln was speaking mainly as a business leader who feared that any war might disrupt the prosperity that was only gradually returning to the nation.

As the nineteenth century was about to give way to the twentieth, Lincoln was starting to show some of the public shyness that would characterize his later life. In late 1897 when a cousin, Mrs. Edwards, asked for his photograph, he answered that he had not had one taken in a dozen years and that he never intended to sit again "and in that way keep out of the vile newspaper cuts."[14] The following spring Lincoln wrote again to Mrs. Edwards and sent two pictures:

> That of "Jack" as we called him, is an enlargement of the last one taken—when he was about 14 years old. The one of myself was taken at about the same time and I send it for that reason, rather than one of this date. It happens to be the last I have had and one made now would be almost exactly at my father's age at his death. I think the collection is more satisfactory in this way.[15]

The subject of photographs again arose in 1903 when the local press requested a likeness of the president of the Pullman Company. Lincoln replied:

> I have your request for a modern photograph of myself for occasional use in the *Tribune*. I read the *Tribune* daily and it is

[13] *Mount Pleasant* (Iowa) *News*, Feb. 24, 1898.

[14] Lincoln to Josephine Edwards, Dec. 14, 1897, ISHL. Evidently she had congratulated him on his new position with Pullman, for his reply was, "The work that has fallen on me is greater than I supposed I should undertake at my time of life. It gives me great anxiety and leaves me no leisure, so that I am hardly to be congratulated."

[15] Lincoln to Josephine Edwards, May 2, 1898, *ibid*.

one of the minor pleasures of life left to me that I can open the paper feeling sure that I am not to be confronted by a portrait of myself.

The letter then concluded with the writer's observation that he was so happy with the present arrangement that he hoped he would be excused for not complying with the request.[16] He did finally give in, however, for he had at least two more formal photographs made.

Over the years Lincoln managed to keep in touch with his various relatives and he was ever interested in their activities. Although there were no Lincoln relations, there were many Todds and they often occupied his attention. He kept up his correspondence with Aunt Emelie Todd Helm and to her he gave a running account of his activities and his troubles. On February 1, 1896, he wrote that for three months his house had been filled with workmen and he had been driven from room to room trying to get out of the way of the workers. In the midst of the confusion a Todd cousin turned up, suffering from a lack of gainful employment, and Lincoln had found him a place in the telephone company.[17] Two years later he sent Mrs. Helm a pass on the Louisville and Nashville Railroad,[18] and two years after that he inquired about a golden wedding anniversary invitation he had received. Aunt Emelie was an authority on the complicated Todd genealogy.[19]

There were also other family matters, more urgent and much closer home. Lincoln's younger daughter, Jessie Harlan, had spent much time at the home of her maternal grandfather, James Harlan, in Mount Pleasant, Iowa, where she met Warren W. Beckwith. The romantic interest that grew between them was frowned upon by the girl's parents. One who knew Beckwith at the time remembers him as the star football player of the Iowa Wesleyan College team.[20] He was moderately well-to-do, and the

16 Lincoln to James Keely, June 22, 1903, CHS.
17 Lincoln to Emelie Todd Helm, Feb. 1, 1896, copy in ISHL.
18 Lincoln to Mrs. Helm, Apr. 5, 1898, copy *ibid.*
19 Lincoln to Mrs. Helm, Oct. 11, 1900, copy *ibid.*

sort of student who disappeared during the spring semester of college, but always was on hand in the fall for the football season.[21] Without warning, Jessie and Warren eloped and were married in Milwaukee, Wisconsin, November 10, 1897. Nearly everyone was taken by surprise. Next day the Iowa Wesleyan team met for practice and "everyone was asking, 'Where is Warny?' as he was our star halfback and indispensable . . . ."[22]

The answer was found in the newspapers. Reporters descending upon Robert T. Lincoln were told:

> About a year ago my daughter and young Beckwith became sweethearts while she was visiting her mother's old home at Mt. Pleasant, Ia. Both Mrs. Lincoln and I objected to the young man. We broke off the attachment, separated the young people, and thought that settled it. While Miss Jessie was in Mt. Pleasant, on a recent visit, it seems the attachment was renewed, unknown to us. We still disapprove of the young man as much as we did at the outset. He is not satisfactory to us to be the husband of our daughter. He is the son of Capt. Beckwith, a good friend of Mrs. Lincoln's family at Mt. Pleasant—and the father is altogether an estimable old man. It is the son, not the father, we are opposed to.
>
> I do not know anything about the details of the ceremony. I do not know what business the young man engages in, but he was in some business or other in Mt. Pleasant. Jessie is now here at home with us. I do not know anything about the whereabouts of Mr. Beckwith nor his plans. We did not know of the secret wedding until Mrs. Lincoln questioned our daughter in her room after dinner, when she admitted having gone to Milwaukee and being married secretly in the afternoon. That's all there is to it.[23]

Despite the evident objections of her parents, Jessie Lincoln Beckwith was in Mount Pleasant on November 17, when Iowa Wesleyan, with Beckwith playing, defeated the Keokuk Medics

[20] Conversation with F. M. Lefforge of Amarillo, Tex., a classmate of Beckwith and Jessie Lincoln at Iowa Wesleyan.

[21] *Ibid.*

[22] *Ibid.*

[23] Lester W. Olson, "Lincoln's Granddaughter Eloped to Milwaukee," *Historical Messenger* (Dec., 1955), 3.

48–0.[24] Three children were born to the Beckwiths: Mary, born August 22, 1898; a still-born child, born in 1901; and Robert Lincoln Beckwith, born July 19, 1904.[25]

IT WAS THE STRANGE LOT of Robert T. Lincoln to have been associated with the first three martyred Presidents of the United States and then finally to lie buried close by the grave of the fourth. In 1901, Lincoln and his family were on their way to Buffalo to visit the exposition when just before leaving the train they heard the news that President William McKinley had been shot. Lincoln visited the wounded Chief Executive and saw Vice-President Roosevelt.[26] Some days later the Pullman president wrote to the new resident at the White House:

> When I had the pleasure of seeing you at Buffalo, neither of us, I think, supposed that the great burden of care which is now yours was so soon to fall upon you. I do not congratulate you for I have seen too much of the seamy side of the Presidential Robe to think of it as a desirable garment, but I do hope that you will have the strength and courage to carry you through a successful administration.[27]

It is said that some years later when another President invited him to lunch, Lincoln remarked referring to his association with presidential tragedies, "If only they knew, they wouldn't want me there."[28] On another occasion, he was supposedly asked if he planned to attend an event where the President was to be and Lincoln's answer was, "No, I am not going and they'd better not invite me because there is a certain fatality about presidential functions when I am present."[29]

IN 1902, ROBERT T. LINCOLN purchased an estate of several hun-

24 New York *Tribune*, Nov. 18, 1897.

25 McMurtry, *The Harlan-Lincoln Tradition*, 15.

26 Speech by Harry J. Dunbaugh to the Fortnightly, Chicago, May 2, 1962.

27 Lincoln to Theodore Roosevelt, Sept. 18, 1901, Theodore Roosevelt Papers, Library of Congress.

28 Clipping in the R. T. Lincoln Papers, Library of Congress.

29 *Burlington* (Vt.) *Free Press*, July 27, 1926.

dred acres at Manchester, Vermont. He had been visiting the area since the Civil War, and his partner Edward Swift Isham had long had a home in the area. Lincoln so enjoyed his summer place that he called it his "ancestral home."[30]

One of Lincoln's great joys and interests in life was golf, which he played as often as the opportunity presented itself. Marshall Field's nephew Stanley was a regular member of Lincoln's golfing group and recalled that he, his uncle, and Lincoln once matched coins to see who would pay the train fare to and from Wheaton where they played. Stanley lost and had to stand the cost out of the meager fifteen dollars a week that his uncle paid him. Marshall Field and Robert Lincoln were much amused by his discomfort.[31] On New Year's Day, 1906, Lincoln, Marshall Field, James Simpson, and Stanley Field, using red golf balls, played eighteen holes despite the bitter cold and the knee-deep snow.

Shortly afterwards Marshall Field left for New York on business with a cold and sore throat. Ultimately he became quite ill and died on January 16.[32] Lincoln visited his ailing friend in New York just before Field died; later Lincoln wrote to his Aunt Emelie of his great personal loss.[33] It must have been not long after Marshall Field died that Lincoln himself became ill. In late March he wrote from Augusta, Georgia, "I have been down here for nearly two months trying to recover from a nervous break-down."[34] In time he became well enough to resume his normal work.

The year 1909 brought the celebrations of the centennial of the birth of Abraham Lincoln, and his eldest son could hardly have remained aloof if he had desired. A major event was being planned in Springfield, and on January 4, 1909, Lincoln wrote to Judge J. Otis Humphrey that he planned to attend but that he must not be asked to participate, which meant to speak in any

30 Lincoln to Henry White, Mar. 19, 1905, Henry White Papers, Library of Congress.

31 Speech by Harry J. Dunbaugh, May 2, 1962.

32 John Tebbel, *The Marshall Fields*, 111–12.

33 *Ibid.*; Lincoln to Emelie Todd Helm, Jan. 25, 1906, copy in ISHL.

34 Lincoln to George N. Black, Mar. 20, 1906, ISHL.

way.[35] Two days later he wrote that he would arrive in his own railroad car.[36] Since there were several dignitaries scheduled to attend, the association in charge of the ceremonies asked for a reduction of railroad fare for the party coming from Washington. This was not possible, but when Lincoln heard of it he sent two hundred dollars to Judge Humphrey to help with the expenses. He asked the Judge to say that the draft came from "a friend, who does not wish his name known."[37] The observance was a great success and was attended by such luminaries as William Jennings Bryan, the British ambassador, Lord Bryce, and the French ambassador, Jusserand. Lincoln wrote Judge Humphrey, "I have said to you before that I was astonished at the splendid way in which Springfield conducted the celebration. It was absolutely perfect, and the work and attention given by everybody there was most affecting to me."[38] The visit was Lincoln's last to the city of his birth.

A few days after the occasion in Springfield, President Theodore Roosevelt spoke at the dedication of the so-called Lincoln Cabin, located on what was once the family farm in Kentucky. Robert Lincoln was not present, and the President's military aide thought he knew the reason when he wrote:

> and if it be true, as I hear, that Bob Lincoln . . . does not relish the perpetuation of this cabin, I cannot blame him. The very thought of it, having seen it once, would make any member of his family shudder with horror. It does not bear the stamp of poverty alone, but degradation and uncleanliness.[39]

Just a few months later Robert Lincoln, although quite ill at the time, attended the celebration held in Hodgenville, Kentucky. The highlight of it was the unveiling of a statue of the Great Emancipator. Lincoln had looked forward to the occasion with eagerness, for he wrote to one who was to accompany him,

[35] Lincoln to J. Otis Humphrey, Jan. 4, 1909, Humphrey Papers, ISHL.
[36] Lincoln to Humphrey, Jan. 6, 1909, *ibid.*
[37] Lincoln to Humphrey, Jan. 21, 1909, *ibid.*
[38] Lincoln to Humphrey, Oct. 20, 1910, *ibid.*
[39] Archibald Butt to Mrs. Lewis F. Butt, Feb. 14, 1909, Lawrence F. Abbott, ed., *The Letters of Archie Butt, Personal Aide to President Roosevelt,* 333–34.

"I trust we shall all be in good trim, and have a pleasant day."[40] The day was May 31, and Lincoln arrived with his aunt, Mrs. Helm, in Hodgenville by his private railroad car. The principal orator of the day was the newspaper editor, Henry Watterson, a long-time friend of Robert T. Lincoln. During the proceedings Lincoln became quite ill and had to be helped off the platform and back to his car.

The celebrations observing the birth of Abraham Lincoln continued as the years passed, but often his son was forced to decline invitations because of his health. President Taft invited Lincoln to travel in the presidential car to ceremonies in Springfield, in February, 1911, but Lincoln wrote that he could not go at all on the advice of his physicians.[41] In November of the same year, the Speed Memorial to Abraham Lincoln was dedicated at Frankfort, Kentucky. Governor Willson of Kentucky wrote inviting Lincoln to attend the dedication. According to the Louisville *Courier-Journal*, if he did come at all, he would not take part in the ceremonies but would be simply a spectator.[42] The state of Lincoln's health, however, was such that he replied to Governor Willson, "The occasion is one of such peculiar interest to me that nothing could have kept me from accepting your most kind invitation but absolute necessity."[43] At Frankfort the Governor read Lincoln's letter to the assemblage, which included President Taft, Henry Watterson, Governor Woodrow Wilson of New Jersey, and other distinguished guests.[44]

Although Lincoln had always considered Chicago his home, in his late sixties he made a change in his residence. As the winter of 1910 approached, he leased for four months the "Atwood residence at 1300 Seventeenth Street northwest," Washington, D.C. For the first time since 1885, he resided in the nation's capital.

Whether he will retain a permanent residence in Washington is

[40] Lincoln to Logan Murray, May 21, 1909, Princeton University Library.
[41] Lincoln to J. Otis Humphrey, Jan. 30, 1911, Humphrey Papers.
[42] Louisville *Courier-Journal*, Nov. 2, 1911.
[43] *Ibid.*, Nov. 9, 1911.
[44] *Ibid.*, Nov. 22, 1911.

not known. Mr. Lincoln has visited Washington several times since he formerly resided here, and often expressed a desire to live part of his time in this city. His professional duties, however, prevented the gratification of his desires. It is believed that if the Washington winter climate is found agreeable he will purchase the Atwood residence and with his family will occupy it a part of each winter.[45]

During that winter Lincoln was only technically in residence in Washington. Privately to his aunt he reported that he had left his wife and Jessie and her children in a "very comfortable house in Washington," but that he did not plan to be there much because he "could not possibly stand the racket of dining out which would come" upon him. Instead he was planning to stay in his old home in Chicago even if it was "a little lonesome."[46] Although Lincoln wrote that his work at Pullman "was in every way pleasant," in May, 1911, he resigned as president of the corporation and became chairman of the board. He resigned, he said, because he would have died if he had not.[47]

That same year Lincoln sold his old home at 60 Lake Shore Drive to Charles A. Monroe, a public utilities official,[48] and purchased a home in Washington. To a friend he wrote: "My residence there is 3014 N Street, in a part of Washington, which was formerly Georgetown. I live in a very old house which is interesting in various ways."[49] The house was a magnificent three-story brick mansion built about 1800 by John Laird to replace an earlier frame house located on the same lot. The Laird house passed into the Dunlop family by the marriage of the original owner's daughter to Judge James Dunlop. Ironically the Judge was removed from office for his southern sympathies by the father of the man who now became the owner of the house.[50] Robert T. Lincoln took a considerable pride in his home and in the history

45 Unidentified newspaper clipping, dated Nov. 13, 1910, Harvard University Archives.

46 Lincoln to Emelie Todd Helm, Dec. 14, 1910, copy in ISHL.

47 Lincoln to George H. Thatcher, May 9, 1912, quoted by Harry J. Dunbaugh, May 2, 1962.

48 Chicago *Daily News*, Oct. 6, 1939.

49 Lincoln to William L. Shearer, in Randall, *Lincoln's Sons*, 317–18.

50 Grace Dunlop Ecker, *A Portrait of Old George Town*, 108–12.

of the area. Thanking a lady for a copy of a history of Georgetown, which interested him greatly, he wrote in 1918, "I shall
look up the original boundary stone in our garden, which you
speak of." Then he regretfully added that he had had to cut down
three very large old oak trees that had died.[51]

The Georgetown home became Lincoln's winter residence,
and with the coming of summer he always journeyed north by his
private railroad car to "Hildene." There he took an interest in
local affairs: he was a trustee of the Mark Skinner Library, president of the Ekwanok Country Club for twenty-two years, and
"active in local charities."[52] The Lincolns would remain at
"Hildene" as long as possible. In November, 1912, Lincoln wrote
Helen Nicolay, "We are all very well and happy up here in the
mountains and all dread being driven away by the cold winter to
come."[53] He added, however, that he would have to leave the
next day for ten days of work in Chicago. Lincoln had a
keen interest in mathematics and astronomy. At "Hildene" he
had installed an observatory, which was described as "well
equipped."[54] Once Lincoln wrote to Nicholas Murray Butler that
his train would pass by a bright spot in the scenery which was the
observatory. There, he continued, "I look nightly into a horizon
where there is no Referendum or Recall and only one body which
is at once powerful and incalculably [erratic?] and though still
influential upon the Tides, is said to be dead. I refer only to the
moon."[55] Robert T. Lincoln had amassed a fortune and from
time to time would shut himself up in his library to go over his
account books and take an inventory of his holdings.[56]

After Lincoln's retirement he had much more time for golf,
playing usually with Robert M. Janney of Philadelphia, George
H. Thacher of Albany, and Horace G. Young of Albany. The

51 Lincoln to Cordelia Jackson, Aug. 3, 1918, CHS.

52 *New York Times*, July 27, 1926; Scott, "Lincoln," *New England Historical and
Genealogical Register*, Vol. LXXXI (July, 1927), 246.

53 Lincoln to Helen Nicolay, Nov. 7, 1912, Nicolay Papers.

54 *New York Times*, July 27, 1926.

55 Lincoln to Nicholas Murray Butler, June 16, 1913, Butler Papers, Columbia
University Library.

56 Mearns, *Lincoln Papers*, I, 97.

group became known as the "Lincoln Foursome."[57] Nicholas Murray Butler reported that Lincoln's "golf game was not of the best . . . , but was good enough."[58] Each year in March, Lincoln's love of golf and good companionship would take him to the Hotel Bon Air at Augusta, Georgia. There he would be joined by several others including Warren G. Harding, Senator Hale of Maine, Senator Hitchcock of Nebraska, Senator Brandegee of Connecticut, Senator Saulsbury of Delaware, Speaker of the House Gillett of Massachusetts, and Governor James M. Cox of Ohio. Known as the "Little Mothers," the group got its name from "a woman who insisted that when the group came together, it was for the purpose of rocking the cradle of the universe."[59] The "Little Mothers" played golf each day and then assembled from ten until midnight at a table for good talk. It was said that Robert Lincoln "told interesting and often amusing stories of his experiences."[60]

Even in retirement Lincoln could not escape public attention, much as he might try to avoid it. In the bitter 1912 presidential campaign Lincoln wrote a strongly worded letter to Theodore Roosevelt condemning his use of the name of Abraham Lincoln to support his "New Nationalism" policies.[61] Robert T. Lincoln was a devout Taft supporter. Twelve years after the 1912 campaign was over, a story was told in the press that involved Lincoln, Taft, and Roosevelt. In the 1912 Republican convention sixty-six Negro delegates held a balance of power between Taft and Roosevelt. Some of them went to General James S. Clarkson of Iowa, regarded as a friend of the Negro since years before when he had been active in the underground railroad, and asked for advice about how they should vote. At first Clarkson had nothing to say, but on the morning that the convention was to nominate a presidential candidate, he had an inspiration. He wrote a ten-page typed appeal addressed to a Negro delegate-at-large from Georgia, Henry Lincoln Johnson,

57 *New York Times,* July 27, 1926.
58 Nicholas Murray Butler, *Across the Busy Years,* I, 380.
59 *Ibid.,* I, 379–80.
60 *Ibid.*

The Robert T. Lincoln family arriving at the dedication
of the Lincoln Memorial, May 30, 1922.
Reproduced from a photograph in the collections
of the Library of Congress.

Chief Justice Taft, President Harding, and Robert T. Lincoln
at the dedication of the Lincoln Memorial.
Reproduced from a photograph in the collections
of the Library of Congress.

Robert T. Lincoln at the dedication of the Lincoln Memorial.
Usually camera-shy Mary Harlan Lincoln can be seen in the
background.
Reproduced from a photograph in the collections of the
Library of Congress.

in which he urged, "You and your sixty-five colleagues join in casting your votes for President for Robert T. Lincoln, the son of the Emancipator and a man fit in every requirement of ability and fidelity to be President . . . ."[62] The General's son, Grosvenor B. Clarkson, who typed the letter, at his father's orders took the letter to Theodore Roosevelt, who read it and said, "This is an inspiration. Go to it as fast as you can."[63] Young Clarkson then attempted to see Henry Lincoln Johnson but could not get into the convention hall; hence, the letter was never delivered. That morning Taft was nominated with 561 votes, while Roosevelt had 107 votes and the support of 344 who refused to vote. Thus Taft had twenty-one more votes than were needed. The assumption was that the Negro delegates voted principally for Taft, but if they had read the letter and only half of them had voted for Lincoln, then Roosevelt would have had the nomination. Grosvenor Clarkson later told the story and he believed that the letter could have prevented the renomination of Taft. There is, however, no additional confirmation for the story. As for Lincoln's views on his nomination for the presidency, he had written in May, 1912, that it was entirely out of the question; after all, he was sixty-nine years of age.[64]

Robert T. Lincoln's animosity toward Theodore Roosevelt lasted on through the campaign of 1916. During that election the Philadelphia merchant John Wanamaker actively worked to bring the former President and his Bull Moose supporters back into the Republican fold to present a united front behind Charles Evans Hughes, who was running against President Wilson. The return was to be made public by a speech Roosevelt would make in behalf of Hughes on the evening of November 3, 1916. The place was to be Cooper Union in New York City, and the rally would, of course, invoke the spirit of Abraham Lincoln who many years before had spoken there. Wanamaker telegraphed

---

61 *New York Times*, July 27, 1926.
62 *Ibid.*, June 1, 1924.
63 *Ibid.*
64 Lincoln to George H. Thatcher, May 9, 1912, quoted by Harry J. Dunbaugh, May 2, 1962.

thirty prominent Republican businessmen, some members of the old guard and others mild progressives, to join with him in inviting the former Rough Rider and President. All but two accepted. Joseph H. Choate said he could not sign. The other person refusing to take part was Robert T. Lincoln, who said that there were "circumstances that made it impossible for him to join in the invitation."[65] Thus, when Theodore Roosevelt spoke in the same room that President Lincoln had and used the same desk and chair that Lincoln had used, Robert T. Lincoln was not among "The flower of Republicanism in the East" that witnessed the "return of Theodore Roosevelt to the Republican party."[66] Lincoln did manage, however, to refer to himself as a friend of the former President. In February, 1916, there was a rumor that Lincoln or Leonard Wood had been an emissary between Roosevelt and Elihu Root in some preconvention matters. Although Lincoln did deny the matter with "a laugh," he also spoke of himself as on good terms with both parties.[67]

In the spring of 1915, Lincoln was again in the public eye, this time in his capacity as chairman of the board of Pullman. The Federal Commission on Industrial Relations held hearings in Washington on the matter of the porters employed by Pullman. The company's position was that since it employed some 6,500 men it was one of the great benefactors of the Negro. Although the corporation had paid out dividends of $161,000,000 within the past year, it paid its porters $27.50 a month. Under questioning, Mr. Lincoln conceded that the porter's job was a "blind alley" with no chance of promotion. Frank P. Walsh, the chairman of the Commission, asked Lincoln if it was true that the complaints of the Pullman employees about their working conditions never reached the Pullman board. The reply was that "it would be rather hard to get the board together for such a purpose."[68] Observing that one porter had testified that his monthly income was $87.50 from tips plus his $27.50 salary, Walsh posed

---

[65] Herbert A. Gibbons, *John Wanamaker*, II, 397–98.
[66] *Ibid.*
[67] *New York Times*, Feb. 20, 1916.
[68] *Ibid.*, May 5, 1915.

the question, "Would you or any self-respecting member of your Board of Directors be willing to take your pay in the same way, Mr. Lincoln?" The reply was, "Oh, no, and I must say that this arrangement of tips is not a nice one at all. But it is an old one." The witness added with a chuckle, "and one to which the colored race is accustomed. The public seems to be fond of it. The little services a porter can do—brush your clothes, see that your dinner is served, or run and get a newspaper—such things seem to justify the tip."[69] Next Lincoln was asked if Pullman had ever considered abolishing tipping, and gave a negative reply. Questioning along other lines elicited the information that Pullman porters were required to purchase their uniforms at Marshall Field and Company, but Mr. Lincoln denied that Chauncey M. Keep, trustee of the Field estate, who also served on the Pullman board, had anything to do with that. On the subject of employer's liability, Lincoln testified that if an employee was injured on the job he could sue the company, but, as a practical matter, Pullman always settled these claims. Speaking of a federal Employer's Liability Act, the witness said that he "would start out in a friendly way toward that proposition." Finally, Robert T. Lincoln "begged to be excused" and that closed the matter.[70] The next day the *New York Times* editorialized that seldom had any employer been as frank as Mr. Lincoln was in admitting that the public paid the wages of its employees with tips. It further noted that while the general public accepted this arrangement and with it the superior-inferior relationship it involved, the newspaper felt that any honorable work should be paid for in agreed-upon wages.[71]

69 *Ibid.*
70 *Ibid.*
71 *Ibid.*, May 6, 1915.

Chapter 15

The Final Decade

Despite the fact that Lincoln was now supposed to be retired, he was in the midst of a remarkably busy schedule. Indeed his activities were limited only by the state of his health, which was at times poor. In October, 1916, he wrote his Aunt Emelie from "Hildene" that he was steadily getting better but that in ten days he would have to go to the annual meeting of the Pullman Company. He was unfortunately dreading the journey, probably in part due to Mrs. Lincoln's health troubles: "Mary concluded to have a little breakdown on her own account a couple of weeks ago, due largely I think to my troubles, but she is having very good care of course and will be on her feet again I think in a very short time." He noted that their daughter Jessie was with them so she could stay with her mother while her father was absent on business.[1] On November 1, Lincoln wrote a friend that he had had "a very uncomfortable summer," but now he seemed to be improving in health.[2] Early the next year, when Aunt Emelie herself was ill, Lincoln wrote to her daughter, "I have myself been much alarmed by the effects of high pressure and nervousness . . . ." He asked her to tell her mother to avoid worry, for "that has been a good while my best medicine and I am glad to say that I am steadily improving with it."[3]

1 Lincoln to Emelie Todd Helm, Oct. 28, 1916, copy in ISHL.
2 Lincoln to Judd Stewart, Nov. 1, 1916, Huntington Library.

In the following months the correspondence between Lincoln and the Helms continued to emphasize health problems. On March 7, 1917, Lincoln wrote that Washington had been in the uproar "always caused by the inauguration business," but he and his wife had taken no part, "for we are not feeling well enough to do so."[4] Still some days later he observed, "I am enjoying life somewhat more."[5] Throughout 1917, Lincoln's condition continued to improve, and in September he reported to Mrs. Helm that he was "a good deal better in health," so that he was trying to get through a backlog of work, and also attempting to get in a daily round of golf. Nothing more than concern over an early frost, which ruined their bean crop and, according to Mrs. Lincoln, threatened the corn crop, now troubled the couple.[6] In November, Lincoln was again bound for Chicago to attend the usual Pullman meeting.[7]

One of his pleasures during this time was being an elector of the Hall of Fame, a position he held from 1910 to 1920. Lincoln took a lively interest in the balloting to choose the distinguished of the past.

All of his life Robert T. Lincoln gave evidence of being fundamentally a kindly and generous individual. Sometimes his concern for others was expressed through an organization, such as his being a member of the incorporating body when Congress granted the American Red Cross a new charter in 1905,[8] or an institution, such as his sending a one-thousand-dollar contribution to the Westminster (formerly Second) Presbyterian Church of Springfield in 1907.[9] Although he generally managed to cover up his good works and deeds, when his sympathy was aroused there were few limits to his willingness to do something for another person. While he was president of Pullman, he called one day at the home of a former servant in his household. In the

---

3 Lincoln to Kate Helm, Feb. 10, 1917, copy in ISHL.
4 Lincoln to Kate Helm, Mar. 7, 1917, copy *ibid.*
5 Lincoln to Emelie Todd Helm, Mar. 19, 1917, copy *ibid.*
6 Lincoln to Mrs. Helm, Sept. 13, 1917, copy *ibid.*
7 Lincoln to Mrs. Helm, Nov. 13, 1917, copy *ibid.*
8 United States Congress, 58 Cong., *U.S. Statutes at Large*, 599–602.
9 Lincoln to Clinton L. Conkling, Jan. 14, 1907, Conkling Papers.

family was a crippled child who had never ridden on a train and longed to do so. Immediately the visitor took the boy to the railroad yards, commandeered a locomotive, and the pair went for a long ride.

Relatives, old friends, former employees, and others who had fallen on evil days found a ready response from Robert T. Lincoln. Typical of this sort of thing was a letter to a man in St. Louis regarding a letter Lincoln had received from a distant relative, Miss Margaret Ann Todd:

> I have had such annoying experiences in many matters of this kind that I am always at a loss if I do not have somewhat accurate knowledge as to just what is right to do in answering applications such as she makes to me. I have much misgiving. I do not remember that I ever met her personally; at least if I did it must have been when I was a small child. I know nothing whatever of her characteristics, and as to whether she is reasonably careful with money when she has it. Of course I do not imagine that she has had very much; but I have known cases where women, however poor they were, seemed utterly reckless in their extravagances, comparatively speaking, with money in their pockets.

Enclosed in the letter was a note to Miss Todd containing a check for one hundred dollars. Lincoln did not consider his duty completed with that, though, for he asked the St. Louisian to tell him what he "ought to do for her in her trouble besides the little present" he was sending.[10]

Family matters of a different nature caused him concern too. In 1914, J. M. Spencer, president of Sayre College, Lexington, Kentucky, wrote a biographical sketch of Mrs. Abraham Lincoln, which he submitted to Robert Sterling Yard, editor of *Century Magazine*.[11] Yard wrote Lincoln to ask his opinion of the matter, and Lincoln wrote in reply:

My dear Mr. Yard:

I was just starting to write to you when your note of yesterday

[10] Lincoln to Daniel Breck, Aug. 5, 1911, Lincoln Memorial University Library.
[11] J. M. Spencer to Robert Sterling Yard, Apr. 10, 1914, New York Public Library.

came and I am returning to you the three pieces of Spencer manuscript. As I have already expressed to you, I appreciate very greatly your action in the matter. I entirely agree with the views you gave in your first letter and on the general subject there is nothing I care to add. Spencer's article contains some trivial absurdities but I confess I was most surprised by its lack of any literary style, that is, good style. I thought him more highly educated than he appears to be. I shall take no steps against or through him to stop its publication, but am very glad that, put in better form or not, it is not to appear in the Century Magazine.

Aside from the consideration you express, I have feelings which spring from my own peculiar position, and the kindness which you have shown me, as did Mr. Gilder some years ago in regard to some of my mother's letters, leads me to write to you in a way in which I would not wish to do to a stranger.

It became evident to me soon after my father's death, that the shock of all the dreadful circumstances had deranged my mother mentally but not at first to a degree which justified me in invoking any judicial action; I could not hold her back from doing many things that distressed me beyond any power of description; advertising her old clothes for sale and writing begging letters by the hundreds, were only a part of what I had to grieve and be mortified about; there was any quantity of newspaper publicity about her actions and writings and much of my time was spent in sadly answering inquiries about her. It all nearly wore my life out.

At last her conduct became dangerous to herself and in June, 1875, acting in concert with some old friends of my father and myself, I presented her case to the proper tribunal in Chicago and she was placed in a private asylum. After a prolonged stay there her health seemed to improve so much that my aunt, her sister, Mrs. Ninian Edwards, of Springfield, undertook to care for her in her own house and this she did until my mother's death in 1882.

You can well understand that I could not be happy in the prospect of a reopening of all the unhappy history the nature of which I am only suggesting.

In April, 1910, Spencer called on me and upon his representation of the needs of his school, I, feeling a little sentimental interest in Lexinton [*sic*], Kentucky, gave him a thousand dollars and he departed seemingly thankful. A year later, when I was in such bad health that I resigned the presidency of the Pullman Company, he turned up again and pressed me to give him one hundred thousand dollars as a "Memorial" of my mother. I declined to do so. He thereupon began to go about among people in Chicago well known to me socially, pressing on them his so-called memorial scheme. I suppose most of these people very naturally wondered why, if I thought well of the memorial, I did not myself pay for it. Having learned that in my absence he was coming to my old office a good deal, and had asked my successor, Mr. Runnells, to head his "Committee," I wrote to my old Secretary, then Assistant to the President of the Pullman Company, to tell Mr. Runnells to have nothing to do with him and to tell Spencer I wished him to keep away from our building as I was highly offended by his conduct. It was and is my belief that Spencer, believing that what he was doing was very annoying to me, schemed that I would stop it by giving him the money. I may be wrong, but that is my belief. Feeling in that way, as I do, I will of course, have nothing to do with him; he has written to me several times and has sent me literature about his scheme but I make no reply to him.

I thank you again for what you have decided to do.

> Believe me,
> Very sincerely yours,
> ROBERT T. LINCOLN[12]

During the latter part of his life, Lincoln became involved in some noteworthy disputes over some statues of his father. Long a man of strong likes and dislikes, he had never hesitated to express his views on representations, artistic or realistic, of the President and his family. He liked, for example, the Brady photograph of the Chief Executive seated with Tad nearby and both looking at what many thought was a Bible. (Robert Lincoln pointed out that it was a photograph album.[13]) When someone sent him another picture for inspection, he returned it with the comment:

[It] seems to be based on some attempted likeness of President Lincoln. If taken as it seems to have been, from a death mask, it

[12] Lincoln to Robert Sterling Yard, Apr. 15, 1914, *ibid.*
[13] Lincoln to Marcus J. Wright, Jan. 6, 1898, ISHL.

has all the disagreeable qualities of such a work, and I can only say it is the worst thing of the sort I have ever seen in the way of a likeness.[14]

As the years passed and the popularity of Abraham Lincoln became world-wide, many more artistic representations were made. To Clinton Conkling, Lincoln wrote in 1917 that he had been amazed to receive a list of the statues of the President that had been erected in the United States. He had not guessed there were so many, but unfortunately no statue to date had really captured a true likeness, as marble and bronze are "utterly different from what is seen in life." As for some of the statues:

> I do not like positively the Vinnie Reme [*sic*] statue in the Capitol here. I do not like the crouching attitude of Mr. Borglum's statue in Newark, N.J. With its pedestal it is all so low that the pedestal and body of the statue are used as a play ground by the hoodlum children of the neighborhood.

Almost ruefully he noted that only twice had he ever been asked for advice regarding statues "before it was too late to have any suggestions of mine adopted."[15]

George G. Barnard executed a statue of Abraham Lincoln to which Robert T. Lincoln greatly objected. The controversy that followed "degenerated to the level of the ranting of demagogues in the fury of a political campaign."[16] To many the statue was a great work of art. Some called it the "stomach-ache" Lincoln, for the President's hands are placed over the area of the anatomy in such a manner as to indicate some sort of internal troubles. Robert T. Lincoln insisted, "I personally never saw my father in such an attitude, that is to say, with the hands crossed on the stomach."[17] To William Howard Taft, Lincoln complained that the sculptor "scorned" photographs of the President, "and took

14 Lincoln to S. Townsend, Apr. 8, 1918, Lincoln National Life Insurance Company.
15 Lincoln to Clinton L. Conkling, Nov. 24, 1917, Conkling Papers. Lincoln's advice had been sought for works by Saint-Gaudens and Daniel Chester French.
16 Lauriston Bullard, *Lincoln in Marble and Bronze*, 228–41, contains an account of the episode.
17 Lincoln to Truman H. Bartlett, Oct. 27, 1917, Boston University Library.

as a model for his figure a man chosen by him for the curious artistic reasons that he was six feet four and one-half inches in height; was born on a farm fifteen miles from where Lincoln was born; was about forty years of age and had been splitting rails all his life." The result was a "monstrous figure."[18] Writing to Isaac Markens, Lincoln said of the statue, "I think it is simply horrible," and he complained that it was also "grotesque."[19]

In June, 1917, the *Art World* had the first of a series of anti-Barnard statue articles.[20] Pleased, Lincoln complimented the editor, F. Wellington Ruckstuhl, although he explained that he had only recently become acquainted with the magazine. "My only excuse is that I have been pretty well occupied in business and that in my recreations I have rather devoted myself to scientific and historical publications.[21] Before long, others had jumped into the argument and other journals were involved pro and con. George Bernard Shaw joined the crowd,[22] as did Theodore Roosevelt. To Ruckstuhl, Lincoln replied that he had not seen an issue of *The Outlook*, but he understood "that Colonel Roosevelt was deelighted [*sic*] at any new thing, as usual."[23] To another, Lincoln aired his views on "The Colonel" and his statements on the statue:

> Confidentially, also, as you were, I am not greatly surprised at anything in regard to the Colonel. He is a very strong and able man. The trouble is that the gun he fires is a very large one, and when it goes off at half-cock it makes a great deal of noise and is apt to cause a great deal of trouble. But for all this, I should gratefully welcome any form of recantation he should authorize. He, however, is not apt to make his recantation as loudly as his original.[24]

Early in the row when Lincoln wrote to William Howard Taft,

18 Lincoln to William Howard Taft, Mar. 22, 1917, Huntington Library.
19 "Robert Todd Lincoln and the Barnard Statue," *Chicago History*, (Summer, 1966), 356.
20 Bullard, *Lincoln*, 229.
21 Lincoln to F. Wellington Ruckstuhl, Sept. 3, 1917, Huntington Library.
22 Bullard, *Lincoln*, 230–33.
23 Lincoln to Ruckstuhl, Sept. 12, 1917, Huntington Library.
24 Lincoln to Judd Stewart, Jan. 8, 1918, *ibid.*

he asked the former President to use his influence with his half-brother, Charles, who was donating the statue to be placed in England, to have something like the Saint-Gaudens erected instead. If used, the Barnard would cause him "sorrow."[25] He was able to take some cheer from the fact that: "There are so many good men working, and so vigorously, against its going to Europe that I have not lost hope of success, although the obstinacy of the London Commissioner will be very hard to overcome."[26] Only a month earlier he had written that he had heard that the statue was in New York, but he doubted that it would ever cross the ocean.[27] In the end, Robert T. Lincoln had his way in part; the Barnard work did cross the ocean and was placed in Manchester, England, but London received a replica of the Saint-Gaudens work. It has been said that it was better for London to have Lincoln the president rather than Lincoln of the prairie.[28]

While the Barnard controversy was raging, another was beginning. The state of Illinois was about to place a statue of Lincoln in front of the capitol at Springfield. This one by Andrew O'Connor was still under way when Lincoln was given an opportunity to view it and make suggestions. He agreed to go to New York on an inspection trip, provided it was not too late to make changes if he saw the need for them.[29] When it developed that it would be necessary for Lincoln to go to Worcester instead, his physician advised against the journey.[30] Early in 1918, Lincoln wrote Conkling that he had seen a photograph of the O'Connor work and it looked relatively satisfactory. However, some items did not please. The collar worn by the President seemed to resemble a misshapen muffler and the waist coat was absurdly wrinkled, to mention only two of the objections he had.[31]

25 Lincoln to William Howard Taft, Mar. 22, 1917, *ibid.*
26 Lincoln to Truman H. Bartlett, Nov. 21, 1917, Boston University Library.
27 Lincoln to Charles T. White, Oct. 19, 1917, Lincoln Memorial University Library.
28 Bullard, *Lincoln*, 238–39.
29 Lincoln to Clinton L. Conkling (telegram) Nov. 27, 1917, Conkling Papers.
30 Lincoln to Conkling, Nov. 30, 1917, *ibid.*; Lincoln to Conkling (telegram), Dec. 1, 1917, *ibid.*
31 Lincoln to Conkling, Feb. 26, 1918, *ibid.*

THE OVERLOAD CAUSED BY THE WORLD WAR coupled with weather conditions had brought American railroads to a state of complete collapse, and Lincoln felt the pressure of his work. On New Year's Day, 1918, the president and other officials of the Pullman Company met at the Washington home of the chairman of the board.[32] Later in the month Lincoln complained, "Everything here is chaotic." and since coal was in short supply for two days he had had none.[33] When spring came the Lincolns again made their journey from Washington to Vermont, although they could not have their usual freight car for baggage owing to the rail situation.[34] In November, 1918, the war ended, and Lincoln could write that he was in as good health as an old man could expect.[35] Unfortunately, neither his good health nor his peace of mind would last long.

Lincoln had never been very fond of Woodrow Wilson, and just prior to the 1917 declaration of war, he had written a friend:

> Just now here, as you can imagine, things are very much disturbed and at the Club, where I usually have a daily outing, there is much discussion and speculation; the general thought being that we may hear of the issuance of something important from the White House at any moment, most of the talkers thinking it will be the announcement of the break in our German relations. I hardly know what to think about what may first happen; perhaps the President will await some disastrous occurrence which is likely to come under the recent German announcement. For one, I wish the government was in the control of men possessing greater ability and statesmanship than is possessed, in my opinion, by those who are now in charge.[36]

In the postwar period Lincoln was a staunch critic of Wilson. In February, 1919, he wrote his aunt that the general condition of the country was worrying him but there was nothing either of

32 Lincoln to Judd Stewart, Jan. 2, 1918, Huntington Library.
33 Lincoln to Clinton L. Conkling, Jan. 25, 1918, ISHL.
34 Lincoln to Emelie Todd Helm, Mar. 22, 1918, copy *ibid.*
35 Lincoln to Mrs. Helm, Jan. 5, 1919, copy *ibid.*
36 Lincoln to Jacob M. Dickinson, Feb. 2, 1917, Dickinson Papers, Tennessee State Archives.

them could do. The trouble was in large part that "Wilson seems to be letting Congress adjourn next Tuesday, himself going to Europe for an indefinite stay—apparently serious affairs don't bother him."[37] Later on in the year he wrote in a similar vein:

> I am, as is everybody except Mr. Wilson, greatly disturbed by the general condition of our public affairs, both from the political & the business point of view. It almost looks as though there is to be a great breakdown in nearly all large business enterprises—but there is no good in worrying.[38]

In September, Lincoln simply observed, "What a mess we are all in!"[39] At least he had been in fairly good health that summer.[40] For the improved health of the country in 1920 he had a suggestion; "I am earnestly in favor of Senator Harding's election and believe that we will all be more happy when Wilson & all his friends are out of the government." Unfortunately, by August of that election year he was bothered by "a nearly constant nervous indigestion," so great as to interfere with his business affairs.[41]

Throughout these years Lincoln was mulling over a problem that had been with him for some time. What should he do with his father's papers still in his possession? The manuscripts were his property since he was the only surviving member of the President's immediate family. As early as 1882, Lincoln was pressed to make a final disposition of the papers but he had side-stepped the issue by saying that he would be happy to do so, "if there was anything of sufficient consequence to include in such a collection."[42] Around the turn of the century, Lincoln wrote:

> If my son was still alive, I should probably leave the papers in his hands, but as it is, I think it my duty to select some depository for them, just what it will be I am not yet prepared to say.[43]

[37] Lincoln to Mrs. Helm, Feb. 27, 1919, copy in ISHL.

[38] Lincoln to Mrs. Helm, July 21, 1919, copy *ibid.*

[39] Lincoln to Judd Stewart, Sept. 26, 1919, Huntington Library.

[40] Lincoln to Stewart, Sept. 14, 1919, *ibid.*

[41] Lincoln to Mrs. Helm, Aug. 20, 1920, copy in ISHL.

[42] Lincoln to Albert D. Hager, secretary of the Chicago Historical Society, Aug. 27, 1882, CHS.

[43] Lincoln to Herbert Putnam, librarian of Congress, Jan. 1902, quoted in Mearns, *Lincoln Papers*, I, 90–91.

For years Lincoln had been willing to give away sample auto-graphs of his father, but in 1909 he was forced to reply to a re-quest that the supply of these had long ago been exhausted and that the papers left were "of such a character that they ought to go to societies, libraries, or other places of record where they can have proper and permanent care."[44]

The papers were not actually in Lincoln's hands. After the completion of the Nicolay and Hay work, they had remained stored in Washington in the custody of Nicolay. Following his death in 1901, they were divided into two lots: one group was stored in a bank vault in Washington, and the other, composed of letters to the President, remained in the custody of Miss Helen Nicolay until Robert T. Lincoln arranged for them to be placed in the vaults of the State Department where John Hay was then secretary. After the death of John Hay, Lincoln took direct charge of the papers and kept them with him. When he went to "Hil-dene" in the summer, they traveled with him and then came back again in the fall to Washington. In November, 1917, he wrote Clinton Conkling that as soon as his freight car arrived he was going to go through his "seven Lincoln trunks."[45]

This he did do, spending the first months of 1918 at the task. In a letter written to Helen Nicolay at the end of March, he mentioned something he had found while cleaning up his father's papers.[46] Not long after, he explained that his reply to a letter was delayed because he was engaged "in the midst of a great deal of other pressing work, in going over and putting into better order a large mass of papers relative to President Lincoln's Ad-ministration."[47]

In connection with the publication of the great collection of papers, David C. Mearns has told in elaborate detail the story of the long campaign carried on by the Library of Congress to secure possession of the Abraham Lincoln papers. At last, on May 6,

44 Lincoln to Mrs. Albert M. Smith, Mar. 3, 1909, ISHL.

45 Lincoln to Clinton L. Conkling, Nov. 17, 1917, Conkling Papers.

46 Lincoln to Helen Nicolay, Mar. 27, 1918, Lincoln National Life Insurance Company.

47 Lincoln to William K. Boyd, Apr. 4, 1918, Duke University Library.

1919, a memorandum was sent to the chief of the mail division, at the Library:

> Please have the wagon call at Mr. Robert T. Lincoln's house, 3014 N Street, N.W., for seven trunks of papers to be delivered unopened to the Manuscript Division.
> The wagon should be there at nine o'clock tomorrow.[48]

One might suppose that the long-awaited transfer of the papers would be a news-worthy item. It was, but no public announcement was made until 1923, due to the following conditions laid down by Lincoln when he put the papers in the Library:

1. That the papers are in the Library is to be kept from the public.
2. One of the officials of the Library is to examine and arrange them under the direction of Mr. Lincoln.
3. The papers are to be consulted only after permission has been granted by Mr. Lincoln.[49]

The papers were to become public property in the event of Lincoln's death.

In January, 1923, Robert T. Lincoln changed the conditions of his gift. He had drawn a document which contained the provision, lacking previously, that the Abraham Lincoln papers were not to be subject to "official inspection or private view until after the expiration of twenty-one years (21) from the date of my death."[50] This famous condition is popularly assumed to have been invoked due to Lincoln's problems with Albert J. Beveridge.

Over the years other legends concerning the papers came into existence. One of the more important came to light in 1939, when Nicholas Murray Butler told of having Horace G. Young, a close friend of Lincoln's, call upon him with the distressing news that Robert Lincoln was burning his father's papers. According to Butler, he went the next day after Young called to see Lincoln and found him sitting in front of a wood fire with a trunk stand-

---

48 Mearns, *Lincoln Papers*, I, 100–101.
49 *Ibid.*, I, 101.
50 *Ibid.*, I, 103.

ing nearby. When Butler asked Lincoln if he was going somewhere, he received a negative reply. Whereupon Butler asked
what the trunk was doing in the room.

> "Well," said Lincoln quietly, "It contains only some family
> papers which I am going to burn."
> "What are you going to do?" I said, in startled fashion. "Burn
> your family papers! Why, Robert Lincoln, those papers do not
> belong to you. Your father has been the property of the nation for
> fifty years, and those papers belong to the nation. That you should
> destroy them would be incredible."

Butler and Lincoln then discussed the matter for an hour, and
at last the latter said:

> "All right, but no one must see them while I live."
> "Very well," I said. "Then deposit them in the Library of Con-
> gress and fix a date before which they shall not be opened."[51]

This story has often been repeated with minor changes in detail, but unfortunately it has one great flaw in it. Butler gave the
date of his conversation with Lincoln as August, 1923, and insisted that the date was correct as late as 1947, the year before
his death.[52] However, the Lincoln papers had been placed in the
Library of Congress in 1919.

Assuming that Mr. Butler did see Lincoln preparing to burn
some papers, the obvious question is what papers did Lincoln
have before him. Perhaps they were his own private papers. Perhaps he was going through some papers that he had not turned
over to the Library of Congress. Another matter, closely related to
this, is whether or not Robert T. Lincoln destroyed any of his
father's papers. Again there is no final answer, nor is there any
evidence to indicate that he did. His granddaughter once saw
him burn some papers, but what they were is not clear.[53] Abra-

51 Butler, *Across the Busy Years*, I, 375–76. Ida Tarbell also feared that Lincoln
would burn the manuscripts. Ida Tarbell, *All in a Day's Work*, 169–70.

52 Butler Papers.

53 Mearns, *Lincoln Papers*, I, 130.

ham Lincoln's papers, it has been observed, are primarily lacking in personal correspondence to and from his family.[54] Once, when pressed for letters from his father, Robert Lincoln answered, "He wrote me a few letters when I was in college, but unhappily I gave them away to begging autograph hunters at the time."[55] In 1916, Lincoln commented that his own "letter press books" were in "perfect order," but that a particular letter for which he was searching had probably been "destroyed with an immense number of old letters and papers when I broke up my residence in Chicago . . . ."[56]

On October 17, 1919, Robert T. Lincoln, taking cognizance of the fact that he was then in his middle seventies, made his will. That same year he established trust funds of approximately one million dollars for each of his daughters.[57] With the first World War over, the nation plunged into the "Roaring Twenties," and Lincoln lived on as a relic of a bygone era. Because of his unique position, he continued to remain in the public's mind. On occasion he would be asked questions about matters of the moment. For instance, where did he stand on the question of a soldier's bonus for veterans of the Great War? His answer was, "I beg that you will excuse me from expressing any opinion at all with reference to that matter."[58] More often the letters were connected in some way with the Lincoln legend. Typical of dozens of the period was a reply on February 5, 1925, to Dr. John Wesley Hill:

> I beg to acknowledge receipt of your kind invitation to be present at a luncheon to be given by the Trustees of the Lincoln Memorial University on Thursday, February 12th at the New

[54] *Ibid.*

[55] Lincoln to Caroline McIlvaine, secretary of the Chicago Historical Society, Feb. 8, 1921, CHS.

[56] Lincoln to Duane Mowry, May 20, 1916, in *Journal of the Illinois State Historical Society*, Vol. XIII, No. 4 (January, 1921), 475.

[57] Estate of Robert Todd Lincoln, *24 Reports of the United States Board of Tax Appeals*, 335.

[58] Lincoln to S. C. G. Watkins, Feb. 20, 1924, Yale University Library.

Willard Hotel, and regret very much that the condition of my
health prevents me from accepting the same.

    With all good wishes for the success of the occasion, believe me,

Sincerely,

ROBERT T. LINCOLN[59]

By 1920, Lincoln's life had settled into a well-regulated routine.
His health was always a major concern. In addition to his other
troubles he suffered from a chronic condition of the eyelids,
which required daily treatment; although "an annoying condition," it in no way endangered his life.[60] "His hearing was unusually acute, and although he wore glasses, his eyesight was good
and he was a constant reader. He played golf until within two
years of his death," and then gave it up only because his physician
was fearful that he might fall on the rough, rocky golf course at
Manchester.[61] A typical day in his life was one in which:

> He took his breakfast in bed and remained there until after his
> physician's visit between 10 and 11 a.m. . . . . He then rose, dressed,
> and went to his library, where he looked over his morning mail and
> attended to his correspondence. . . . . This occupied the time until
> luncheon, which was served at 1:30. . . . .
> Lincoln rested about half an hour after luncheon and almost
> daily, unless the weather prevented, went for a drive, saw his friends
> at the country club, or made calls on them. Returning home, he
> either rested or read until dinner, dined with his family, joined
> them in the library until 10 p.m. and then went to bed. Ordinarily
> he read until 11 or 12 o'clock before turning out his light.[62]

Lincoln did not entirely give up all business activities, for at
his death he was still a director of the Continental and Commercial Bank of Chicago, the Commonwealth Edison Company,
also of Chicago, and the Pullman Company. He continued as
chairman of the board of Pullman until January 14, 1922, and
only ten days before his death he volunteered to go to New York

---

[59] Lincoln to John Wesley Hill, Feb. 5, 1925, Lincoln Memorial University Library.
[60] Estate of Robert Todd Lincoln, 336.
[61] *Ibid.*
[62] *Ibid.*, 337.

258

for a company meeting in order to assure a quorum of the board of directors.[63]

Lincoln's connections with Illinois were, for the most part, severed. He had not been in Springfield since 1909.[64] In 1920 he wrote, "I have really been absent from Chicago and Illinois for so many years that I feel like a stranger there."[65] Almost wistfully he noted, "Since the death of Mr. Conkling and later of Mr. George Latham, there is not now in Springfield, I feel quite sure, a single one of my old men friends or even acquaintances who might write to me."[66] When the question arose of who the custodian of the Lincoln home was to be, Robert T. Lincoln wanted it to be his cousin, Mary Edwards Brown. If she were forced to move out, he said, "the house will be left entirely naked, and possibly some future manager will ornament it—as a former one did—with a picture of Wilkes-Booth on the Mantel piece."[67]

In Kentucky there remained Mrs. Helm and her family, and Lincoln's letters to them were full of the details of his ill health, always a safe subject to correspond about with relatives. In June, 1921, he complained, "I have been in great trouble from nervous prostration," but he did feel a little better. Of his wife he wrote, "Mary is happily, quite well and takes the best possible care of me. None of our children or grandchildren are with us as things are getting where very little bother unduly troubles both of us."[68] A year later he was struggling to get to "Hildene": "I do not anticipate a very pleasant summer there in the condition of my health."[69] The doctors told him his trouble was "nervous dyspepsia," and in February, 1923, he wrote Mrs. Helm that he had suffered a "severe attack."[70] However, in 1924 and 1925 his health improved a little, and in May of the latter year, he wrote his cousin Kate that he would leave for Vermont on May 27 to stay

63 *Pullman News*, Aug., 1926.
64 *Illinois State Journal*, July 26, 1926.
65 Lincoln to Mary Edwards Brown, Dec. 27, 1920, ISHL.
66 Lincoln to Mary Edwards Brown, Mar. 16, 1921, *ibid.*
67 Lincoln to Mary Edwards Brown, June 24, 1921, *ibid.*
68 Lincoln to Emelie Todd Helm, June 24, 1921, copy *ibid.*
69 Lincoln to Mrs. Helm, June 24, 1922, copy *ibid.*
70 Lincoln to Mrs. Helm, Feb. 26, 1923, copy *ibid.*

there until late October or November, "as usual." He was as well as a man of eighty-two could expect, "though, as you know, I am not exactly 'spry.' "[71] From Vermont he wrote his aunt Emelie that he was having a pleasant time and that his daughter Mrs. Isham was in Manchester, while his granddaughter was staying at "Hildene."[72]

The last major public appearance of Robert T. Lincoln was on the occasion of the dedication of the memorial to his father in Washington. The weather was good May 30, 1922, and a large crowd, including Mary Harlan Lincoln, was in attendance. "Applause greeted arriving dignitaries; the ovation of the day was bestowed on Robert Todd Lincoln as he walked to his seat on the platform."[73] William Howard Taft spoke of the history of the building of the memorial; the president of Tuskegee Institute delivered an oration; Edwin Markham read "Lincoln, The Man of the People"; and President Warren G. Harding also spoke.[74] Because of his age and poor health, plus his personal inclinations, the son of the honored President did not speak. The memorial pleased Robert Lincoln; it was said that whenever he went out for a drive in the capital "the itinerary always included a turn around the temple on the Mall, and that as the car approached the steps he would call to the chauffer, 'Stop the carriage, stop the carriage!' and looking up at that luminous, brooding figure, he would exclaim, 'Isn't it beautiful?' "[75]

Lincoln was very proud of the honors paid to his father. In acknowledging receipt of some books, he wrote: "They are very gratifying indications of the public regard in which my father's memory is held, and I am, of course, very grateful for it. You would be surprised to know how widely extended these indications are; never a day comes that I do not get some letter relating to him, and the books which come are also numerous."[76]

---

71 Lincoln to Kate Helm, May 18, 1925, copy *ibid.*
72 Lincoln to Mrs. Helm, Aug. 5, 1925, copy *ibid.*
73 Bullard, *Lincoln*, 340.
74 Allen C. Clark, *Abraham Lincoln in the National Capital*, 171–72.
75 Mearns, *Lincoln Papers*, I, 108–109.

Occasionally he still spoke out to defend his father's memory. In 1922 he denied that his father had ever made anti-Catholic utterances or had been anti-Catholic in thought. In a letter to the editor of a Knights of Columbus publication, he observed that the President's name had become "a peg on which to hang many things." Specifically, Lincoln insisted:

> I know of no anti-Catholic utterance made by my father. The only instance known to me of my father's referring in any way to the subject is in a letter to Archbishop Hughes of New York, in which he requested the Archbishop to give him the name or names of suitable persons of the Catholic Church whom he might with propriety designate as chaplains in our military service.

However, Lincoln did note that a United States senator was currently quoting Abraham Lincoln's statements on the question which the member of Congress had obtained through the "report of a spiritualistic medium."[77]

Once in a while Lincoln had distinguished visitors either in Vermont or Washington. In July, 1923, Governor Alfred E. Smith called at "Hildene."[78] Later in the year the train carrying David Lloyd George, former prime minister of England, passed through Vermont and stopped at Manchester. Lincoln boarded it and chatted a few minutes with the British statesman.[79]

The year 1926 began routinely enough. Lincoln was present in February when his mother's portrait was presented to the White House.[80] In March and April, to cut down on his income tax, he gave to his wife of fifty-seven years over one million and one-quarter dollars in securities, consisting of stocks and bonds.[81] On May 11, somewhat early for them, the Lincolns left Washington for Manchester.[82] Lincoln reported that the trip, made in the

76 Lincoln to Clarence H. Howard, Feb. 1, 1921, Lincoln Memorial University Library.

77 *New York Times*, Feb. 12, 1922.

78 *Ibid.*, July 16, 1923.

79 *Ibid.*, Oct. 7, 1923; Frank Owen, *Tempestuous Journey*, 669.

80 *New York Times*, Feb. 19, 1926.

81 Estate of Robert Todd Lincoln, 335–36.

82 Lincoln to Clive Runnells, May 27, 1926, CHS.

Pullman car "Advance" was "very comfortable indeed."[83] Upon arriving at "Hildene," the Lincolns assumed their normal routine. Lincoln took frequent drives, perhaps in the Rolls-Royce automobile that Mary Harlan Lincoln had given him as a birthday present the previous August.[84]

On Sunday, July 25, 1926, Lincoln took his customary ride, "dined with his family in good spirits, and went upstairs with his valet and to bed, as usual. . . . The next morning when the butler went in with . . . breakfast, he found him in bed, dead."[85] The family physician at Manchester, Dr. C. M. Campbell determined that death was due to "cerebral hemorrhage induced by arteriosclerosis." Robert Todd Lincoln had lived a life just short of eighty-three years.

As it always had been throughout his life, Lincoln was remembered in death more as the son of his father than as a person in his own right:

> Though he refrained from public appearances and studiously went out of his way in his effort never to capitalize the fact that he was the Emancipator's son, Mr. Lincoln was a warm-hearted, charming and lovable gentleman of culture who had many close personal friends in Washington. He was a delightful conversationalist, full of anecdote, a trait probably inherited from his father. Though second to none in admiration of his great father so many of the persons he met in life wanted to talk with him about President Lincoln that he early developed a reticence on that subject.[86]

However, probably Lincoln would have preferred the editorial of the New York *Herald Tribune*:

> Robert T. Lincoln did not live in the shadow of his father's greatness. He carved out a career for himself, mostly apart from the controversies of politics. He was a hard worker in his profession and rose to eminence in it. As an advisor to large business enterprises and a director in their operation he made an enviable place for

83 *Ibid.*
84 Estate of Robert Todd Lincoln, 335.
85 *Ibid.*, 337.
86 *New York Times*, July 27, 1926.

himself and became a conspicuous figure in the life of the Middle West. He was a modest, conscientious, capable and successful American, absorbed in his work and standing on his own feet.[87]

In faraway London, the *Times* noted the death of the former American minister and observed:

> Seldom do sons of the great achieve the distinction and the glory of their fathers. Fortune, perhaps, had favoured Robert Lincoln too highly, and nature had not endowed him with the rugged grandeur and the human sympathy that the father had learned in the hard school of life. Yet in his way Lincoln served his country well in more than one high position, and in old age he had won the respect and esteem of all who knew him.[88]

It was also said, "In the death of Robert Todd Lincoln the nation's capital not only lost a distinguished citizen but one of her most picturesque residents."[89] Personal tributes poured in from many. President Coolidge spoke of Lincoln as an "outstanding American who had served his country well and helped advance good business methods."[90] Other letters and telegrams came from Secretary of State Frank B. Kellogg, John Hays Hammond, E. F. Carry, president of Pullman, and Frank O. Lowden.[91] Alfred E. Smith also spoke of his regard for Robert T. Lincoln and of his regret at his passing because "of my delightful associations with him."[92] The acting secretary of war, Hanford Mac-Nider, announced the death of the former head of the War Department to the army and ordered flags at military posts to be at half mast.[93]

At four o'clock the afternoon of July 28, the Reverend D. Cunningham of the Congregational Church of Manchester, conducted funeral services for Lincoln at his beloved "Hildene." One reporter observed that there had been no ostentation in his

87 New York *Herald Tribune*, July 27, 1926.
88 *The Times* (London), July 27, 1926.
89 *New York Times*, July 27, 1926.
90 *Ibid.*, July 28, 1926.
91 *Ibid.*
92 *Ibid.*, July 27, 1926.
93 Sec. of War, G.O. No. 16, July 26, 1926, National Archives.

life, and there was none at his funeral. The services were private and were attended only by the family and a few friends. Lincoln's grandsons, two of his attorneys, and members of the Isham family carried his body from "Hildene" for the last time, as it was borne to Dellwood Cemetery, located near the gate of the estate. There he was laid to rest in a vault to await removal to Illinois.[94]

Robert T. Lincoln was not buried in the magnificent Lincoln tomb in Springfield, although the reason why is not entirely clear. In November, 1922, Lincoln had written Nicholas Murray Butler that one day he would be buried there,[95] but it is presumed that Mrs. Lincoln preferred instead Arlington National Cemetery. There the final interment took place on March 14, 1928, and on May 27, 1930, Abraham Lincoln II, after being removed from the vault in Illinois, was reburied near his father.[96]

Following the death of her husband, Mary Harlan Lincoln continued to live in Washington and Manchester. Mary Lincoln Isham, widowed in 1919, came to live with her and had her own apartment within the large home in the Georgetown section of Washington.[97] On March 31, 1937, Robert T. Lincoln's widow died in Washington and was buried at Arlington. Mrs. Isham died in New York City, November 21, 1938.[98] Jessie Lincoln Beckwith had been divorced from her husband in 1907 and in 1915 she married Frank Edward Johnson, from whom she was divorced a decade later. The following year she married Robert J. Randolph. On January 4, 1948, the last surviving child of Robert T. Lincoln died in Bennington, Vermont.[99] The next generation of the family was composed of Lincoln Isham, who in 1919 married Leahalma Correa; Mary Beckwith, who did not marry; and Robert Lincoln Beckwith, who in 1927 married Hazel Holland Wilson. There have been no further generations of the family.[100]

[94] *New York Times*, July 29, 1926.
[95] Lincoln to Nicholas Murray Butler, Nov. 15, 1922, Butler Papers.
[96] Records of Arlington National Cemetery.
[97] Edith Benham Helm, *The Captains and the Kings*, 284.
[98] *New York Times*, Nov. 22, 1938.
[99] *Ibid.*, Jan. 6, 1948.

There is no doubt that Robert T. Lincoln was deeply appreciative of the greatness of his father, and if at any point he ever resented his own secondary role in history, he came in his mature and later years to revere the great President who was also his father. However much he loved his father, one suspects that if Robert Lincoln had his personal choice in the matter, he would have wished to be excepted from the Lincoln legend so that he might have lived his own life. Many benefits came to him because of his parentage, but at the same time he was denied the fundamental right to succeed or fail in life purely on his own merits. In any attempt to assess the worth of the younger Lincoln in relation to the political, legal, and economic record of his own age, there is always present the shadow of the preceding generation. For this reason, Robert T. Lincoln could never be clearly and freely a man in his own right.

100 McMurtry, *Harlan-Lincoln Tradition*, 10–11. For a gossipy, "human interest" type of newspaper article on the grandchildren of Robert T. Lincoln, the type their grandfather so hated, see *The Sunday Star* (Washington, D.C.), Feb. 8, 1931.

Bibliography

Mention of Robert T. Lincoln may be found in a great number of published works, but generally it is brief in length and limited in scope. The surviving letters to and from Lincoln are scattered. Few libraries have enough to constitute a collection. Aside from manuscripts perhaps the most important source of biographical material is newspapers. The Chicago *Tribune* is especially useful for the years of Lincoln's residence there.

Manuscripts

Boston University Library.

Nicholas Murray Butler Papers, Columbia University Library, New York City.

Chicago Historical Society.

Jacob M. Dickinson Papers, Tennessee State Archives, Nashville.

Duke University Library, Durham, N.C.

Harvard University, Cambridge, Mass.
   College Library
   University Archives

John Hay Papers, Brown University Library, Providence, R.I.

Rutherford B. Hayes Library, Fremont, Ohio.

Historical and Philosophical Society of Ohio, Cincinnati, Ohio.

Historical Society of Pennsylvania, Philadelphia.

Henry E. Huntington Library, San Marino, Calif.

Illinois State Historical Library, Springfield.
  Humphrey Papers
  Conkling Papers
Indiana University Library, Bloomington.
Library of Congress, Washington, D.C.
  James A. Garfield Papers
  Herndon-Weik Manuscripts
  Abraham Lincoln Papers
  Robert T. Lincoln Miscellaneous Papers
  John A. Logan Papers
  John G. Nicolay Papers
  Theodore Roosevelt Papers
  Philip Sheridan Papers
  Elihu Washburne Papers
  Henry White Papers
Lincoln College Library, Lincoln, Ill.
Lincoln Memorial University Library, Harrogate, Tenn.
Lincoln National Life Insurance Foundation, Fort Wayne, Ind.
National Archives, Washington, D.C.
  Dispatches from United States Ministers to Great Britain,
    1889–93
  Letters sent by the Secretary of War, 1881–85
New Hampshire Historical Society, Concord.
The Newberry Library, Chicago.
New York Public Library, New York City.
  Andrew Carnegie Papers
  Levi P. Morton Papers
New York State Library, Albany.
Princeton University Library, Princeton, N.J.
Tarbell Lincoln Collection, Allegheny College, Meadville, Pa.
University of Chicago Library.
  William E. Barton Collection
  Robert T. Lincoln Miscellaneous Papers
Vermont Historical Society, Montpelier.
Yale University Library, New Haven, Conn.

GOVERNMENT PUBLICATIONS

Caemmerer, H. P. *Washington, The National Capital*. Washington,
  Government Printing Office, 1932.

Messages and Papers of the Presidents. Washington, Government
Printing Office, 1897.
Annual Reports of the Secretary of War. Washington, Government
Printing Office, 1881–85.

NEWSPAPERS

Chicago *Times*, 1861–65.
Chicago *Tribune*, 1865–1959.
Illinois State Journal (Springfield), 1858–81.
New York *Herald*, 1861–1924.
New York *Tribune*, 1861–1924.
New York *Herald-Tribune*, 1924–26.
Washington *Evening Star*, 1868–85.

BIOGRAPHIES AND MEMOIRS

Abbott, Lawrence F., ed. *The Letters of Archie Butt, Personal Aide
to President Roosevelt.* New York, Doubleday, Page & Company,
1924.
Adams, Henry. *The Education of Henry Adams.* Popular edition.
Boston, Houghton Mifflin Company, 1927.
Anderson, Isabel, ed. *Larz Anderson, Letters and Journals of a Diplomat.* New York, Fleming H. Revell Company, 1940.
———, ed. *The Letters and Journals of General Nicholas Longworth
Anderson.* New York, Fleming H. Revell Company, 1942.
Angle, Paul M. *Lincoln, 1854–1861, Being the Day-by-Day Activities
of Abraham Lincoln from January 1, 1854 to March 4, 1861.* Spring-
field, The Abraham Lincoln Association, 1933.
———, and Earl S. Miers, eds. *The Living Lincoln.* New Brunswick,
Rutgers University Press, 1955.
Asquith, Herbert Henry. *Memories and Reflections, 1852–1927.* 2
vols. Boston, Little, Brown and Company, 1928.
Bancroft, Frederic, ed. *Speeches, Correspondence and Political
Papers of Carl Schurz.* 6 vols. New York, G. P. Putnam's Sons, 1913.
Barnard, Harry. *"Eagle Forgotten," The Life of John Peter Altgeld.*
Indianapolis, Bobbs-Merrill Company, 1938.
Barrows, Chester L. *William M. Evarts, Lawyer, Diplomat, States-
man.* Chapel Hill, University of North Carolina, 1941.
Basler, Roy P., ed. *The Collected Works of Abraham Lincoln.* 9 vols.
New Brunswick, Rutgers University Press, 1953.

268

Bayne, Julia Taft. *Tad Lincoln's Father*. Boston, Little, Brown and Company, 1931.

Beale, Harriet S. Blaine, ed. *Letters of Mrs. James G. Blaine*. 2 vols. New York, Duffield and Company, 1908.

Beer, Thomas. *Hanna*. New York, Alfred A. Knopf, 1929.

Bowen, Catherine Drinker. *Yankee From Olympus*. Boston, Little, Brown and Company, 1944.

Bowers, Claude G. *Beveridge and the Progressive Era*. Boston, Houghton Mifflin Company, 1932.

Browne, Francis Fisher. *The Every-Day Life of Abraham Lincoln*. Chicago, Browne & Howell Company, 1914.

Busey, Samuel Clagett. *Personal Reminiscences and Recollections*. Washington, n.p., 1895.

Butler, Nicholas Murray. *Across the Busy Years, Recollections and Reflections*. 2 vols. New York, Charles Scribner's Sons, 1939–40.

Caldwell, Robert G. *James A. Garfield, Party Chieftain*. New York, Dodd, Mead & Company, 1931.

Carpenter, F. B. *Six Months at the White House with Abraham Lincoln*. New York, Hurd and Houghton, 1866.

Chidsey, Donald Barr. *The Gentleman from New York: A Life of Roscoe Conkling*. New Haven, Yale University Press, 1935.

Cullom, Shelby M. *Fifty Years of Public Service*. Chicago, A. C. McClurg & Company, 1911.

Davis, George T. M. *Autobiography of the Late Colonel George T. M. Davis*. New York, Press of Jenkins and McCowan, 1891.

Dennett, Tyler. *John Hay, From Poetry to Politics*. New York, Dodd, Mead & Company, 1933.

Dennis, Charles H. *Victor Lawson, His Time and His Work*. Chicago, University of Chicago Press, 1935.

Depew, Chauncey M. *My Memories of Eighty Years*. New York, Charles Scribner's Sons, 1922.

Dingley, Edward N. *The Life and Times of Nelson Dingley, Jr.* Kalamazoo, Ihling Brothers and Everard, 1902.

Dodge, H. Augusta, ed. *Gail Hamilton's Life in Letters*. 2 vols. Boston, Lee and Shepard, 1901.

Donald, David. *Lincoln's Herndon*. New York, Alfred A. Knopf, 1948.

Eisenschiml, Otto. *The Celebrated Case of Fitz John Porter*. Indianapolis, Bobbs-Merrill Company Inc., 1950.

Evans, W. A. *Mrs. Abraham Lincoln, A Study of Her Personality and Her Influence on Lincoln.* New York, Alfred A. Knopf, 1932.

Fehrenbacker, Don E. *Chicago Giant; A Biography of "Long John" Wentworth.* Madison, Wisc., The American History Research Center, 1957.

Ford, Worthington C., ed. *Letters of Henry Adams, 1858–1891.* 2 vols. Boston, Houghton Mifflin Company, 1930.

Freeman, Douglas Southall. *George Washington, A Biography.* 7 vols. New York, Charles Scribner's Sons, 1948.

Garraty, John A. *Henry Cabot Lodge, A Biography.* New York, Alfred A. Knopf, 1953.

Gernon, Blaine Brooks. *The Lincolns in Chicago.* Chicago, Ancarthe Publishers, 1934.

Gibbons, Herbert Adams. *John Wanamaker.* 2 vols. New York, Harper & Brothers, 1926.

Goltz, Carlos W. *Incidents in the Life of Mary Todd Lincoln.* Sioux City, Press of Deitch & Lamar Company, 1928.

Greely, Adolphus W. *Reminiscences of Adventure and Service.* New York, Charles Scribner's Sons, 1927.

———. *Three Years of Arctic Service.* New York, Charles Scribner's Sons, 1894.

Gresham, Matilda. *Life of Walter Quinton Gresham.* 2 vols. Chicago, Rand McNally & Company, 1919.

Hale, Edward Everett. *James Russell Lowell and His Friends.* Boston, Houghton, Mifflin and Company, 1899.

Harrison, Carter H. *Stormy Years: The Autobiography of Carter H. Harrison.* Indianapolis, Bobbs-Merrill Company, 1935.

Haupt, Herman. *Reminiscences of General Herman Haupt.* Milwaukee, Wright & Joys Company, 1901.

Hay, Clara, ed. *Letters of John Hay and Extracts From His Diary.* 3 vols. Washington, printed but not published, 1908.

Hazen, Charles D., ed. *The Letters of William Roscoe Thayer.* Boston, Houghton Mifflin Company, 1926.

Helm, Edith Benham. *The Captains and the Kings.* New York, G. P. Putnam's Sons, 1954.

Helm, Katherine. *The True Story of Mary, Wife of Lincoln.* New York, Harper & Brothers, 1928.

Herndon, William H. *Life of Lincoln.* Angle edition. New York, Albert and Charles Boni, 1930.

Hertz, Emanuel. *The Hidden Lincoln*. New York, The Viking Press, 1938.

Hoar, George F. *Autobiography of Seventy Years*. 2 vols. New York, Charles Scribner's Sons, 1903.

Howe, George F. *Chester A. Arthur: A Quarter-Century of Machine Politics*. New York, Dodd, Mead & Company, 1934.

Howe, M. A. De Wolfe, *James Ford Rhodes, American Historian*. New York, D. Appleton and Company, 1929.

Howe, Mark De Wolfe. *Justice Oliver Wendell Holmes: The Shaping Years, 1841–1870*. Cambridge, The Belknap Press of Harvard University Press, 1957.

Huidekoper, H. S. *Personal Notes and Reminiscences of Lincoln*. Philadelphia, Bicking Print, 1896.

Hunt, Thomas. *The Life of William H. Hunt*. Brattleboro, E. L. Hildreth & Company, 1922.

Hutchinson, William T. *Lowden of Illinois; The Life of Frank O. Lowden*. 2 vols. Chicago, University of Chicago Press, 1957.

Johnson, Claudius O. *Carter Henry Harrison I*. Chicago, University of Chicago Press, 1928.

Keckley, Elizabeth. *Behind the Scenes*. New York, G. W. Carleton & Company, 1868.

King, Willard L. *Lincoln's Manager, David Davis*. Cambridge, Harvard University Press, 1960.

———. *Melville Weston Fuller*. New York, The Macmillan Company, 1950.

Kirkland, Caroline. *Chicago Yesterdays, A Sheaf of Reminiscences*. Chicago, Daughaday and Company, 1919.

Leale, Charles A. *Lincoln's Last Hours*. N.p., 1909.

The Letters of Queen Victoria. 3rd ser. 3 vols. London, John Murray, 1931.

Lewis, Lloyd. *Myths After Lincoln*. New York, Readers Club, 1941.

Lincoln, Robert T. *Speech of the Honorable Robert T. Lincoln Made at the Celebration of the 38th Anniversary of the Lincoln-Douglas Debates, Galesburg, Illinois*, October 7, 1896. New York, privately printed for Charles T. White, 1891.

Logan, Mrs. John A. *Reminiscences of a Soldier's Wife, An Autobiography*. New York, Charles Scribner's Sons, 1913.

McClure, Alexander K. *Our Presidents and How We Make Them*. New York, Harper & Brothers, 1900.

McCormack, Thomas J., ed. *Memoirs of Gustave Koerner, 1809–1896.* 2 vols. Cedar Rapids, The Torch Press, 1909.

McCulloch, Hugh. *Men and Measures of Half A Century.* New York, Charles Scribner's Sons, 1900.

McDonald, Forrest. *Insull.* Chicago, University of Chicago Press, 1962.

McElroy, Robert. *Levi Parsons Morton.* New York, G. P. Putnam's Sons, 1930.

McMurtry, R. Gerald. *Ben Hardin Helm.* Chicago, privately printed, 1943.

———. *The Harlan-Lincoln Tradition at Iowa Wesleyan College.* Mount Pleasant, Iowa, The Harlan-Lincoln Restoration Commission, 1959.

Martin, Edward S. *The Life of Joseph Hodges Choate.* 2 vols. New York, Charles Scribner's Sons, 1920.

Martin, Frederick T. *Things I Remember.* New York, John Lane Company, 1913.

Mearns, David C. *The Lincoln Papers.* 2 vols. Garden City, New York, Doubleday & Company, 1948.

Mende, Elsie Porter. *An American Soldier and Diplomat, Horace Porter.* New York, Frederick A. Stokes Company, 1927.

Mitchell, William. *General Greely.* New York, G. P. Putnam's Sons, 1936.

Morse, John T., Jr. ed. *The Diary of Gideon Welles.* 3 vols. Boston, Houghton Mifflin Company, 1911.

Nevins, Allan. *Henry White; Thirty Years of American Diplomacy.* New York, Harper & Brothers, 1930.

———, ed. *The Letters and Journal of Brand Whitlock.* 2 vols. New York, D. Appleton-Century Company, 1936.

Nicolay, Helen. *Lincoln's Secretary: A Biography of John G. Nicolay.* New York, Longmans, Green and Company, 1949.

Nicolay, John G., and John Hay. *Abraham Lincoln, a History.* 10 vols. New York, The Century Company, 1890.

Oberholtzer, Ellis P. *Jay Cooke, Financier of the Civil War.* 2 vols. Philadelphia, George W. Jacobs & Company, 1907.

Owen, Frank. *Tempestuous Journey: Lloyd George, His Life and Times.* New York, McGraw-Hill Book Company, Inc., 1955.

Page, Elwin L. *Abraham Lincoln in New Hampshire.* Boston, Houghton Mifflin Company, 1929.

Paine, Albert Bigelow. *Mark Twain, a Biography.* 3 vols. New York, Harper & Brothers, 1912.

Pease, Theodore C., and James G. Randall, eds. *The Diary of Orville Hickman Browning.* 2 vols. Springfield, Illinois State Historical Library, 1925.

Pendel, Thomas F. *Thirty-Six Years in the White House.* Washington, The Neale Publishing Company, 1902.

Perling, J. J. *Presidents' Sons.* New York, Odyssey Press, 1947.

Poore, Ben: Perley. *Perley's Reminiscences.* 2 vols. Philadelphia, Hubbard Brothers, 1886.

Porter, Horace. *Campaigning With Grant.* New York, The Century Company, 1897.

Pratt, Harry E. *Lincoln, 1840–1846; Being the Day-by-Day Activities of Abraham Lincoln, from January 1, 1840 to December 31, 1846.* Springfield, Abraham Lincoln Association, 1939.

———. *The Personal Finances of Abraham Lincoln.* Springfield, The Abraham Lincoln Association, 1943.

Putnam George H. *Memories of My Youth.* New York, G. P. Putnam's Sons, 1914.

Randall, Ruth Painter. *Lincoln's Sons.* Boston, Little, Brown and Company, 1955.

———. *Mary Lincoln, Biography of a Marriage.* Boston, Little, Brown and Company, 1953.

Richardson, Leon Burr. *William E. Chandler, Republican.* New York, Dodd, Mead & Company, 1940.

Roberts, Octavia. *Lincoln in Illinois.* Boston, Houghton Mifflin Company, 1918.

Rogers, Henry Munroe. *Memories of Ninety Years.* Boston, Houghton Mifflin Company, 1928.

Roosevelt, Theodore, and Henry Cabot Lodge. *Selections from the Correspondence of Theodore Roosevelt and Henry Cabot Lodge, 1884–1918.* 2 vols. New York, Charles Scribner's Sons, 1925.

Ruggles, Eleanor. *Prince of Players, Edwin Booth.* New York, W. W. Norton & Company, 1953.

Sage, Leland L. *William Boyd Allison, A Study in Practical Politics.* Iowa City, State Historical Society of Iowa, 1946.

Saint-Gaudens, Homer, ed. *The Reminiscences of Augustus Saint-Gaudens.* 2 vols. London, Andrew Melrose, 1913.

Sandburg, Carl. *Abraham Lincoln; The Prairie Years.* 2 vols. New York, Harcourt, Brace & Company, 1926.

――――. *Abraham Lincoln: The War Years.* 4 vols. New York, Harcourt, Brace & Company, 1939.

――――, and Paul M. Angle. *Mary Lincoln, Wife and Widow.* New York, Harcourt, Brace & Company, 1932.

Schley, Winfield S., and J. R. Soley. *The Rescue of Greely.* New York, Charles Scribner's Sons, 1885.

Searcher, Victor. *The Farewell to Lincoln.* New York, Abington Press, 1965.

Seward, Frederick W. *Reminiscences of a War-Time Statesman and Diplomat.* New York, G. P. Putnam's Sons, 1916.

Smith, Theodore Clarke. *The Life and Letters of James Abram Garfield.* 2 vols. New Haven, Yale University Press, 1925.

Stevens, Walter B. *A Reporter's Lincoln.* St. Louis, Missouri Historical Society, 1916.

Stoddard, Henry L. *As I Knew Them: Presidents and Politics From Grant to Coolidge.* New York, Harper & Brothers, 1927.

Tarbell, Ida. *All in a Day's Work, An Autobiography.* New York, Macmillan Company, 1939.

Tebbel, John. *The Marshall Fields.* New York, E. P. Dutton & Company, Inc., 1947.

Thayer, William Roscoe. *The Life and Letters of John Hay.* 2 vols. Boston, Houghton Mifflin Company, 1915.

Thomas, Benjamin P. *Abraham Lincoln.* New York, Alfred A. Knopf, 1952.

Thomas, Benjamin P., and Harold M. Hyman. *Stanton, The Life and Times of Lincoln's Secretary of War.* New York, Alfred A. Knopf, 1962.

Thoron, Ward, ed. *The Letters of Mrs. Henry Adams, 1865–1883.* Boston, Little, Brown and Company, 1937.

Timmons, Bascom, ed. *Charles G. Dawes; A Journal of the McKinley Years.* Chicago, The Lakeside Press, 1950.

Todd, A. L. *Abandoned: The Story of the Greely Arctic Expedition 1881–1884.* New York, McGraw-Hill Book Company, 1961.

Townsend, William H. *Lincoln and His Wife's Home Town.* Indianapolis, Bobbs-Merrill Company, 1929.

Villard, Henry. *Lincoln on the Eve of '61.* New York, Alfred A. Knopf, 1941.

Volwiler, Albert T., ed. *The Correspondence Between Benjamin Harrison and James G. Blaine, 1882–1893*. Philadelphia, The American Philosophical Society, 1940.

Waddington, Mary King. *Letters of a Diplomat's Wife, 1883–1900*. New York, Charles Scribner's Sons, 1911.

Wall, Joseph Frazier. *Henry Watterson, Reconstructed Rebel*. New York, Oxford University Press, 1956.

Warren, Louis A. *Lincoln's Parentage and Childhood*. New York, The Century Company, 1926.

Weigley, Russell F. *Quartermaster of the Union Army: A Biography of M. C. Meigs*. New York, Columbia University Press, 1959.

Williams, Charles R., ed. *Diary and Letters of Rutherford Birchard Hayes*. 5 vols. Columbus, Ohio State Archeological and Historical Society, 1922–26.

Wilson, Rufus R. *Intimate Memories of Lincoln*. Elmira, N.Y., The Primavera Press, Inc., 1945.

———. *Lincoln Among His Friends*. Caldwell, Ida., Caxton Printers, 1942.

Woldman, Albert A. *Lawyer Lincoln*. Boston, Houghton Mifflin Company, 1936.

Younger, Edward. *John A. Kasson, Politics and Diplomacy from Lincoln to McKinley*. Iowa City, State Historical Society of Iowa, 1955.

OTHER PRIMARY SOURCES

Bullard, Lauriston. *Lincoln in Marble and Bronze*. New Brunswick, Rutgers University Press, 1952.

A Catalogue of the Officers and Students of Harvard University for the Academical Year, 1860–1861. Cambridge, Sever and Francis, 1860.

Fuller, Frank. *A Day with the Lincoln Family*. Rare booklet in the collection of Illinois State Historical Library, Springfield.

Gookin, Frederick William. *The Chicago Literary Club*. Chicago, printed for the club, 1926.

Harvard College. *Class of 1864, Secretary's Report*. Number 2, 1864–1867. Boston, printed for the class, 1867.

Number 6, 1864–1889. Boston, printed for the class, 1889.

Number 8, 1864–1914. Boston, printed for the class, 1914.

Mackey, T. J. *The Hazen Court-Martial.* New York, D. Van Nostrand, 1885.

GENERAL HISTORIES

Allen, H. C. *Great Britain and the United States.* New York, St. Martin's Press, 1955.

Andreas, A. T. *History of Chicago.* 3 vols. Chicago, A. T. Andreas Company, 1886.

Andrews, E. Benjamin. *The History of the Last Quarter-Century in the United States, 1870–1895.* 2 vols. New York, Charles Scribner's Sons, 1896.

Angle, Paul M. *"Here I Have Lived": A History of Lincoln's Springfield.* Springfield, The Abraham Lincoln Association, 1935.

Bishop, Jim. *The Day Lincoln Was Shot.* New York, Harper & Brothers, 1955.

The Centennial History of the Harvard Law School. N.p., The Harvard Law School Association, 1918.

Church, Charles A. *A History of the Republican Party in Illinois, 1854–1912.* Rockford, Ill. Wilson Brothers Company, 1912.

Clark, Allen C. *Abraham Lincoln in the National Capital.* Washington, W. F. Roberts Company, 1925.

Colman, Edna M. *Seventy-Five Years of White House Gossip.* Garden City, N.Y., Doubleday, Page & Company, 1925.

Corliss, Carlton J. *Main Line of Mid America: The Story of the Illinois Central.* New York, Creative Age Press, 1950.

Crosbie, Laurence M. *The Phillips Exeter Academy, A History.* Norwood, Mass., The Plimpton Press, 1923.

Cunningham, Frank H. *Familiar Sketches of the Phillips Exeter Academy and Surroundings.* Boston, James R. Osgood and Company, 1883.

Currey, J. Seymour. *Chicago: Its History and Its Builders.* 5 vols. Chicago, The S. J. Clarke Publishing Company, 1912.

Cuthbert, Norma B. *Lincoln and the Baltimore Plot, 1861.* San Marino, Calif., The Huntington Library, 1949.

Dedmon, Emmett. *Fabulous Chicago.* New York, Random House, 1953.

Ecker, Grace Dunlop. *A Portrait of Old George Town.* Richmond, Garrett & Massie, Inc., 1933.

Flower, Frank A. *History of the Republican Party*. Springfield, Union Publishing Company, 1884.

Green, Thomas Marshall. *Historic Families of Kentucky*. Cincinnati, Robert Clarke & Company, 1889.

Harper, Robert S. *Lincoln and the Press*. New York, McGraw-Hill Book Company, Inc., 1951.

Hill, George Birkbeck. *Harvard College by an Oxonian*. New York, Macmillan and Company, 1895.

History of the City of Chicago, Its Men and Institutions. Chicago, Press of the Blakely Printing Company, 1900.

Josephson, Matthew. *The Politicos, 1865–1896*. New York, Harcourt, Brace and Company, 1938.

Knoles, George H. *The Presidential Campaign and Election of 1892*. Stanford, Stanford University Press, 1942.

Leech, Margaret. *Reveille in Washington, 1860–1865*. New York, Harper & Brothers Publishers, 1941.

Lindsey, Almont. *The Pullman Strike*. Chicago, University of Chicago Press, 1942.

Milton, George F. *Age of Hate*. New York, Coward-McCann, Inc., 1930.

Moses, John, and Joseph Kirkland, eds. *History of Chicago*. 2 vols. Chicago, Munsell & Company, 1895.

Palmer, John M., ed. *The Bench and Bar of Illinois*. 2 vols. Chicago, Lewis Publishing Co., 1899.

Peck, Harry Thurston. *Twenty Years of the Republic, 1885–1905*. New York, Dodd, Mead & Company, 1907.

Pierce, Bessie L. *A History of Chicago*. 3 vols. New York, Alfred A. Knopf, 1937–57.

Pratt, Julius W. *A History of United States Foreign Policy*. Englewood Cliffs, N.J., Prentice-Hall, Inc., 1955.

Singleton, Esther. *The Story of the White House*. 2 vols. New York, The McClure Company, 1907.

Williams, Myron R. *The Story of Phillips Exeter*. Exeter, N.H., The Phillips Exeter Academy, 1957.

Williams, T. Harry. *Lincoln and His Generals*. New York, Grosset & Dunlap, 1952.

Willson, Beckles. *America's Ambassadors to England, 1785–1928*. London, John Murray, 1928.

ARTICLES AND ESSAYS IN PERIODICALS

Ayres, Philip W. "Lincoln as a Neighbor," *Review of Reviews*, Vol. LVII, No. 2 (February, 1918).

Batchelder, Samuel F. "Old Times at the Law School," *Atlantic Monthly*, Vol. XC (November, 1902).

Bullock, John M. "President Lincoln's Visiting-Card," *Century Magazine*, Vol. LV (February, 1898).

Butler, Nicholas Murray. "Lincoln and Son," *Saturday Evening Post*, (February 11, 1939).

Darrin, Charles V. "A Lincoln Family Friendship," *Journal of the Illinois State Historical Society*, Vol. XXXXIV (1951).

Evjen, Harry. "Illinois State University, 1852–1868." *Journal of the Illinois State Historical Society*, Vol. XXXI, (March, 1938).

Grimsley, Elizabeth Todd. "Six Months in the White House." *Journal of the Illinois State Historical Society*, Vol. XIX (1926–27).

Hall, Reverend Newman. "My Impressions of America," *Journal of the Illinois State Historical Society*, Vol. XXXVII (1944).

Lewis, Lloyd. "Lincoln and Pinkerton," *Journal of the Illinois State Historical Society*, Vol. XXXXI (1948).

Olson, Lester W. "Lincoln's Granddaughter Eloped to Milwaukee," *Historical Messenger*, Milwaukee County Historical Society (December, 1955).

"Pullman, Inc." *Fortune*, Vol. XVII, No. 1 (January, 1938).

Scott, Henry Edwards. "Hon. Robert Todd Lincoln, L.L.D.," *New England Historical and Genealogical Register* Vol. LXXXI (July, 1927).

Temple, Wayne C. "Mary Todd Lincoln's Travels," *Journal of the Illinois State Historical Society*. Vol. LII (Spring, 1959).

Index

Adams, Charles Francis: 174
Adams, George E.: 156
Adams, Henry: 41, 192
Adams, Mrs. Henry: xv
Adams, John Quincy: xi
Agassiz, Louis: 42
Allen, H. C.: 214
Allison, William B.: 167
Altgeld, John P.: 215–16, 218
American Railway Union: 218
American Red Cross: RTL a member of the incorporating body (1905), 245
Anderson, Fred P.: 56
Anderson, Larz: 197, 198, 199, 203, 209–10
Anderson, Nicholas Longworth: 146, 197, 209
Arnold, Isaac N.: 95
Arthur, Chester A.: 112, 120, 121, 122, 123, 127, 132, 134, 135, 139, 140, 141, 142, 143, 147, 148, 152–53, 160, 169, 194
Ayer and Coles (Chicago law firm): 102

Badeau, Adam: 105, 113, 133
Barnard, George G.: 249, 250, 251
Barr, Thomas F.: 104, 126, 167
Bartlett, Truman H.: 186
Bayard, James A.: 213, 214
Beale, William G.: 97, 194, 197
Beckwith, Jessie Lincoln: 90, 149, 196, 232–34, 238, 264
Beckwith, Mary: 234, 264

Beckwith, Robert Lincoln: 234, 264
Beckwith, Warren W.: 232–34
Benn, George W.: 31
Beveridge, Albert J.: xiii, 191, 255
Beveridge, John L.: 110
Bixby letter: 77
Blaine, James G.: 117, 118, 119, 122, 123, 142, 143, 145, 146, 147, 161, 167, 175, 176, 193, 202, 203, 204, 205, 206, 208, 214
Blaine, Mrs. James G.: 123, 203
Blair, Albert: 33
Blatchford, E. W.: 158
Bledsoe, Sophie: 8
Booth, Edwin: 70–71
Booth, John Wilkes: 69, 70, 88, 259
Borglum, Gutzon: 249
Boutwell, George S.: 147
Brandegee, Frank S.: 240
Brewster, Benjamin H.: 122, 134
Brooks, Noah: 79
Brown, Mary Edwards: 259
Browning, Orville H.: 49, 56, 72, 74
Bryan, William Jennings: 229, 236
Bryce, Lord: 200, 236
Burns, Ruth: 11
Butler, Nicholas Murray: 69, 191, 239, 255–56, 264

Caldwell, Ervin W.: 167
Cameron, J. Donald: 114
Campbell, C. M.: 262
Canedy, P. C.: 22

Canisius, Theodore: 109
Cannon, Joseph G.: 155
Carnegie, Andrew: 194, 196
Carpenter, F. B.: 79
Carry, E. F.: 263
Carson, Mrs. William W.: 202
Caton, John D.: 93, 150
Chalfin, S. F.: 65
Chandler, William E.: 117, 122, 135, 136, 141, 144, 145
Charnwood, Lord: 191
Chase, Salmon P.: 53–54
Cheyenne, Wyo.: RTL visits, 88
Chicago: in period of RTL's residence there, 95ff.
Chicago Bar Association: 95–96
Chicago Club: 95, 177
Chicago Edison Company: 217
Chicago Elevated Railways: 98
Chicago Great Western Railroad: 218
Chicago Historical Society: 96, 181, 221
Chicago Literary Club: 95
Chicago Telephone Company: 217
Chicago, University of: 91
Child, Francis James: 82
Choate, Joseph H.: 198, 214, 242
Cilley, Bradbury Longfellow: 27
Clarke, Mr. and Mrs. Samuel B.: 28
Clarkson, Grosvenor B.: 241
Clarkson, James S.: 241–42
Cleveland, Grover: 140, 147, 148, 149, 151, 157, 160, 162, 169, 170, 210, 212, 213, 218, 228
Cleveland, Mrs. Grover: 160
Cluskey, Henry: 32
Cockrell, Francis M.: 130
Columbian Exposition, Chicago: 201–202, 210
Commonwealth Edison Company: 98, 258
Confederate battle flags, RTL and: 149
Conkling, Clinton L.: 249, 251, 254, 259
Conkling, Roscoe: 164
Cooke, Jay: 66
Coolidge, Calvin: 263
Coolidge, T. Jefferson: 214
Cox, James M.: 240
Crerar, John: 158
Crosby, (Chief clerk, War Department): 131

Cullom, Shelby M.: 110, 114, 172, 173, 175, 176, 196
Cunningham, D.: 263

Daniel, John W.: 224
Darrow, Clarence: 219
Davis, David: 13, 16, 34, 41, 72, 73, 80–82, 84, 85–86, 92, 93, 94, 101, 106, 123, 132, 152, 180
Davis, George T. M.: 18
Davis, Jefferson: 131
Dawes, Charles G.: 226
Debs, Eugene V.: 218, 219
Depew, Chauncey M.: 173, 228
Dingley, Nelson, Jr.: 198
Dixon, Mrs. Elizabeth L.: 70
Doane, J. W.: 222
Dodge, William E.: 53
Doty, Duane: 221–22
Douglas, Stephen A.: 24; monument to, 110
Douglas, Stephen A., Jr.: 110, 111, 112, 170
Douglass, Frederick: 166
Drum, Richard C.: 104, 131
Dunlop, James: 238

Eagan, J. M.: 218
Edmunds, George F.: 145, 146–47
Edwards, Elizabeth Todd (Mrs. Ninian W. Edwards): 5, 49, 247
Edwards, Josephine: 231
Edwards, Ninian W.: 5
Ekin, James A.: 129
Ekwanok Country Club, Manchester, Vt.: 239
Eliot, Charles W.: 41, 151
Endicott, William C.: 140, 148
Evarts, William M.: 64, 108, 109, 173
Everett, Edward: 57

Fairbank, Nathaniel K.: 226
Farwell, Charles B.: 155, 172, 173, 175, 176
Field, Marshall: 98, 151, 158, 171, 198, 222, 226, 235
Field, Stanley: 235
Field, Stephen J.: 148
Fifer, Joseph W.: 196
Folger, Charles J.: 122, 141
Foraker, Joseph B.: 160, 224–25

Index

Force, Manning: 133
Foster, Charles: 211
Fowler, Asa: 31
Freeman, Douglas Southall: xi
Frelinghuysen, Frederick T.: 122
Fuller, Melville W.: 153, 157
Fuller, Samuel W.: 91

Gage, Lyman J.: 151
Garfield, James A.: 112, 114, 115, 116, 117, 118, 134, 142, 143, 146; assassination of, 119ff.; death and funeral, 121-22
Garfield, James R.: xi
"General Tom Thumb": 51
Gilder, Richard Watson: 247
Gillett, Frederick H.: 240
Gladstone, William E.: 193
Globe Tavern, Springfield, Ill.: 6, 7
Gourley, James: 12
Grant, Frederick D.: 110, 167-68, 174
Grant, Ulysses S.: 64, 65, 66, 73, 74, 107, 108, 109, 110, 111, 113-14, 120, 143, 144
Grant, Ulysses S. III: 168
Gratz, Simon: 130
Gray, Asa: 42
Greeley, Horace: 108
Greely, Adolphus W., and Arctic expedition: 134ff.
Gresham, Walter Q.: 122, 141, 147, 152, 168, 169, 213, 219
Grigsby, Sarah Lincoln: 4
Grimsley, Elizabeth Todd: 47, 74
Grosscup, Peter S.: 219

Hale, Frederick: 240
Hale, John P.: 88
Hall of Fame: RTL an elector of, 245
Halstead, Murat: 211
Hamilton, Gail (Dodge, Mary Abigail): 118, 203
Hamilton, John M.: 155
Hammond, John Hays: 263
Hancock, Winfield S.: 139
Hanna, Mark, 218
Harding, Warren G.: 240, 253, 260
Harlan, James: 67, 68, 88, 89, 90, 93, 116, 196, 210, 232
Harlan, John M.: 213

Harper, William R.: 221
Harris, Ira: 61
Harrison, Benjamin: 169, 170-71, 172, 173, 175, 176, 209, 213, 227
Harrison, Mrs. Benjamin: 203
Harrison, Carter H., Sr.: 155, 156
Harrison, Carter H., Jr.: xv, 155, 224, 225
Harrison, Mrs. Russell B.: 199, 203
Harvard: 24, 25, 26, 41ff., 56ff., 194
Harvard Law School: 62-64
Hatton, Frank: 122
Haupt, Herman: 141
Hawley, Joseph R.: 147
Hay, John: 23, 38, 39, 46, 48, 52, 55, 56, 59, 67, 69, 70, 71, 79, 96, 97, 101, 107, 108, 112, 115, 116, 120, 123, 142, 148, 149, 173, 178ff., 192, 195, 196, 199, 214, 215, 217, 229, 254
Hayes, Rutherford B.: 64, 108, 109, 133, 145
Haymarket riot: 215
Hazen, William B.: 134, 136, 137, 138, 139, 140
Helm, Emelie Todd (Emily, Mrs. Ben Hardin Helm): 19, 60-61, 66, 118, 132, 232, 235, 237, 244, 245, 259, 260, 261
Helm, Kate: 244-45, 259
Henry, Anson G.: 83
Henry, C. B.: 136
Herndon, William H.: 9, 10, 12, 81, 83-85, 100, 180, 185ff.
Hill, John Wesley: 257
Hitchcock, Gilbert M.: 240
Hitt, Robert R.: 171, 172
Hoar, George F.: 175, 214
Holland, J. G.: 83
Holmes, Oliver W.: 42
Holmes, Oliver W., Jr.: 63
Hoxie, Vinnie Ream: 249
Howard, Oliver O.: 139
Howe, Frank E.: 50
Howe, Timothy O.: 122
Hoyt, Joseph Gibson: 28
Hughes, Charles Evans: 241
Hughes, John: 261
Hulbert, H. C.: 222
Humphrey, J. Otis: 235, 236
Hunt, William H.: 117, 119, 122, 123
Huxley, Thomas H.: 200

Illinois Central Railroad: RTL a trustee of, 110; Golden Jubilee celebration, 225
Illinois State University: 22–23
Indian uprisings (1880's): 126
Ingalls, Rufus: 129
Insull, Samuel: 217
Isham, Charles: 197, 206
Isham, Edward S.: 96–97, 115, 198, 235
Isham, Lincoln: 198n., 264
Isham, Mary Lincoln: 90, 104, 118, 149, 169, 194, 195, 196, 197, 210, 216, 264
Isham, Ralph N.: 100, 102

James, Thomas L.: 117, 119, 122, 227
Janney, Robert M.: 239
Jewett, John N.: 172
Johnson, Andrew: 71, 72, 73, 74, 106
Johnson, Henry Lincoln: 241–42
Judd, Norman B.: 88, 106
Jusserand, Jean Jules: 236

Kasson, John A.: 173
Keckley, Elizabeth: 75
Keep, Chauncey M.: 243
Keep, Henry H.: 114
Kellogg, Frank B.: 263
King, Willard L.: 13
Kirkwood, Samuel J.: 117, 122
Knights of Columbus: 261

Laird, John: 238
Lamon, Ward H.: 38, 53, 86, 132
Lamphear, Orpheus T.: 32
Langdell, Christopher C.: 62
Latham, George: 25, 28, 29, 31, 259
Latham, R. B.: 129
Lee, Robert E.: 46, 52, 68
Leggett, M. D.: 145
Lehmann, Frederick W.: 24
Lincoln, Abraham (great-grandfather of RTL): 3
Lincoln, Abraham (father of RTL): early life, 4; marriage, 5; absence from home, 6; debts and financial struggles, 7; purchases home, 8; thoughts on RTL, 9, 78–79; as a parent, 11 ff., 18; as a congressman, 13, 14; and Illinois Central Railroad, 21; interest in RTL's schooling, 23–24; visits RTL at Exeter, 30–33; inauguration trip of, 36–39; assassination of, 69–70; birthday celebrations, 145; reburial of in 1901, 220–21; statues of, 249–51
Lincoln, Abraham II ("Jack," son of RTL): 90, 118, 149, 194, 195, 196, 197, 231, 264
Lincoln, Edward B.: 8, 14, 15, 16
Lincoln, Mary Harlan (wife of RTL): 67, 68, 75, 88–90, 91, 93–94, 118–19, 148, 149, 150, 151, 171, 196, 203, 210, 212, 213, 233, 238, 244, 245, 259, 260, 262, 264
Lincoln, Mary Todd (mother of RTL): early life and background, 5, 6; marriage, 5; problems with child rearing, 10; servant troubles, 11; visits Kentucky, 14, 15; travels as First Lady, 35–36, 46, 47, 50, 55; concern over RTL entering army, 60–62; grief at murder of husband, 70ff.; dealings with Herndon, 84–85; return from Europe with Tad, 94–95; later emotional instability and insanity trials, 99–105
Lincoln, Nancy Hanks: 3, 4, 132
Lincoln, Robert Todd: no desire for a biography, xii; birth, 6; early home life, 8ff.; and father, 9, 12; visit to Kentucky and Washington, D.C., 13ff.; early schooling, 16; bitten by "mad dog," 17; eye injury, 17; learns social graces, 19; baby sitter for brothers, 20; member of the Springfield cadets, 20; student Illinois State University, 22–23; applies to Harvard, 24–25; at Phillips Exeter, 26–30; visited by father at Exeter, 30–33; receives news of father's presidential nomination, 33; reads Declaration of Independence, 35; shyness as a young man, 34–35; "Prince of Rails," 37; inaugural trip to Washington, 36–39; the lost inaugural address, 37–38; criticisms of as son of the President, 39–40; college student, 41 ff.; relations with father during Civil War, 48, 52–55; as member of Harvard Alumni Association, 57–58; generosity of, 57–58; question of entering the army, 60–62; at law school, 62–64;

army service, 64–68; murder of father, 69–70; funeral of father, 70–73; resigns from the army, 73–74; newspaper criticisms of during war, 76–77; settlement of father's estate, 79–82; marriage, 88–90; attends University of Chicago, 91; admitted to the bar, 92; first law partnership, 92; activities in Chicago as young attorney, 95–96; forms new partnership with Edward S. Isham, 96–97; ability as a lawyer, 98–99; difficulties with mother, 99–105; drawn into politics, 108ff.; declines Federal appointments, 108–109; town councilman, 110; presidential elector (1880), 112; appointment as Secretary of War, 112ff.; press reaction to cabinet appointment, 117ff.; presence at shooting of Garfield, 119–20; as member of the Arthur administration, 122ff.; description of RTL in 1880's, 125; and Fitz-John Porter case, 133ff.; and Greely arctic expedition, 134ff.; and Hazen court-martial, 136–40; and Republican presidential nomination (1884), 142, 147; resumes Chicago law practice, 149; social life in Chicago, 150–52; spoken of for Senate vacancy, 154–55; and election of 1888, 159ff.; views on tariff, 169–70; appointment as Minister to England, 171–76; and biographers of father, 178–91; arrives in England, 193; death of son, 194–95; as Minister to England, 198–208; and Bering Sea controversy, 205–207; and election of 1892, 209–12; returns home to Chicago (1893), 215; as special counsel for Pullman Company, 217; and Pullman estate, 221; as president of Pullman Company, 222ff.; and election of 1896, 227–29; views of sinking of the *Maine*, 230–31; fondness for "Hildene," 234–35; last visit to Springfield, 236; moves to Washington (1910–1911), 237–38; resigns as president of Pullman and becomes board chairman, 238; interest in astronomy, 239; love of golf, 239–40; and election of 1912, 240–41; and election of 1916, 241–42; appearance before Federal Commission on Industrial Relations (1915), 242–43; ill health, 244ff.; and statues of father, 249–51; views on Woodrow Wilson administration, 252–53; final disposition of father's papers, 253–57; continued business activities, 258; daily routine in old age, 258; dedication of Lincoln Memorial (1922), 260; death and funeral, 262–64

Lincoln, Samuel: 3
Lincoln, Sarah Bush Johnston: 4, 182n.
Lincoln, Thomas (grandfather of RTL): 3, 4, 132, 182
Lincoln, Thomas ("Tad," brother of RTL): 9, 16, 18–19, 59, 68, 70, 74, 79, 80, 82, 87, 89, 94–95, 190, 249
Lincoln, William W.: 8, 14, 16, 190
Lincoln Memorial University: 257
Lloyd George, David: 261
Lodge, Henry Cabot: 145, 173
Logan, John A.: 110, 111, 112, 113, 114, 115, 120, 123, 128, 146, 147, 149, 152, 153, 154, 155, 160–61
Logan, Mrs. John A.: 198
Logan ("Old Judge"): 93
Long, John D.: 167
Lowden, Frank O.: 220, 221, 226, 263
Lowell, James Russell: 24, 42–43, 151, 193, 203
Luce, Cyrus G.: 166

McCagg, E. B.: 91
McCormick, Robert S.: 177
McCoy, Amasa: 94
McCulloch, Hugh: 89, 122
McKee, Mrs. James R.: 199, 203
McKinley tariff: 204
McKinley, William: 227, 229, 234
MacNider, Hanford: 263
McNulta, John: 158
MacVeagh, Franklin: 150
MacVeagh, Wayne: 117, 122, 128

Manchester, Vt.: RTL's first visit to, 55; RTL purchases estate there, 234–35; RTL's love of his home there, 239
Manierre, William R.: 225
Markens, Isaac: 250
Markham, Edwin: 260

Mark Skinner Library, Manchester, Vt.: 239
Marshall Field and Company: 98, 243
Marshall, John: 176–77
Martin, Mrs. Bradley: 199–200
Maybrick, Mrs. Florence E.: 203, 204
Meade, George G.: 52
Mearns, David C.: 104, 180, 189, 254
Meconkey, Dick: 35
Medill, Joseph: 98, 112, 115
Meigs, Montgomery C.: 129
Miller, John F.: 128
Monroe, Charles A.: 238
Morgan, Edwin D.: 129
Morgan, J. Pierpont: 223
Morrill tariff: 211
Morton, Levi P.: 210
Murchison letter: 172

Neill, Edward D.: 71, 72
New, John C.: 171, 204
Newberry, Walter L.: 98, 158
Nicolay, Helen: 54, 180, 190, 239
Nicolay, John G.: 46, 48, 50, 55, 86, 107, 149, 150, 178ff., 217, 254
Northern Pacific Railroad: 141
Norton, Charles Eliot: 82
Norton, Daniel S.: 72

O'Connor, Andrew: 251
Oglesby, Richard J.: 73, 155, 196, 226
Ord, Edward O. C.: 66
Orne, Mrs. Sally: 103

Page, Walter Hines: 214
Palide (Venezuelan diplomat): 207
Palmer, George H.: 41
Palmer, John M.: 154, 228
Palmer, Potter: 150, 151
Palmer, Mrs. Potter: 211
Parker, Joel: 63
Parsons, Theophilus: 63
Paton, Walter: 50
Pendel, Thomas F.: 69
Pettis, S. Newton: 143
Phelps, Edmund J.: 193, 214
Phillips Exeter Academy: 26–30, 194
Phoenix, Ariz.: RTL visits, 226
Pinkerton, Allan: 61
Pomeroy Circular: 54
Ponsonby, Sir Henry: 202

Porter, Fitz-John: 133ff.
Porter, Horace: 98, 219, 226
Pratt, Harry E.: 15
Pulitzer, Joseph: 145
Pullman Company: 98, 217ff., 222, 223, 258
Pullman, George M.: 150, 151, 171, 217ff.; death of, 220; will and estate of, 221
Pullman strike: 217–20
Pullman Universalist Memorial Church, Albion, N.Y.: 221

Quay, Matthew S.: 211–12

Ramsay, Alexander: 72, 89
Randall, Ruth Painter: 7, 10, 15
Ream, Norman B.: 221
Ream, Vinnie: *see* Hoxie, Vinnie Ream
Reed, H. R.: 222
Reed, John: 50–51
Reid, Whitelaw: 173, 214
Republican state convention, Illinois (1880): 111–12
Roche, John A.: 157
Rockwell, Julius: 41
Rogers, Henry M.: 48
Roosevelt, Franklin D.: 213
Roosevelt, James R.: 213
Roosevelt, Theodore: 145, 173, 214, 234, 236, 240, 241, 242, 250
Root, Elihu: 242
Rosebery, Lord: 213
Rucker, D. H.: 129
Ruckstuhl, F. Wellington: 250
Runnells, John S.: 217, 219, 222, 223, 248
Rutledge, Ann: 84–85, 188

Sackville-West, Sir Lionel: 172
Saint-Gaudens, Augustus: 154, 251
Salisbury, Lord: 193, 201, 203, 204, 207, 208
Sandburg, Carl: 76
Saulsbury, Willard: 240
Scammon, Charles T.: 92
Scammon, Jonathan Y.: 91, 96
Schley, Winfield S.: 138
Schneider, George: 109
Schofield, John M.: 139, 151
Schomburgk, Sir Robert: 207

Schurz, Carl: 146
Scribner, Charles: 187–88
Second Presbyterian Church, Chicago: 96
Seward, Frederick W.: 53
Seward, William H.: 53
Shaw, George Bernard: 250
Sheridan, Philip: 126, 127, 141
Sherman, John: 142, 145, 147, 161, 167, 173, 211
Sherman, William T.: 126, 127, 128
Shouler, James: 189
Sickles, Daniel E.: 61
Simpson, James: 235
Simpson, Matthew: 88, 89
Smith, Alfred E.: 261, 263
Smith, Clark M.: 84, 152
Smith, William Henry: 108, 109
Smyth, Frederick: 31
Snow, Marshall S.: 29
Soule, Gideon Lane: 26, 27, 29, 30
Southall, John W.: 224
South Chicago, town of: 110
Speed, Joshua Fry: 6, 9, 83
Spencer, Christopher M.: 54
Spencer, J. M.: 246–48
Sprague, O. S. A.: 222
Springfield cadets: 20
Stager, Anson: 149
Stanton, Edwin M.: xiv, 50, 55, 58, 65, 70, 72, 89, 131
Stanton, Edwin M., Jr.: 72, 89
Stephens, Alexander H.: 129
Storrs, Emery A.: 115
Stuart, John T.: 73, 101
Stuart, John T., Jr.: 19
Sumner, Charles: 46, 47, 70, 83
Swett, Leonard: 110

Taft, Charles P.: 251
Taft, Robert A.: xi
Taft, William H.: 237, 240, 241, 249, 250, 260
Tarbell, Ida: xii, 190
Taylor, Richard: xi
Teller, Henry M.: 122
Terry, Alfred H.: 151
Thatcher, George H.: 239
Thompson, John: 200
Thomson, Frank: 196
Todd, Eliza Ann Parker: 4

Todd, Margaret Ann: 246
Todd, Mattie: 109
Todd, Robert S.: 4, 5, 7, 13
Treat, Samuel H.: 18
Tree, Lambert: 151
Trumbull, Lyman: 49, 53, 106, 151, 157
Tuck, Amos: 28, 34, 35
Twain, Mark (Samuel L. Clemens): 127–28

Union League Club: 176, 177

Vanderbilt, Frederick K.: 223
Vanderbilt, William K.: 223
Van Voorhis, John: 128
Vest, George G.: 141
Victoria, Queen: 176, 193, 202, 203, 213
Villard, Henry: 141

Waddington, Mary King: 209
Waddington, William Henry: 213
Wagner Sleeping Car Company: 223, 225
Waite, Morrison R.: 121, 157
Walker, James: 26
Wallace, Frances Todd (Mrs. William S.): 17, 87
Wallace, William S.: 87
Walsh, Frank P.: 242
Wanamaker, John: 241
Washburn, Emory: 63
Washington, George: xi
Watterson, Henry: 237
Weik, Jesse W.: 186, 187
Welles, Edgar T.: 89, 181, 196, 213
Welles, Gideon: xiv, 89, 90, 107, 181
Wentworth, George Albert: 27
Wentworth, John: 106
Western Edison Light Company: 216–17
Westminster Presbyterian Church, Springfield, Ill.: 245
White, Henry: 43, 191, 192, 193, 195, 197, 198, 207, 213
White, Horace: 187
Whitlock, Brand: 188
Wickes, Thomas H.: 222
Wilde, Oscar: 200
Wildes, Frank: 138
Williams, Norman: 93, 222
Willson, Augustus E.: 237

Wilson, Woodrow: 237, 241, 252

Windom, William: 117, 119, 122

Wood, Leonard: 242

Wormley, J. H., Jr.: 89

Yard, Robert Sterling: 246

Yellowstone park: RTL visits with President Arthur, 141

Young, Horace G.: 239, 255

HILDENE

As soon as Robert T. Lincoln's summer home at Manchester, Vermont, was enough finished so that the family could occupy it, the beautiful estate became the center of life for all the living descendants of President Lincoln. Robert Lincoln was there as much as his work permitted him to be. Until he retired from the presidency of the Pullman Company he managed that firm from his first floor office in Hildene. Indeed toward the end of his management of the corporation he was surprisingly little in Chicago anymore and instead when not in Vermont or Washington, D.C., was in New York City where he maintained an apartment or stopped at a hotel. If possible, Mary Harlan Lincoln came to love Vermont even more than her husband did. While the winter weather could drive him south, she at times remained in the place which she had named. Chicago was never one of her favorite cities and while she did spend, even after the death of her father, some time in Mt. Pleasant, Iowa, she more and more tended to think of Manchester as her principal residence.

At the time her parents had Hildene built, Mary Lincoln Isham and her husband, Charles, bought a residence in Manchester which is now known as the "1811 House." There they spent their summers while maintaining their principal home in New York City. Lincoln Isham, their son, was often a visitor at Hildene and was one day allowed to drive his grandfather's 1905 Thomas automobile which he upset near the carriage barn and the chauffeur had a great deal of explaining to do. Jessie Lincoln Randolph often came with her children to Hildene and indeed their absence from her first husband, Warren W. Beckwith, was the principal factor in their divorce. Mary ("Peggy") and Robert ("Buddy") Beckwith were practically raised at Hildene. One may today see the screen in the nursery which has pasted on it illustrations from well known children's stories. Their grandfather, it is said, bought a book, cut it apart and himself pasted the pictures on the screen.

Although they all visited or lived there at times the mistress of Hildene until her death in 1937 was the matriarch of the family, Mary Harlan Lincoln. The house and grounds were not included in the trusts which Robert T. Lincoln and his wife created and after the death of her mother Hildene became the property of Mary Lincoln Isham. She began to redecorate the home, especially the dining room, but her own death only a year and a half later terminated her stewardship. Mary Harlan had specified that after Mrs. Isham ownership would pass to her granddaughter, Mary Lincoln Beckwith, who had often resided with her. "Peggy," a woman of many interests including flying, photography, fencing and sculpting determined to make Hildene a working farm. In this she was successful. At times she sold some of the land originally included in Robert T. Lincoln's purchase in 1902. An individual who did not particularly care for publicity, she had many friends and later would be remembered for her acts of charity and kindness.

Lincoln Isham and his wife eventually settled in Dorset, Vermont. He was a talented amateur musician and his wife wrote children's stories. She died in 1960 and he lived until September 1, 1971, when he died in Bennington, Vt. Their relations with their Beckwith cousins were described as "cordial but not close." Despite her avoidance of the limelight Miss Beckwith agreed to christen the nucleur submarine U.S.S. Abraham Lincoln in 1960 and she later wrote to its captain "I must confess that I'm thrilled to be associated with her." She lived alone in Hildene except for domestic help and her dogs. When the last three animals became too old to negotiate the stairs to the second floor of the house they were transported up and down in the dumb waiter. The last private owner of Hildene died July 10, 1975, survived only by her brother, Robert.

Over the years the three members of the last generation of the descendants of Abraham Lincoln had followed their grandfather's admonition to never traffic on the family name. In so doing they had acquired a reputation of being unapproachable. Such was not always the case. Ralph G. Newman, life long Lincoln student, collector and publisher, had corresponded with the trio and although the health of Lincoln Isham and Mary Beckwith did not permit them to travel in their later years in 1965 Robert Beckwith went to Illinois to participate in ceremonies to commemorate the ending of the Civil War a hundred years before. There he met James T. Hickey, another life long Lincoln student and curator of the Lincoln collection at the Illinois State Historical Library, who would play an important role in the collection of family artifacts following the death of the last mistress of Hildene.

Robert Todd Lincoln Beckwith became very conscious of his role as the last living member of his family. Unfortunately after the death of Lincoln Isham many of his possessions had been auctioned and Lincoln family momentos were lost to the public view. Beckwith wished to make certain that the story was not repeated. He and James Hickey spent weeks and months going through trunks and storage boxes at Hildene. The long missing letter books of Robert T. Lincoln were found in good condition in a closet off the downstairs bedroom in which he died. They were transferred to a permanent home in the Illinois State Historical Library. Other items were distributed to libraries and historical societies. Robert Lincoln had kept a careful record of family and personal possessions. He had burned the letters sent to him personally, in the belief that to do otherwise was an intrusion on the privacy of those who had written to him, but he collected and carefully maintained other items.

His work done, Robert Beckwith lived quietly until his death near Saluda, Virginia, December 24, 1985. He was survived by his widow, the former Margaret Fristoe, to whom he had been married in later life. Beckwith had spent most of his adult life living in Maryland and Virginia. He inherited the estate, "Woodstock," not far from Williamsburg which his mother had originally purchased in 1920. A friend said of him that he appreciated most in life good food, fast automobiles, boats, and beautiful women. Unfortunately he did not have a sufficient appreciation for the Rolls Royce which Mary Harlan Lincoln had given her husband on his last birthday. When it was about fifteen years old Beckwith drove it to Virginia, sold the motor to power a boat, and scrapped the rest.

In her will Mary Beckwith provided that after her death the Church of Christ Scientist would own Hildene and it would "be used and maintained as a rest home and/or as an historical museum which shall be open to the public. . ." The arrangement did not work; the church was not interested in the project and it looked as though the house and grounds were in for dark days. Fortunately there were people in the area who were interested in saving Hildene and restoring it to its former grandeur. The "Friends of Hildene, Incorporated," a non-profit trust was organized and took control of the estate July 1978. Although professional consultants had advised that it was not practical to do what the group hoped to accomplish, fortunately their advice was not heeded, and today the home of Robert T. Lincoln is now restored and stands as a memorial to the family which lived there for three generations.

ROBERT TODD LINCOLN
A Man in His Own Right

ROBERT TODD LINCOLN, the eldest son of President Abraham Lincoln, might well have been President of the United States himself had he sought the office. An able secretary of war under Presidents Garfield and Arthur and minister to Great Britain under Benjamin Harrison, he was in private life a successful corporation lawyer and president of the Pullman Company from 1897 to 1911.

Measured in the traditional American materialistic terms, the life of Robert Todd Lincoln was one of great accomplishment. It was also one of great tragedy. His father was cut down by an assassin's bullet, his mother was mentally ill for years, and his only son, to whom he was obviously devoted, died just as he was approaching manhood. Few have speculated in print about the success of the Robert Lincoln—Mary Harlan marriage, but there are persistent rumors that even though it lasted for more than half a century, it was subject to more than the usual difficulties. Moreoever, for sixty years Robert Lincoln lived in a glare of publicity which he constantly sought to escape. He died in 1926, at the venerable age of eighty-three.

Most of the publications dealing with Abraham Lincoln have all but ignored his eldest son. A millionaire lawyer and businessman of decidedly conservative views is difficult to reconcile with the Lincoln legend, and not until now has he found a biographer of his own. At last Robert Todd Lincoln is revealed as an interesting and capable adult, whose career paralleled and was part of the rise of the great railroad corporations in America.

THE AUTHOR

JOHN S. GOFF is chairman of the Social Science Department of Phoenix College, Arizona. He became interested in Robert Todd Lincoln not because of the Lincoln story, but as a result of investigations into the history of late nineteenth-century America.